# THE POST-PANDEMIC
# LIBRARY HANDBOOK

# THE POST-PANDEMIC LIBRARY HANDBOOK

Julie Todaro

ROWMAN & LITTLEFIELD

Lanham • Boulder • New York • London

Published by Rowman & Littlefield
An imprint of The Rowman & Littlefield Publishing Group, Inc.
4501 Forbes Boulevard, Suite 200, Lanham, Maryland 20706
www.rowman.com

86-90 Paul Street, London EC2A 4NE

British Library Cataloguing in Publication Information Available

**Library of Congress Cataloging-in-Publication Data**

ISBN 978-1-5381-5374-1 (cloth)
ISBN 978-1-5381-5375-8 (pbk.)
ISBN 978-1-5381-5376-5 (electronic)

# Dedication

Although there are many ways to say "thank you," there are some people for whom "thank you" is never enough. But when trying to write this dedication, I looked only at my pandemic months, and during this time I have been closer to only a few people—more so than usual—and their help really stood out.

My first category of "thank you for all of your help" is reserved for those who provided answers to my questions during my evenings, weekends, and holiday writing sessions. Our discussions focused on what they were doing in their libraries or what they were reading about in their area of our profession (Louise stands out but is really friend and family) during this most difficult and unprecedented time in our work and home life. I also want to commend the practitioners I work with because daily they power through, against all odds, to protect their staff and serve their communities. And most importantly, they made their choices and decisions based on their values first rather than on fears, and that was not an easy thing to do.

The second group for my thanks is much smaller and is for those people who gave me direct assistance. Some close friends, like Rosa—who is both friend and family and who has worked with me for almost ten years—and Evan and Caitlin—my children and incredibly smart adults who, probably no thanks to me, not only are incredibly accomplished but also consistently make good choices. Also—as Todaro women do—I want to thank my dog for his support and being a non-complaining, boon companion. For this second much-smaller list, though, my sister Jetta is number 1 for many reasons but especially for one of her many talents: her cooking and then delivery, errands, and caring not only for me but also for our other family and extended family members.

The last category for thanks has only one person on the list: my partner (because I am too old to call him my boyfriend and too young to call him my gentleman friend), who for the last five years has startled me daily with just how similar we are, how loving he is, how smart, clever, and funny he is, and—in general—how unfailingly supportive he is—and for being my best friend ever, every day.

# Contents

# Preface

From the first rumor of a pandemic, I did what any respectable researcher does: I started to update my research on the topic, which—based on my other two emergency books—was a great deal for emergency events that I *could* apply but precious little just on pandemics, other than personal experience (so read on). I also had two pandemic documentaries on PBS (horrifying) and three months in 2019 of descriptive warnings from a work colleague that I never really actually believed or understood, given my lack of in-depth knowledge on pandemics. And—of course—I wasn't alone; I began to collect opinions from other professionals, but no one came close to what I thought was an actual plan with projected timelines like "out in March and back in June or midsummer." I did feel relatively comfortable planning for changed facilities and many precautions but always expected "back in September" or—for me—the start of the fall term. Little did I know I was half right—and we *are* back in September, but one year later.

So—because we *weren't* ready—my initial research included a review of my two previous books, and I was pleased to see that they are helpful (and this is not a plug), but the reality was and is the uniqueness of the conditions and consequences were so much more serious, and although there are things that I could use, I had a number of gaps. With more of a full realization of the situation (I think it hit at the end of April 2020), I certainly began to know what I didn't know, so I used my paradigms, grids, and the processes to complete these. I ended up, however, with much more on a few of them—clearly in the area of business continuity—and those few significantly more in-depth ones included a paradigm shift on cleaning products and practices and paradigms on each service we continued to offer—with new, added categories that focused on "completely online."

As we all do though, I had a long list of what I thought would work, but many things my organization (community college) could not or would not choose to do; therefore, I ended up with a great deal of information that wasn't going to apply to me. I used some of it in webinars I was asked to do (association with vendor events) and made it clear I did not intend to make it a "Gee, I don't know; what about you?" event or participate in complaining about my work environment nor serve on a panel in a program that just collected questions—primarily because I observed that no one—post-event—answered those dozens of questions. In addition, although a large number of vendors stepped up to offer incredible support during these past few years (deals, packages, delayed and structured payments, free information), I didn't feel comfortable and wasn't asked to recommend one product.

With all of this information seemingly "left over," *The Post-Pandemic Library* was born, to provide to some—and I hope many—information, recommended processes, and possible solutions on the breadth of issues, the pervasiveness of the effects (basically every library function), dealing with fears (with many workers and users exhibiting emotional and mental concerns), and with realizations of the presence and importance of related impacts (literally the majority of those in the global society are deeply involved and ultimately connected) and—of course—something that the research from earlier pandemics did not dwell much on: the local, state, and national political issues that (in my opinion) extended the timing and severity and exacerbated the economic impact of the pandemic.

And—while most people in our profession do not dwell on the cause of the event itself or, in this case, the virus—I had to do just that, as much like during a forest fire, a fire scientist studies the fire (what causes it, how it moves, why it spreads, and how to stop it), I had to study the virus at the heart of the pandemic, and at the time, there was very little out there. So I rewatched the documentaries of the 1918 pandemic (barely making it through children literally playing on the coffins that lined the streets), and I created a structure—organized in a variety of ways—by physical facility, services, resources, workers, users, and so on, or most if not all facets of a library organization.

I started by matching up what people did know, quickly had to change it to track by stages, and—most importantly—picked the information centers I trusted (CDC and FEMA primarily). And while I thought that our 1918 hindsight of our profession *would* have provided something to build on, the vast majority of that information is actually imbedded in internal documents of public institutions at the time, and even this—given some press and reports of the time—focuses on consequences and impact on usage, numbers, and very little information—for example—on health practices recommended for frontline workers in very public environments during good times, much less bad or catastrophic ones.

What is fascinating—with "doomed to repeat it" echoing in my head—is that newspaper articles and public health edicts within news outlets stated that masks, washing surfaces, washing hands, distancing, and isolating were primarily recommended then (sound familiar?), but many ignored them. No surprise, but no warnings ended up being enough to stop the end-of-1918-end-of-the-war celebrations with thousands of people (images show few masks) crowding the streets. So why did it happen again? What was different about that pandemic included: how the virus moved by age of victims, limited (of course) public information, very different travel and transportation, and generational housing with crowded families and many densely populated neighborhoods. Of course, sophisticated treatments were not available, and ultimately people rebelled—against the exact same restrictions, many for the same reasons but with one crushing difference for today: the speed and multiple delivery methods, written by everyone but researched by few, of 21st-century communication, resulting in a nonstop conveyance of almost everything bad that happened during the 2020 pandemic. Ultimately, information (much of it false) is proving to be what holds us back from faster and responsible personal *and* workplace recovery.

What do we need to look at in the pandemic and post-pandemic library? While my intuition and past research have continued to provide information to answer this question, I have also learned by finding out what others don't have and have been honored this past year to be a speaker in a number of venues. Finding out from planners what their audiences needed has been very helpful, and I have answered calls to help those in practice elsewhere—one very new librarian who had just been asked to join the university's response team, librarians desperate to clearly represent the work their staff would be doing from remote locations, those seeking help in opening and others seeking help in closing yet continuing to serve, and those needing specific wording on moving money, requesting support, and justification and accountability in general.

In looking at all that I gathered and placing it in order of information that should be presented and when, this content covers:

- an initial focus on in-person activities and facilities, how we deliver services, and how we maintain our behind-the-scenes spaces and the storage spaces we actually have and what we need;
- our assets (and yes, our workers are our primary asset) as public and private monies spent on materials or collections and resources;
- methods of assessment and accountability and not only the data needed but also the questions we need to ask with suggestions on how to use it;
- our human assets or human resources, and the training, education, and development needed to make every effort to keep them employed, successful, and safe while at work;
- the critical communication needed to support existing and new activities internally as well as the communication needed to reach external audiences during emergency events;
- necessary management techniques for working with people and within the organizational structures needed during emergency events;
- the necessary leadership focus—different from management techniques—needed during emergency events;
- typical and inevitable pitfalls, problems, mistakes, and complete failures—completely recoverable—that are always prevalent but especially during emergency events;
- general service access and delivery during emergency events;
- the required infrastructure of public relations, marketing, and branding, with concern for every aspect of the pandemic and post-pandemic periods; and
- the necessary issues surrounding "returning to begin again" with recommendations—because that what's we do, and we often need help with the roadmap to begin again.

Finally, while the information in this book isn't required cover-to-cover reading for everyone, we all know that every area of the profession can and should use content for accountability: justifications for budget building and budget requests, educating board members (governing and advisory) on not only needs but also similarities and differences of library spaces, training frontline staff as well as spurring discussion and input from those who—literally—do the work in so many of our areas (middle managers and all levels of leaders), and finding content not only to agree but also to disagree with.

And a primary audience must be the related professions with special focus on moving forward—architects and builders for design and delivery of new, refreshed, or renovated areas for our physical spaces that aren't like the others they build and aren't completely coming back as they were before. If we thought that those who design our spaces didn't understand or design with our services and workers in mind, much less users—it's going to get worse. We must get other professions to step back and take an honest look at not only what we have but also what we don't have, which includes money, workers, and space, much less clear understanding of what we do in our public and behind-the-scenes spaces. If just one chapter or chart helps librarians convey the fact that we don't "read all day" but neither do we stand around in public all day or just need to "touch down" a few times a day; that our services are vital and—although typically never the most important service—extremely important; that we need safe, responsible office spaces for adults; that our users want dramatically different things from "just fun," including old-fashioned quiet for study and research; that different libraries serve different needs and different populations; that—for goodness' sake—we need storage (I mean who doesn't?); that we aren't able to share space with just anyone to make it less expensive for them; and that many showplace ideas from other edifices they have built or really want to build simply don't translate to our service reality, then I feel my work here is done.

# Introduction

THERE ARE A VARIETY OF TECHNIQUES authors use for introducing content. I prefer to provide as much context as possible—so that information is relevant, more easily understood, memorable, and then applied. In my previous emergency-management publications, I chose to use scenarios for introducing content so that the content is accompanied with specific techniques and practices to address issues and problems—and specifically and typically, those problems and issues raised in scenarios. One of the reasons I felt this technique worked well is because the emergency-management topic is *very* broad and scenarios assisted in narrowing down the breadth and depth of primarily unknown or recently introduced information to managers who need to apply it—often as quickly as possible.

Post-pandemic content, however—although broad and uncharted territory we *must* address across all types and sizes of libraries—*is* more of a single snapshot or issue in this particular time and place in which we all now find ourselves. In fact, much like monographs focusing on specific functions in libraries such as collection management, post-pandemic practices present almost universal or similar—if not identical—issues for moving forward. Although a crisis of heretofore unmet proportions, it *is* more commonly felt than people would have imagined.

So working with the reality that our standard practices and processes will never be the same, I choose the before-and-after approach with the premise "What if we *had* been ready?" In choosing to pose the "impossible question," I found the majority of library managers struggling with the enormity but—overall—in much better shape for addressing issues than most of those around them. Why?

- For decades, libraries have been adapting emergency plans of counties and cities to their own environments, and in many locales they have played and still play a pivotal role—given their size, hours, and environment—in being designated a shelter-in-place for many types and sizes of community or institutional emergency events.
- Libraries have been responsible for disaster planning and preparedness for collections and resources for many years.
- Librarians have played a major role as first responders for large-scale issues such as hurricanes, fires, explosions, and so on. In fact, many recovery funding opportunities—deemed available for application based on first-responder criteria, have included librarians as eligible designees.
- Early plans for library strategic planning have been adapted from and have adopted the emergency-management professional rubric for designing responses based on planning, prevention, response/business continuity, and recovery.
- Long proponents of online resources and services available remotely, libraries have long offered significant content online 24/7.
- As a primary "support" profession, in educational, general public/community, and commercial and government settings, libraries have been positioned to expand support and often lead in supporting their umbrella institutions and entities as they grow in digital and online directions.

In identifying what we would have done *if we had been ready*, I want people to see that they actually have more than they think they do for dealing with the post-pandemic library world and the process and path for moving on, and that by having many of the "cards in the deck," as it were, taking inventory and then action in revising and shuffling the cards may get them much farther than they thought they could get—much more quickly.

# 1

# The Pre-Pandemic Library

## *If We Had Been Ready*

### Pre-COVID

EARLY IN DECEMBER 2019, a colleague came into my office and said—literally—"it's coming." I can remember the look on his face, my first thoughts, and then my concerns about *his* mental and emotional condition. Then—for at least a month—he leaned into my office each time he passed the door, spouting numbers about the move of the virus, the rumors of where it was coming from, and the rapid move of it—as well as the various public theories: "It was created in a lab as part of germ warfare and escaped," and so on. Before that month, I knew him relatively well and greatly admired—and still do—his abilities, his work ethic, and his rational approach to workplace issues; but, while he updated his facts, gave me websites to visit, and became increasingly more (what I thought was) paranoid in his behavior, I can distinctly remember telling my boss when she asked me about it—"Have you *heard* him?"

One night, however, early in February—I watched a documentary on the pandemic of 1918—a terrifying and almost unbelievable look at the United States for more than two years when, intermittently, but for days at a time, "occupied" coffins were stacked on sidewalks in front of homes, waiting to be picked up by funeral homes who brought wagons through the streets. They then piled coffins on the wagons as high as they could, then returned later for those left behind. I silently (and incorrectly now—obviously) comforted myself with the thought that the America of 1918 didn't have the infrastructure for fighting contagions and certainly in 2020, we were ready, so it couldn't happen here or now.

But even more terrifying than the documentary as it unfolded was my realization at the end of the program that the pandemic itself never came to a specific ending or conclusion. So I immediately sought information and research on "how a pandemic ends." This content focused on the strides—or lack of—that scientific professions and specifically medicine have made since 1918, the ambiguity of answers to "how a pandemic ends," the number of people infected in 1918 (one-third of the world that we know of), and directions from public officials that were startlingly similar to the diverse views in 2020 and 2021 but that *did* include wearing a mask, washing your hands, isolating and quarantining those infected, not gathering in crowds of people who know or don't know each other, and closing public spaces and schools.

Frankly, I can't remember the exact moment when or even why I realized my work colleague was right, but I did, and then I turned a corner and began to prepare in earnest. So, with little or no frame of reference other than my own medical history, my emergency-management (EM) work, and the recent content I found on influenza outbreaks and pandemics, I began to build instructions for staff cleaning and then instructed the cleaning to begin on February 7, 2020. And during that same week, although I didn't fill my *garage* with sanitizing products, I began to stock up on cleaning supplies both at work and at home. In the second week of February, one of my managers expressed concern based on what she was hearing and asked if we shouldn't have our frontline staff also begin to wear masks—which I thought at the time was one of the hardest decisions I had to make.

Coincidentally in March, the second edition of my EM book—published in late fall 2019—arrived. I had already been using the forms, templates, and checklists from my first book and had used both the first and second edition for additional forms and a pandemic definition and information. Looking back now, I had given the event equal attention as other emergency events: no more than two pages and it focused on the category of a pandemic event but offered very little. One of my sentences stood out, however (and I ask *not* to be judged by that now): "Although the United States is typically not at risk for some of the more global pandemic issues, there are elements of pandemics to be concerned with including influenza viruses and other viruses such as severe acute respiratory syndrome (SARS)."

Luckily, I reassured myself that the rest of my "pandemics" section was right on point, and I continued to use the content as the outline for my 2020 activities. I soon realized, however, that the:

- cleaning information was good;
- forms, templates, and checklists provided a solid foundation for the approach to managing any event and specifically the pandemic event; and
- the basic communication plan still worked, *but* the book didn't go anyway near far enough to envision a situation so uncontrolled that the world would close—repeatedly—and that many Americans would alternately stay at home and work as usual while others would repeatedly deny reality.

In addition, it was clear that I felt that the 2020 management and leadership infrastructure *was* equipped to either step into or find someone else who could step into emergency-management and leadership roles, but instead quickly saw—during the spring of 2020—chaos in all areas.

When I realized in late March that we needed to move even more quickly, I was also forced to embrace the fact that the profession (and obviously many other professions) was unsure of how to move into uncharted waters for—among other things—ways to balance safety for staff and the public while carrying out methods for ensuring we were meeting our obligations for providing the core values of providing spaces, digital access and infrastructure, information and research, and recreational and cultural content for constituents, so I began to look for more information.

Although I had already reviewed the emergency-management professional literature and content on disaster management for my previous publications and research, I had established a series of steps for myself for not only content from the emergency-management world and the library and information profession but also content in other professions where I felt similar information could be found. From the few very valuable areas I tracked (and still track) with good, specific content, five should be identified: (1) the hotel/motel world under the broad category of "travel industry," (2) workplace infrastructure information found in OSHA content, (3) worker guidance from the world of human resources, and vendor content for not only disas-

ter repair and recovery but also (4) public health and (5) public health crises information.

In tracking these areas—and as librarians do—I categorized the information and research and it was clear that before January 1, 2020, the library and information profession had extensive content on some of the *specific* areas we were facing; there was older but specific information from (what led me to write my books initially) 9/11, Oklahoma City, and the Olympics, and when reviewed for looking at the big picture, it was clear:

- the library and information profession offered best practices content on disaster planning (primarily) for library materials (model management documents including strategic plans, model budgets, preventive policies, and procedures) and facilities recovery from fire, water, and pestilence, and so on;
- library and information professionals had been and continue to be identified as experts in preservation and conservator facility issues and materials/resources;
- specific vendors had been identified in multiple incidents with recommended products, services, practices, and training;
- safety and security research and information had a strong focus on protection from mischievous and criminal behavior—with a focus on terrorism—as well as online safety for users (all ages), for user data, organizational data, and data safety in general;
- some prevention activities were recommended with a focus on the health of workers and users for flu and cold "seasons" with concern for cleaning keyboards and cleaning phones in public spaces (if there are any, anymore!); and
- professional development curriculum (disaster preparedness—with a *resource* and services recovery focus) was available for education for workers and users on materials handling, materials recovery, data safety, general business continuity, and customer service in difficult times.

Particularly helpful content was and still is available and presented effectively using scenarios and case study methods for chronicling *specific* events, discussing business continuity, and offering steps to recovery with preventive information. Also, the profession had and continues to have a growing body of content on specific events or activities taking place not only in new facilities but also in historic, aging, and flawed buildings as well as in shared spaces and repurposed buildings (e.g., a big box store to a library, a renovated mall for city services including public library, shared computer facilities, etc.). Additional helpful content was and is still available covering issues on staff and user safety and focusing on the presence of or recovery from problems such as mold, air quality, and pestilence and—among other things—cleaning product issues (mixing chemicals from mixing product, etc.) as well as the types of materials used for cleaning and handling resources.

Library and information professional literature also had and continues to provide current and replicable planning examples (benchmarks, effective practices) from operational, short-term, and long-term strategic plans and content, institutional and staff goals, and content built into mission, vision, and value statements. Also available and generally required for training workers were plans from umbrella institutions, community content, and peer entities on active shooter issues (the fastest-growing area) and major weather issues—many new in their intensity and severity—for hurricane, storm, and tornadic incidents and thus flood planning in private and public K–12 school districts, city and county governments, institutions of higher learning, and the support services within them as well as special libraries located within entities such as hospitals, government agencies, and commercial entities. Other unique but helpful area plans—pre-2020—include plans to use library spaces qualifying as shelters-in-place for communities and victim and community support services that include library staff as first responders.

Other pre-2020 library projects and services content included librarians:

- providing infrastructure identification of standard nomenclature for all stages of disasters and emergency situations;
- aggregating information on disaster and emergency activities such as the causes of these activities and content (guidelines, standards, policies and procedures, and government documents) for users on individual and community economic recovery; and
- designing information and access pathways linking patrons to accurate and timely information and research.

So, why didn't libraries—or many others for that matter—learn from the past because, of course, the pandemic wasn't our first disaster and—in fact—wasn't our first pandemic or public health crisis that either global society or U.S. society had dealt with. Looking at what we had experienced, however, the world hadn't seen such a widespread crisis, and certainly the United States had not.

The primary "recent" and most similar event in its breadth and depth, the 1918 pandemic, produced a little content on public health and use of public spaces but understandably—given the date—little if anything on library public *spaces*. The more recent and much smaller related events (general viral influenzas, H5N1, the 1997 viral avian or bird flu) did not cause *widespread* problems for libraries, with no more than one thousand cases occurring in the United States. There is also very little found regarding libraries (of any type) addressed in the general news or in pandemic literature for either the 1918 pandemic or contagion issues since.

## Post–March 1, 2020

When pandemic issues and specifically life-and-death public health issues came into focus as a living, breathing, and virtually uncontrollable situation in March of 2020, libraries overall may have been better prepared than most to face the situation facing the world based on their previous disaster planning—but primarily only for resources. In fact, library leaders—having created plans and experienced events to manage and mitigate many disaster and emergency resource situations as well as continuity, recovery, and "return to normalcy" in the past—could rely on some existing content, some designed for them and available from local, state, and federal entities. Very quickly, however, major issues were identified as needing attention in 2020 regarding facilities and resources as well as worker and user safety within the space. These issues included:

- spaces with closely placed, shared furniture (event space, study space, research workstations, leisure reading, and cultural spaces);
- close proximities for services assistance and programming;
- individual technology workstations positioned closely due to limitations not only on space but also on facility power support and older wiring;
- hardwired user workstations not easily moved;
- lack of ubiquitous wireless;
- spaces within the libraries' already smaller spaces such as departments for unique users, small study spaces, and small innovation spaces;
- services based on touching resources for the exchange of materials;
- shared technology in large but primarily smaller spaces;
- materials and resources designed for touch (children's area resources, gaming, topical and heavily used periodicals, newspapers, etc.);
- the "browsing" service—deliberately planned and executed for users in small spaces;
- close exchanges with workers assisting at public desks/services; and

- programs designed for primarily small and medium-sized groups.

And—although occupancy restrictions are adhered to in terms of furniture, footprints, and floorplans—libraries are typically smaller than needed, are busy, and often find themselves filled to capacity and beyond. The nature of the client or user is one who—typically—has frequent comings and goings at their convenience, making the identification of high-use and low-use periods of time difficult to design, and increasing the difficulty of offering staggered worker schedules and "down time" as well as limiting availability for scheduled in-depth cleaning—challenging for even the largest of spaces meeting distancing guidelines required, recommended, or used based on good business practices.

Obviously these determinations, information, and research pieces weren't all produced after 2020 began. Instead, my review of pre-2020 content and of content for "now" vs. projected information needed was an attempt to determine if *any* content was going to be helpful in providing the path forward for the post-COVID library. I determined that although some usable content is available, it is important to first identify the important roles that we know libraries and librarians *do* play. With those roles in mind, I compiled content that librarians can use specifically related to general information on public health crises. As issues progressed in 2020 and 2021, usable content included information and research around:

- librarians' roles in working as contact tracers;
- exploring facilities issues from school library umbrella institutions including relaxed school district guidelines, rules, and regulations (all K–12) for wireless accessibility such as a federal determination that wireless access can vary for greater service distance;
- tracking E-rate dollars guidelines, rules, and regulations (primarily school with some public libraries) that expand to creating or expanding wireless hotspots;
- illustrating the need for access issues regarding open libraries for copiers, free federal forms, and the subsequent possible need—if closed—for temporary delay/suspension of requirements for tax deadlines, and so on;
- tracking budget issues such as broadband funding initial and expanded costs to public institutions;
- identifying specific ongoing needs for the federal definition of public libraries as "essential" and "educational" institutions;
- identifying approved subject headings and keyword terminology for the classification and indexing of pandemic information, data, and research;

- identifying the need for pandemic data aggregation for the design and delivery of pathways of information and research;
- providing ongoing assistance for combating "fake news" specifically relating to contagion events;
- assistance with copyright issues with specificity to online posting, correct attribution of accurate information, and so on;
- identifying issues with the need for expanded e-resources and specifically e-book issues such as cost of content needed for employment assistance, lifelong learning, all levels of academic/school information with home schooling, self-help materials, DIY information, pandemic recovery content, and so on;
- supporting equitable access to hardware and software to address digital have-nots;
- supporting subject-specialist and community librarians as first-responder teams for pandemic assistance related to information and services; and
- maintaining access to multiple-format (including print/paper) materials through services such as contactless resource delivery.

In 2020 and 2021, library managers and leaders quickly realized gaps and needed resources as well as necessary content and data for solutions to issues and situations—many of which have never been fully addressed and more that have never been realized in libraries worldwide.

In addition, in reviewing benchmark disaster plans and strategic plans, most do not cover or even allude to the enormity of the pandemic situation. Even worse, infrastructures did not and still do not move quickly enough to provide either decisions or the information for others to make decisions—in part because pandemic event components changed so often that plans were quickly and repeatedly outdated, often multiple times a week. In addition, many critical, formal partnerships (local EM departments and response teams, etc.) were *not* in place prior to March 2020 except for some weather-related groups. It was hard to put groups together during events as well as educate them, and many (some will say *most*) library and information decision makers (boards, councils, administrators, government structures, partnership leaders, and managers) simply did not know what to do and continued to both flounder and founder.

### What If We Had Been Ready?

The best way to envision the other side of a very bad situation is to design a scenario that—in very general terms—uses the premise that we all know what it looks like now, but how would it look if we had been ready?

Or prepared? Or really prepared? Or—at the very least—more prepared than we were?

This book strives to say just that, across the wide spectrum of issues brought about by the pandemic. So rather than saying outright, "Do these ten things," this content provides a look at areas such as "services" and "communication" and states that if we had been ready to go when March 2020 began, here's what the "landscape" of our work would have looked like—with a critical understanding that one size does *not* fit all.

Providing this more complete and positive way of looking ahead provides both managers and leaders with the chance to not only see the way it should be but also determine—given what they have—how close they were to "being ready" and determine how long—after the pandemic began—it took to provide at the very least a workable plan. And—as in all things—it's a matter of degrees—that is, we have policy "a," but even though it only covers the first and second critical thing needed, what is important to realize is "at least we have policy a." And, realizing that this situation, no matter how difficult, is not overcome through addressing issues tabula rasa, instead libraries need to review their own complete content, partial content, or benchmarked content from their own or other types of library settings; content from publications; and finally, content from consultants as well as other related businesses and similar settings.

Basically the following seven statements provide an outline of what an organization could and should have in order to move quickly or at the very least to begin to work steadily throughout the event to plan for a future of changes that, although significantly better, will absolutely include new protocols, practices, and even policies to cover other emergency events. What is needed include the following:

1. Employees have a high level of trust in managers and leaders.
2. The organization's human resources—library workers and related groups—must be prepared to quickly shift user or constituent support—through existing or new roles and responsibilities and spaces—and provide an infrastructure to meet the needs of workers who, for example, have been surveyed and identify as needing support.
3. Emergency training is in place and workers successfully completed basic training for decision making for those working in or in charge of frontline services.
4. Workers have articulated job descriptions and departmental and individual goals; however, workers also have special projects for both individual work and work in small, assigned groups.
5. Emergency-management content in the business-continuity phase provides shutdown and closure plans articulated as separate plans or within other emergency, risk, or related plans, and plans that provide direction for both short and longer time periods.
6. Measurement and assessment for standard/basic data gathering and—as needed—immediate and higher-level data remains in place or is quickly put in place using existing forms and practices designed for changing or new situations and for continued, meaningful, data gathering.
7. All organizational plans reflect basic handling of emergency issues and activities including sustaining basic functions, communication, and technology infrastructures as well as those parts of infrastructure tasked with delivering the backbone for business continuity's sustaining or alternate plans.

In looking at chapters, the library's functional areas as well as services, HR content, and other critical areas are reviewed for pandemic information along with lists of items and actions necessary to be ready. At the close of each chapter there is a section that offers new content on smaller environments and complements earlier content on smaller environments as well as a summative list of what would be in place if we had been ready.

The following information summarizes the primary functional areas and services covered as well as content on resources.

## Service Spaces, Support Spaces, and Storage Spaces

Libraries are an interesting combination of environments when looking at their physical spaces. These spaces—historically to present day—range from standalone buildings designed and built exclusively by them and for them, spaces within other structures designed or constructed by them and for them, buildings and spaces renovated for library use, and buildings and spaces given to libraries where they "make do" with what they have. Any combination of the above spaces includes space given to libraries, but *not* planned by or with input from librarians (which, of course, happens frequently but is never recommended).

And, while libraries should have a commitment to designing the best spaces for workers, the primary focus of the profession and those who plan libraries remains to be the success of the *user* through design to meet diverse and ever-changing needs of users (often identified as design thinking). For public service spaces, support spaces, and storage spaces, if we had been ready:

- Public-service user spaces are focused on flexibility with areas designed and able to be customized to situations, events, and user patterns for individual use and collaborative spaces.
- Library furniture for users is chosen to allow for distancing through flexible design (wheels, handles, etc.) and with minimal, if any, cloth upholstery or covering, making it possible to clean surfaces often and systematically. This includes *any* upholstered areas or materials being minimized or (preferred) nonexistent on more physical contact locations such as chair arms and head "rest" areas.
- Technology-driven spaces for users are not (primarily) hardwired but instead supported by power and ubiquitous wireless.
- Worker spaces are focused on flexibility with spaces able to be customized to changing work flows, staff scheduling, collaborative space, and project management and group membership.
- Library furniture for workers (as for users) is chosen to allow for distancing through flexible design (wheels, handles, etc.) and with minimal, if any, cloth upholstery or covering, making it possible to clean surfaces often and systematically. This includes *any* upholstered areas or materials being minimized or (preferred) nonexistent on more physical contact locations such as chair arms and head "rest" areas.
- Technology-driven spaces for workers are not (primarily) hardwired but instead supported by power and ubiquitous wireless.
- Public-service points between users and workers allow for short-term distancing and alternative connection opportunities, then return to one-to-one service connections post-event.
- Safety supplies (facilities/worker cleaning materials, area dividers, stanchions, guiding "ropes" or "police tape," floor standing signage, directional labels, user cleaning materials and supplies, etc.) are plentiful, up-to-date, support maximum sanitizing of resources (chosen for safely mixing during use), and are available through easily accessible storage for workday or post-service-hours cleaning.
- Storage areas are designed to accommodate one person safely, and practices are in place to standardize access (few or one at a time) and use including sign-in sheets and material-removal identification.
- Storage spaces within libraries are available, and if not, libraries invest in secure cabinets for storing materials.
- Storage areas (whether built-in or freestanding and lockable) are of a size to accommodate larger numbers of protective supplies going forward, permanently.

- Content on roles and responsibilities establishing and maintaining safe environments is integrated into the institution's value statements, policies and practices, human resources materials (position descriptions, goals, outcomes, strategies, and tasks), and training curriculum.

After the 2020–2021 pandemic, the reality is that user and worker spaces, policies, and practices will not return to pre-COVID normalcy. So in both short- and long-term recovery and future planning, libraries will use specific distancing numbers for the maximum use of space that withstands public health concerns on the pandemic scale as well as the more common, frequently occurring (even annual) communicable disease or cough, cold, and flu seasons.

## Scenarios for Collections and Resources

For decades, libraries have been striving to find the perfect balances of print/paper vs. digital. Accomplishing this feat is an ongoing challenge, and there are a variety of balances based on not only funding available but also size and type of library and user profiles. Being ready for a pandemic, however, does not mean the library is already perfectly balanced nor that it can be quickly balanced; instead any collection building is as an ever-evolving exercise that is accomplished through an acquisitions evidence-based model that focuses on collection assessment and a review and integration of accepted standards that are articulated and regularly evaluated. This evaluation—a well-thought-out measurement and assessment—is of not only a *perceived* need but also the need for relevance and accountability with the use of data for overall usage, identified needs, and the impact of societal issues, changing access, content, and formats. Specifically:

- Managers—overall and during emergency times—must articulate rationale and justifications for expenditures as well as reasons for moving money among accounts. *(Organizations are guided by and may also be hampered by the umbrella organization's accounting practices, state laws, federal law, and other laws governing funding.)*
- Vendor partnerships are identified and established and—when needed—shift to support new populations and different access and user needs, with changes such as bundled costs, temporary access to resources, and billing practices (blankets, delayed billing, etc.) to assist the library in moving among acquisitions practices.

- The library's collection-management policy allows for contingency changes to address issues including hiatus on practices such as acceptance of gifts and donations; immediate turnaround of materials, gifts, donations; materials in open-access areas and browsing availability; subscription models providing fewer than twelve-month billing/accessibility periods; general use of materials such as circulation and access to resources unable to be adequately cleaned such as periodicals, maps, sheet music, jackdaws, kits, realia, media, games, toys, flashcards, rare materials, special collections or materials on loan—to name examples of types and formats.
- The library's resources—designed to connect users to materials (guides, pathfinders, bibliographies, etc.)—are available online for digital access or checkout.

If we had been ready:

- The library explores and maintains a variety of collection acquisitions and expenditure models to meet the variety and diversity of user needs.
- Vendor partnerships exist to support flexible acquisitions operations models.
- The library has up-to-date management documents including a collection-management policy and extensive, in-depth collection user guides.

### Assessment and Accountability

Libraries have long been known for counting many aspects of their work such as the number of resources, facilities visits/users, service usage, and resource usage. Now libraries continue their practices of one-dimension counting of the number of resources, services, and users but also measure many levels and elements of resources, services, and users as well as staff expertise, measures of success of programs, resources, and other sources, as well as levels of success of user interactions and user learning outcomes. In today's libraries:

- The majority of decisions are or should be data-driven, evidence-based decisions.
- All levels or nuances of service delivery and resource use as well as worker expertise, impact, value, benefit, and worth are identified, articulated, measured, and assessed.
- Space usage is clearly defined, measured, and assessed.
- Librarians regularly identify, communicate, and measure their specific goals and outcomes in user success.

- Libraries use a variety of measurement and assessment tools uniformly throughout the institution.
- Measurement and assessment data-gathering tools can be quickly customized for emergency situations that suspend standard access, practice, and services.

Although libraries had primarily left behind the need to articulate the specific rationale for their *basic* existence annually ("Why should we give you *any* money?"), pandemic issues have brought back the need to rearticulate and alter—as necessary—why and how services and resources will be delivered in the future, continued use of space, need for new space and physical resources, and even more contemporary issues such as why and how libraries are defined as first responders.

Libraries need to revise their existing value, worth, benefit, and impact definitions and aggregate data to craft proactive content on library existence and funding needs. Unique assessment and accountability areas must be identified and integrated (worker time spent on existing and new roles and responsibilities, and remote roles and uses). Libraries must create snapshots and—as possible—continue to aggregate data on what staff do remotely specific to user success. In addition, libraries must maintain their ongoing focus on user needs—focusing on the haves and have-nots—and the need to, in post-COVID initial recovery phases, continue to justify why it is critical to return to in-person user services.

If we had been ready:

- Pandemic decisions are tracked and explained with data and evidence.
- Service delivery, resource use, staff expertise, and impact, value, benefit, and worth are identified, articulated, measured, assessed, and used in reporting and marketing continuing or short-term changes as well as long-term changes.
- Space usage is clearly defined, measured, and assessed with paradigm shifts designed to visualize and explain situations pre-event, during the event, and post-event.
- Library, departmental, and individual goals and outcomes are scheduled to be reviewed post-event.
- Measurement and assessment tools are used uniformly throughout the institution with the evaluation timeline set for post-event.

### Maintenance, Upkeep, and Safety

When library-management problems are articulated at the highest levels, few list maintenance, upkeep, and safety (related to health) or even "cleaning" as a major detriment to user or worker satisfaction. The reality is, however, that library buildings—no matter the user profile, location, or size or type—are hard to clean and maintain as clean, especially during public health crises. Not only do libraries routinely fight for general facilities cleaning, but also library *materials* have their own set of cleaning problems and—of course—public health can be very seriously at risk.

In today's libraries, the majority of all types and sizes of facilities have protocols in place for cleaning facilities (typically daily before and after open times) with additional practices for regularly scheduled, in-depth or "deep" cleaning for resources, equipment, shelving, upholstered furniture, and wall and floor coverings. Libraries with realia, toys, games, and so on, clean materials between circulations, and children's services or workers at library locations where families with children come to the library will routinely clean any items kept in children's environments. Prepared organizations are also ready for cold and flu season and individual contact issues such as transmissions of poison ivy, and—for many years—libraries had hand sanitizer walls mounted and stand-alone or tabletop units throughout the facility. In addition, public buildings have long had cleaning statements in bathrooms and kitchens regarding washing hands (at the very least), while others have instructions for cleaning work areas between uses such as sinks, public desks, and keyboards.

Ongoing problems do, however, exist in public buildings with every model of maintenance: subcontracted cleaners are not thorough and do not know the nuances needed; regularly hired cleaning staff do not maintain facilities as needed given the size and needs of most environments, and usage-driven cleaning issues; aging structures becoming increasingly harder to clean; and buildings are hard to maintain as—if nothing else!—pest-free zones. Also, libraries typically don't design, request, or require *intensive* sanitizing or cleaning protocols to be completed during a day for either the public or for workers. Nor do libraries require or even create signage to create significant awareness or need for sanitizing protocols for the health of users. Instead, libraries have focused on not eating food in spaces as well as how to keep books clean and the cleaning issues that are likely if these guidelines are not adhered to: destruction of books, permanently stained floor coverings, and pests.

Dealing with the present and getting ready for the future, readiness now requires different and better and—in many cases—standards for immediate safety cleaning as well as overall maintenance of all spaces and resources with which workers and the public come in contact.

If we had been ready:

- Library-management documents (policies, position descriptions, values, customer service practices, etc.) integrate maintenance and health and safety content.
- Signage for users and staff outline individual roles and responsibilities for visiting and using libraries, services, and resources.
- Cleaning and sanitizing protocols are consistent and required, roles are clearly defined, and customer service interactions parallel signs, policies, and practices.
- Protective gear for users and staff is normalized and—when appropriate—required.
- Organizational facilities and resources are systematically cleaned and maintenance contracts outline cleaning protocols for—for example—HVAC units and ducts and public-service equipment such as copiers.
- Cleaning materials are identified and budgeted for and inventories maintained for user and staff cleaning activities for resources and facilities for public-service and staff workspaces and overall interactions.
- Organizations enact strict protocols (when appropriate) for facility entry and exit practices.
- Library spaces (user and worker) are designed for safe distancing for general times as well as designed and ready to deploy (with systematic assessment) for emergency situations.

### Staff Members, Library Workers, and Supporters

Librarians, library workers, volunteers, stakeholders, partners, and—to some perceived extent—vendors have been in upheaval due to the 2020–2021 pandemic. This unprecedented-in-our-time-pandemic (pre, during, and post) upheaval is particularly difficult to deal with because typically our organizations have little "dramatic change" in any given year, much less any given month or week!

It is safe to say then that society—and especially libraries as busy public places—should not expect a simple return to normal. In fact, it is highly unlikely that much and in some cases most of library operations, resources, and services—and especially facilities—will return to our definition of *normal*—in the short term—*because* all types and sizes of libraries and organizational infrastructures (community, institution, organization) have changed along with global society itself.

As leaders, sustaining our employees and workers—both individuals and workgroups—must be a priority throughout any unique times and beyond. The more unique the situation, as pandemics prove to be, the more leaders strive to not only sustain but also motivate and nurture. It is equally as important, however, in a manager role, to reassess all Human Resources (HR) management content aspects including overarching vision and mission statements; values statements; policies and procedures (even down to the task level); primary and secondary documents; individual goals and strategies; and especially measurement and assessment including all data such as user information and resource data but—with HR in mind—especially in-person and remote work, shifts and changes, behaviors, expectations, and documents tracking performance such as activity completion, and so on. Additional areas for concern are training, staff communication, risk issues and protocols for employees, workplace resource use on- and off-site, and safety for employees.

If we had been ready:

- All organizational overarching management documents integrate commitment to, concern for, and practices supporting the health and safety of employees, library workers, and stakeholders.
- HR management content such as policies and procedures, primary and secondary documents, individual goals and strategies, and performance-driven measurement and assessment include content regarding the safety and health focus of staff as well as staff and user interaction protocols.
- The organization regularly surveys staff and workers to determine satisfaction levels with position roles and responsibilities, public-service space, and support space environs and organizational culture.
- The organization maintains a robust program that focuses on workplace motivation.
- The organization maintains an orientation, training, and continuing-education program with curriculum for EM, risk, and—specifically—serious public health risks such as pandemics.
- There are opportunities for critical continuity and recovery activities, orientation, training, continuing education, and professional development.

In today's libraries, training and educating staff focuses on primary and secondary or basic roles and responsibilities for library operations and functions. Intermediate-level roles and responsibilities focus on obviously more complex aspects of resources and services as well as the customization designed to support unique user profiles. Advanced training and education content includes specialized work occurring in expanding, new, and unique areas of the organization. In the past decades, the greatest variety of training and education integrated into libraries has been in the design and delivery of unique technology (hardware and software) tools and their impact on policies and practices and varying needs to keep pace

with societal changes, EM focusing on resource recovery, and specialized customer services. In today's pandemic situation, training and educating all workers is especially critical, as behaviors as well as practices must change. Also, behaviors are best changed through changes in attitude and opinion—which require different training and education materials.

Although existing training and education can be adapted to critically needed pandemic changes in some ways, managers must identify aspects and activities surrounding pandemic continuity and recovery categories that expand dramatically across the breadth and depth of existing and new work roles and responsibilities, changing technology, business locations, service and resource flow, and dramatically different access and delivery of resources and staff expertise. Given the rapidly changing nature of pandemic situations as well as how a single pandemic changes during its "life," it is difficult and in some cases unreasonable to expect to have a pandemic curriculum "ready to go" not only for immediate need but also for the most serious aspects of health situations.

Solutions for identifying and integrating new content quickly include managers pre-identifying the *changes* that must be made, matching up what is already in place, and then identifying sources to go to that provide updated curriculum. In addition, orientation, training, continuing education, and professional-development training that introduces new content or illustrates position changes or new or expanded roles and responsibilities must be accompanied with paradigm shifts of old jobs to new—sometimes including revised position descriptions, paradigm shifts of old to new spaces and old to new services and how staff deliver services, as well as timelines for learning new roles, scenario or case-method pedagogy, and pre-assessments and post-assessments (perceptions, attitudes, trust, etc.).

If we had been ready:

- Services and resources policies and practices are supported by current, up-to-date policies and practices manuals, online for—as needed—extrapolation and updating for unique, new, and revised situations.
- Emergency resources for new or revised content are identified and can be easily integrated into curriculum.
- HR materials (position descriptions, etc.) are current and can easily and quickly be updated to reflect changing roles.
- Communication plan distribution for HR practices includes all workers in all departments as needed (all employees involved were informed prior to activities

taking place with alternate plans put into effect and necessary training completed).

- Timelines for learning new and revised roles and responsibilities are addressed within basic staff and worker curriculum.
- As applicable, managers must take care to consider HR concerns such as union contracts, issues such as 24/7 facilities, challenges by staff on additional work roles being normalized, and staff concerns on safety during public health crises.

## Communication: Standard Operation and Unique Models

Although the key to any successful environment is good communication, the most critical times for excellence in communication for internal and external individuals and groups is during difficult times and specifically during *uniquely* difficult times. Given the importance of good communication—which can literally mean life and death during a pandemic—ongoing institutional success, and/or the success of management and leadership, initial communication plans or "A" plans must be accompanied with alternate plans including a plan B for more temporary but serious events as well as a plan C for serious and more long-term—if not permanent—changes in the organization and its workers and relationships, resources, services, and facilities.

Even with today's communication departments and workers devoted to the practice of communication as well as the plethora of available communication tools, techniques, and trainings, many organizations struggle with communication. Those that do struggle often have underlying inabilities to deal with management and leadership issues in the organization, and these issues—left alone—cannot be ignored or smoothed over by adequate communication. A spotlight on these issues as well as an exacerbation of the problems caused by these issues is especially problematic during serious events. The 2020–2021 pandemic exposed flaws in systems and infrastructures as well as flawed leadership and management. Although one can't easily or unilaterally bypass or fix leadership and management issues, one can put in a multi-leveled set of communication plans designed to structure successful solutions to problems, allow for performance to be corrected, and improve the overall practices of the organization in general as well as provide a path for the organization to get through the event.

If we had been ready:

- Organizations have staff whose primary job is to focus on general communication with equal but different focus on alternate approaches for communicating during pandemics, in the worst of times.
- The organization's basic communication plan is accompanied with plans A and B ready to deploy as characteristics of the unique, emergency event are revealed and assessed.
- Workers, stakeholders, vendors, and so on, are familiar with communication-plan structures and are aware of underlying and changing communication tools and techniques designed to support the event.
- Libraries maintain communication plans derivative of the organization's communication plans as well as structures to integrate alternate plans into all departmental activity, and departments within the library may need their own communication plans.
- HR management documents include language to define and require worker roles and responsibilities in communication.

## Management: Roles and Responsibilities for Unique Issues and Stepping Up and Stepping In

Management roles and responsibilities vary in times of crises, and during times of *unique* crises, they vary dramatically. In addition to management changes, leadership roles change as well, and there has never been a more important time for leaders to lead than during emergency—and specifically pandemic—events.

Along with changing management and leadership roles, it is important for organizations to identify where management, coordinator, or directive roles could be *shared* and especially a time to identify opportunities for leaders to step up for the first time or to expand their pre-COVID leadership roles. To accomplish this—especially due to the need for organizations to focus on sustaining and, more than likely, nurturing and motivating HR at every level—organizations must, as they do with communication plans, have both management opportunities to include activities such as delegating, ad hoc group work, design of management documents, and project management as well as explore additional leaders and leadership opportunities for motivating workers to keep going and speak up as needed and to focus on sustaining a positive organizational culture overall and a positive culture for the pandemic emergency response team as well as ad hoc or temporary pandemic project and service groups or teams.

If we had been ready:

- Management roles and responsibilities are clearly defined in general and during emergency times/situations.

- Leadership roles and responsibilities are clearly defined in general and during emergency times/situations.
- Position descriptions identify shared aspects of management and leadership roles at appropriate levels.
- Additional management and leadership roles and opportunities are identified in the organization.
- Pathways into management and leadership roles, in general, but especially during emergency times, are clearly defined for workers along with opportunities articulated and training identified for expanding worker-management and leadership-competency toolkits.
- Emergency plans for organizations identify both individual and shared management and leadership roles.
- The emergency orientation, training, continuing education, and professional development required to take advantage of management and leadership roles, responsibilities, and opportunities are identified in emergency plans.
- Measures of performance success for short-term and long-term individual and shared management and leadership are defined for emergency situations including timelines and methods of evaluation.

## Leadership: Roles and Responsibilities for Unique Issues and Stepping Up and Stepping In

There are many aspects of pandemics that call for leadership roles and responsibilities to be separated from management roles and responsibilities, carefully articulated, delegated to someone else in the organization, or identified as appropriate for assistance from external persons—such as stakeholders or community peers. Because of the seriousness of the pandemic as an emergency event, the need for leadership is critical and must be continuous and systematically applied. In addition, in pandemics in general, spokespeople must be knowledgeable about the event itself, including what a pandemic is, what it "does," how it progresses, and how the situation affects workers as well as users.

And because of the seriousness and immediacy of medical issues in pandemics, leaders creating new information or using templates or benchmark information must have core knowledge, including an awareness of the behaviors of the contagion or virus, necessary preventive behaviors of organizations, effects of viruses on users, effects on workers, transmission between and among workers and users, requirements for maintaining viral-free facilities, and consequences of the variety of treatments. And—although most of this content comes

from management directives—leaders need to be able to be specific on organization culture and issues that drive morale of workers and users.

If we had been ready:

- Leadership roles and responsibilities critical for emergency events are clearly defined.
- Ad hoc/temporary leadership roles and opportunities are identified and matched to professional-development content and program goals.
- Emergency orientation and training identifies processes required to support and take advantage of leadership roles as well as providing guidelines on including or transitioning to accept leadership roles.
- Measures of performance success for short-term and long-term leadership are defined for emergency situations including timelines and methods of evaluation.

## Organizational Design Immediate, Short-Term, and Permanent Changes

Although making significant changes to the organization and its structure isn't required nor recommended during emergencies or unique situations such as pandemics, managers must inventory practices to make sure existing services and operations are going to be successful within any changed departments, services, and so on. In the absence of identified roles and responsibilities or in the case of the organizations where there is a perceived inability that a group or department cannot be successful *or* at the determination that—for whatever reason—the processes in place are not successful, administrators should consider alternate routes for operations for—at the very least—the pandemic time period.

At that time, organizations can consider shifting roles and responsibilities within the existing structure as well as creating short-term, long-term, or permanent workgroups. And, although existing workgroups should be able to address all issues for the well-organized environment, issues surrounding the most unique situations may necessitate unique training or roles and responsibilities for existing groups or revisiting goals and strategies early in the timeline.

The better the administration, and the management and leadership within the organization, the more likely it is that this will be done appropriately with an open discussion of issues, a variety of choices identified, and pilot or trial periods. Even within the shortest of timelines for the pandemic and even with the most flawed performances, the administrator should not do this in a vacuum nor in the absence of individuals who are involved. Poor decision-making processes, poor communication about processes, and badly deployed changes result in trust issues and greatly reduce the possibility of success of any new or changed approaches to the organization's operations.

If we had been ready:

- Organizational structures have a well-articulated operating plan (A); a plan B with a plan for emergency short-term actions, activities, and so on; and a plan C for emergency long-term actions.
- Departments and services throughout the organization have their performance routinely assessed for satisfactory levels of operations.
- Organizational issues and problems that need to be solved are discussed with a variety of departments, managers, and leaders, and short-term or long-term plans are enacted to achieve satisfactory performance levels.
- The timelines to deal with pre-COVID and during-COVID issues exist in templates to provide a structure for planning for pandemic and post-pandemic issues and successful processes for solving problems.

## Mistakes, Pitfalls, Failures, and Recovery

It is not unusual in unique, emergency times for workers, administrators, stakeholders, leaders (if separate from managers), or other designees to make a mistake, experience a pitfall or failure, and—given the gravity of the situation—need to recover quickly. Organizations should also be aware that mistakes should be immediately dealt with if there are ongoing issues known to the organization, including issues such as:

- a lack of or misplaced organizational trust;
- negative perceptions of organization and control;
- worker performance;
- user success;
- violation of the institutions' guidelines;
- possible violation of local, state, regional, federal, program, or discipline-related practices;
- failures in services and resource delivery;
- performance in organizational standards; and
- performance of existing organizational and departmental staff.

An important part of EM is the identification of existing, recommended processes for managing mistakes, or if there are no articulated processes or there isn't one for handling issues like mistakes, the administration has to establish new practices for recognizing, gathering information, and then handling mistakes quickly and appropriately.

If we had been ready:

- The climate of the organization is routinely assessed for the presence or lack of presence of trust.
- Organizational problems are identified and integrated into continuity and recovery.
- Mistakes are considered an acceptable part of management, leadership, and taking risks, with a focus on learning from mistakes.
- Policies and processes in the organization are in place to identify mistakes without threat of retribution or sanction.
- Failure plays a role in the organization and is used as a catalyst for discussion, recovery, and learning.

## Service Access and Delivery

The foundational services are often among the first services to disappear or be delayed in difficult times. And there are many reasons for the delay or disappearance of core areas such as service access and delivery, but libraries struggle with decisions for delay, as the overarching themes inherent in these services include the critical role services play in the community and in the lives of the community members. In addition, at the heart of these services is the overall commitment to providing lifelong learning, access to educational support, recreational materials and programs, culture resources, and—in general—core educational content and access to research and information. Libraries committed to serving their patrons find it hard to discontinue, delay, or downsize—even though public health issues may well affect library staff and workers.

In fact, and in an increasing number of emergency situations, with one of the most serious times being the pandemic, the role of libraries and librarians is the role of the first responder on the frontlines who provides technology for workers but specifically users when there is none, offers assistance to individuals for their recovery, and maintains the community infrastructure including the destination. These services are necessary to remain open and enabled by libraries when other support areas in the community are limited, when increased costs are required, or when partner or competing services have failed.

If we had been ready:

- Library collections represent balanced, broad content of e-resources and print/paper content to ensure access while the library is closed.
- Library services offer the opportunity for users to "check out" and take equipment and connectiv-

ity home to provide access to resources while the library is closed.

- Service access and delivery for electronic and print/paper materials, reference, information and instruction expertise, and other resources such as realia are the library's foundational services. These services and their delivery are available during emergencies due to expert design of digital content pathways/gateways, strong redundancies of infrastructure, partnerships, and commitment to 24/7/365 user needs.

## Public Relations, Marketing, and Branding

The role of marketing and branding during possibly more lengthy difficult pandemic situations and post-pandemic cannot be minimized. And while a new/newer image and content do not supplant the institution's central or core mission, it is often valuable because:

- the library's existing role or value remains a stated focus and commitment to users;
- a new approach of a new brand for justification or accountability reaffirms the institution's assistance role in community member lives;
- new approaches with a defining brand recharacterize libraries and often provide new content and evidence for continued or new funding requests for resources and services;
- a rebrand may assist in continuing to define and focus on employee expertise; and
- ongoing marketing and public relations for users or customers are critical to communicating to the user and potential user.

If we had been ready:

- Marketing content for core activities is flexibly designed to include up-to-date continuity issues such as pandemic requirements, care of resources, and facilities design.
- A secondary and possibly temporary brand to advertise continuity of services and resources is identified and deployed quickly.

## Users

Although most if not all of the content in library monographs addresses users (e.g., selecting materials for users; user access to resource services and facilities; designing spaces with users in mind), pandemics—with a focus on COVID-19—cause managers and leaders to take ad-

ditional steps in business continuity and the future in all types and sizes of libraries. And, although different types and sizes involve different aspects of issues, there is a common set of issues for "now" and for "moving forward."

To manage these issues (planning and maintaining for and around these issues), first they must be realized—especially because most of them are new to library environments. *Note:* Most of these concerns are also felt by workers and stakeholders and must be addressed for healthy workplaces—environments, practices, culture, and teamwork—with slightly different issues.

The list of issues related to users includes: fear, lack of value, anger/entitlement, and ignorance/lack of awareness. And, although many of these aspects are completely foreign to users or potential users or funders of library settings and services, managers must address these for business-continuity operational planning, incident data and issue aggregation, and on-the-job training. In addition and simultaneously, managers must begin work for post–COVID-19 operational and strategic planning, on-the-job and service culture assessment and training, annual and longer-term budgeting, data and issue/incident collection, evaluation and outcomes, and new environmental scanning to design profiles for meeting the existing and future needs and overall accountability for users, potential users, stakeholders, decision makers, and advisory and governing bodies. In addition, libraries must assess their public relations, marketing, and branding to address and correct—as much as possible—causes, issues, reactions, and responses.

If we had been ready:

For some time, libraries have sought to position themselves as safe havens for users and potential users. These safe havens are not only for people who think differently and need information but also for those who want to feel comfortable in asking for and discussing issues that are socially difficult and—in many ways—may be dangerous to address. This positioning has been "played out" by language used in creating slogans, branding, and the image of the library including physical spaces, content, expression, and support. Terminology used in public relations, marketing, instructions, and labeling, and so on, now carries messages that can be called into question during and after COVID-19. If we had been prepared, issues would be easier to manage, and "better prepared" looks like:

- Library brands, slogans, and logos can be quickly adjusted to convey different messages to users.
- Physical spaces are balanced (privacy vs. flexibility for visibility/line of sight) to offer opportunities to focus but avoid potentially difficult encounters.
- Based on systematic scanning and identification of influential contacts, outreach and collaboration

practices are in place for library managers to connect with external assistance to deal with new or expanded social issues.

- Issues addressed in strategic plans as well as the design of advisory groups and community contacts include addressing and combatting fear of public spaces, other users, and so on; value of library resources and services addresses the range of print/paper, online, and specifically unique expertise of staff; influencers are prepared to step in to educate and diffuse user anger and entitlement issues; and the library's new services and approaches to services are recognizable and easy to address to stakeholders (for advocacy) and decision makers.

### Returning to Start Over

It may be easier to return to our libraries, or—if you are already back, or if you have never left—it may be easier to look ahead than we think. But is it a reality that many changes are here to stay? And what *is* different about this emergency event—the pandemic? What did we learn from these difficult last months?

### Where Is the Good News?

(With a little not-so-good news, and then some bad news at the end.)

Libraries—during normal or typical operations—have long had a variety of practices for workers, users, and resources regarding the very broad issues of "health" and "safety." And while these practices have taken into account many aspects of practices and issues, the key word to focus on in this process is *variety* because there are many practices (and some have been intermittent) with few—if any—sets of "required" or recommended practices. And while the lack of required actions and the variety of situations and practices exist (*not* necessarily a bad thing), the early days of the pandemic should have taught us a lesson when—literally—hundreds of people tuned in to dozens of online meetings, forums, "trainings," and webinars that resulted in fewer shared ideas or recommendations and many more shared feelings of angst with "I don't know—what are *you* doing?" moments.

But in trying to identify "good," what *was* extraordinarily good were those events by OCLC's Project REALM, where the information was always timely, current, evidence-based, and understandable and provided real answers to questions as well as the myriad suggestions in areas that simply hadn't been considered. Most managers, however, had *many* different kinds of

questions and were left to call on those both internal and external people who they felt knew more, or those in similar settings or those who had successfully weathered previous events with specific practices. Besides these experts, many entities stepped in with good but often more statewide or otherwise localized webinars, blog postings, online guides, and information pathfinders.

In addition, although also primarily used for interpreting statewide and federal information, county-level FEMA operations with widely representative emergency response teams (ERT) were helpful with internal and external experts from both the emergency-management world and a more specialized world of recovery. These ERTs weighed in to assist institutions as they sought answers to the possibilities and hazards for open, hybrid settings as well as closed settings with or without services such as curbside or contactless delivery of resources.

In addition to these practices, library managers took action based on activities from past situations—when it was determined that relevant behaviors could once again be adapted and successful. These included:

- libraries focusing on materials and resource preservation and conservator work (the most expert and in-depth work);
- cleaning product safety issues for use when writing procedures for making decisions for purchasing, storage, application, mixing, and so on;
- the need for workers to wear protective coverings during major cleanings and handling of materials;
- the need for workers (including groups such as book-sale volunteers) to wear protective coverings for safety when handling older or possibly damaged materials;
- the need for workers in rare books settings to wear protective clothing to protect both themselves and rare materials;
- "well building" issues in general for temperature, circulation, HVAC; and
- related "well building" facility issues regarding renovations, repairs, remodels, and new facilities.

These previously used, very wide range of practices after intermittent and more global issues included lessons learned from past events: print/paper mail protocols and ricin poisonings; extreme weather events causing destruction; fires with fire and water and smoke-related damages; vandalism; pestilence damages; and general health and trauma and well-being issues for workers and users found in blogs, sustainability discussions, and association online guides.

Other good news from 2020–2021 includes:

- Almost "overnight," libraries experienced an unprecedented shakeup of long-standing practices where ongoing and typical approaches—often believed to be sacrosanct—became "not the norm," and many policies, procedures, and practices were halted, overhauled, or ceased in practice.
- Returning to more normal or more standard practices after alternate approaches were taken makes it easier for libraries to keep or make changes—now based on comparisons and data—that work better for them and directly and indirectly fixing existing issues and in the long run moving forward.
- Major changes as well as quantum leaps were experienced not only in umbrella organizations but also in communities that previously were moving too slowly toward twenty-first-century changes. Post-COVID practices, however, find that many strides have been made whether it was redirected funding; already-altered, fixed, or expanded technology infrastructure; and uniquely authorized COVID-19 recovery funding; as a result, many libraries feel they do not have as far to go to be able to continue to progress quickly while sustaining positive changes.
- Managers now have opportunities to rebuild and redesign organizations and existing teams or build new teams and organizations—with quickly but effectively trained new managers and leaders.
- Worker roles and responsibilities in both large and small organizations were updated—almost overnight—with much teaching and learning already taking place for use of expanded technology-driven hardware and software.
- Continuing education and staff development were not only focused on but also integrated into the organization both to learn new resources and to expand or enhance skillsets.

## Where Is the Bad News?

It stands to reason that in a well-managed organization with current management operational documents, communication *and* emergency plans in place would assist us for emergency-event business continuity, recovery, and ultimately return. Not necessarily, however, and unfortunately bad news post-COVID comes from any one of a number of issues, most of which were unrecognized, partially or completely out of our control.

- During these unprecedented public-health concerns, we quickly realized—early on—that there was an expectation that "frontline" organizations would remain open, which obviously to us meant there was an

risk to frontline staff. Many library workers then, attracted to work in libraries because of audiences with lower-risk and low-conflict services, found themselves with few choices—out in front with fewer-than-needed protective plans, knowledge-based practices, and resources in place, with all users being identified as "high risk" and all service exchanges—worker to worker as well as user to worker—ripe for conflict. And—whether you are working in closed conditions with some services, business continuity, or within first-time return to physical facilities, high-risk and conflict issues remain and will for some time.

- Library workers, among the lowest paid and often without insurance, were asked to—and in some cases expected to—work without incentives or reduced work (in a world where many people returning to work received incentives and bonuses). Instead they were expected to work in jobs (often completely new ones) that they weren't hired for and that they didn't choose and were told to be grateful that they had jobs—and were *not* always told in the nicest way. And while those deciding and communicating were often not their library managers, few tried to focus on processes that *would* explain it better while realizing these workers were among the most vulnerable of workers providing face-to-face support in environments (city, county, educational settings, etc.).
- Public and nonprofit administrators are often not able to and some not prone to mandating that user behaviors be limited in certain ways based on local, state, and federal legal issues, and that will continue. Many libraries do not have either enough of their own workers or safety and protective employees (police, security, etc.) available to manage problems created by requiring PPE or limiting at points of entry. And—frankly—library staff do not have an interest in, the skillset for, or the authority to turn people away at the door.
- Frontline staff—often many people of color—are risking their health and possibly life through fear of losing their jobs or their commitment to helping users on the front lines. Clearly—given the disproportionate number of people of color we often see on the front lines—it is an equity issue and must be treated as such.

More bad news is:

- Managers of organizations are ill-equipped—given the dramatic differences between pandemics and many other emergency situations—for going back in or returning to more standard services, since as much as 100 percent of their time needs to be spent on recovery issues and worker well-being, retraining, and possibly reassigning. In fact, it would be more honest to say returning to a more normal environment must include rebuilding organizational culture, rebranding teams, and rebuilding trust in organizational decision making—or, quite simply, "all" things human resources.

- Managers will have to handle more things—at least in the beginning—that we have less control over than we would like, including: umbrella organizations mandating same or increased hours or timelines for reinstating services; users pushing for taxpayer services to reopen; users seeking greater access and bandwidth; groups needing support for group activities that may be unavailable (study rooms, community room use, instruction, programming); users seeking more technology as well as no- or low-cost technology; users seeking relaxed rules for protective measures; and budget cuts due to pandemic-caused economic downturns.

Meanwhile, it is of critical importance for managers and leaders to be as transparent as possible in decision making and to use established communication and enhanced tools as well as—as much as possible—cross-level and cross-functional design teams to plan based on sound standards for design-thinking principles, "group think," and collegial decision making.

Table 1.1 illustrates what would have happened if we had been ready in larger libraries.

**TABLE 1.1**
**If We Had Been Ready**

| Chapter and Area | If We Had Been Ready (in-text statement list) | Process Owner/Creator Can Be One or More of the Following: | Have/Last Review Date |
|---|---|---|---|
| The Pre-Pandemic Library: If We Had Been Ready | Managing change—and specifically change related to emergency situations—is integrated into roles and responsibilities for all managers in the organization. | administration, human resources, area managers, HR advisory employee group | annual review, fall review for pandemic specificity and safety |
| | EM training has been identified; individuals and groups have attended and successfully completed basic training for decision makers and those in charge of frontline services. | emergency management coordinator, risk manager, training coordinator, area managers, human resources | initial/required ongoing training and departmental training monthly with a weekly review of content needed |
| | Emergency-management content in the business-continuity phase provides shutdown and closure plans articulated as separate plans or within other emergency, risk, or related plans. These plans are also designed to provide direction for both short and longer periods. | emergency management coordinator, risk manager, area manager representatives, administration as appropriate, ad hoc frontline employees group representatives | annually; March [date] and weekly; May–August every two weeks; September to the present—monthly; application is required for return to annual review |
| | All organizational plans reflect basic handling of emergency issues and activities including sustaining basic library functions, communication, and technology infrastructures as well as those parts of infrastructure tasked with delivering the backbone for business-continuity sustaining or alternate plans. | area managers, external services as needed/appropriate, ad hoc frontline employee group | annual review, early review in [month]; annual review suspended; during COVID, review every 6 months |
| | The organization's human resources—employees, workers, and library and related groups—are prepared to quickly shift patron services—existing or new roles and responsibilities—within a variety of locations. | area managers, ad hoc frontline employees group, administration | updated plan approved and implemented [date]; annual review suspended; during COVID, review every 6 months |

| Chapter and Area | If We Had Been Ready (in-text statement list) | Process Owner/Creator Can Be One or More of the Following: | Have/Last Review Date |
|---|---|---|---|
| | Employees have articulated job descriptions and departmental and individual goals with special projects completed when primary work is done. (Both individual and small group projects are available.) | area managers, HR advisory employee group, project-area managers | implemented [date]; annual review |
| | Measurement and assessment for standard/basic data gathering and—as needed—immediate and higher-level data remains in place with existing forms and practices. Forms are currently designed for changing or new situations—available for continued meaningful data gathering. | area managers, assessment team, ad hoc frontline employee group, administration | April review; January review and update as necessary |
| | Employees have a high level of trust in managers and leaders. | administration, human resources, area manager, union team, employee committee representatives | fall update of internal organizational cultural survey; data for fall announced January; May survey update scheduled |

## Smaller and Solo Environments

If we had been ready:

A large number of library and information settings today are smaller environments, and many of these are solo librarian settings. These smaller settings—in terms of space, number of workers, number of titles/volumes of print/paper materials, capacity/seating, and hours of service—are not in any one area of the profession but throughout academic, public, school, and special. In fact, while some might characterize smaller library settings as being in more K–12 school and special library environments, these settings represent a large number of not only K–12 school (public and private) but also higher-ed/academic and community public libraries.

A generalized overview of smaller space issues includes spaces operated only by one or two designated librarians (or even one full time and one part time), with one identified as the manager, both with varied schedules and offering diverse hours of service. Smaller spaces face the same "hours open" issues and represent many different "open" scenarios including using either self-serve environments or student workers and/or volunteers to maintain those open in limited areas with individual computer workstations, study space, browsing, use of personal technology and seeking power, and wireless use as well as libraries with later-in-the-day or weekend hours.

And more specifically:

- the academic commons, productivity center, or study space that serves as a remote or off-campus "library" setting;

- the public or academic library (leisure reading, community hangout, freshman collaboration space, graduate focus space, medical or law commons or innovation space, etc.) that opens a smaller first-floor overnight commons, productivity center, study space, computer center, or personal device wireless-use space and monitors the space and users with hourly workers and open 24/7;
- the academic library—open 24/7 or extended hours—that opens a first-floor overnight-only commons, productivity center, study space, computer center, or personal device wireless-use space and monitors the space and users with hourly workers; and
- the school library—with one librarian with either a school-schedule work week or school/after-school schedule that opens with volunteers to maintain hours open when library workers are not there.

Making no recommendations for these approaches but with these different smaller and often not traditionally staffed environments in mind, physical spaces, resources, and service issues during pandemics and often into post-pandemic and recovery times are basically the same across all sizes and types of libraries and their public-service areas. The common bad news is smaller and solo library environment managers have—obviously—fewer if any people to assist with making decisions, implementation, and—overall—the changes needed. During pandemics, specific different characteristics include:

- when contagion transmission is the issue, these smaller spaces are—literally—too small to remain open/in service;
- when transmission is the issue, no matter the size or the possibility of expanded space (out of doors, into a meeting room, etc.), the furniture cannot be moved or cleaned if moved, and so on; therefore, there is not the support (furniture, power, HVAC, etc.) needed for (if possible) expanded/greater space use; and
- when libraries are trying to maintain key services, available workers (volunteers, hourly workers) are not able to maintain critical aspects of key service (lack of training, expertise, liability, etc.).

And, while one might think that managers of smaller environments have more latitude (and they might for general *daily* operations) the big decisions on open or closed spaces and services are more out of their control and in the hands of umbrella organizations, managers of the larger physical facilities in which they exist, governing groups, peer agencies or entities (district schools, the company or business, county services, city services, or even a landlord, etc.), or the "community" in general.

### Recommendations

Most of the charts included in this book contain ranges of content with the smallest areas or the fewest access points or possible changes represented in each one; therefore, managers in smaller or solo environments can—using this content and their own expertise—create scenarios of possibilities for their resources, services, and users as well as potential users who may need assistance during an event. Having these scenarios provides alternatives and avenues for managers to take some of the control they need in making their case (if needed) for choosing how they will operate during and after events or business continuity. To create scenarios instead of—for example—individual summaries of services, managers should:

- survey peer, similar, or adjacent locations on what they are doing and see if there are common factors supporting the decisions made or being considered—these factors can be then used to define the same or similar scenarios described below;
- review the recommended ranges in charts and coupled with credentialed content available in the library profession *and* local and peer organizational decision scenarios that offer a summative look (with articulation of the values inherent in providing the smaller service environments), and—although

events and user needs vary dramatically—identifying and sharing this content in scenarios can provide choices that work as a unit or single approach to deciding hours, services, and so on;
- maintain an emergency planning document (with vendors, supplies, etc.) for assisting in managing events and using benchmark documents to make sure the scale is translated to the smaller scale needed for the plan;
- identify existing user needs and support possibilities;
- identify new support possibilities (e.g., emergency response teams) emanating from umbrella organization or landlord environments;
- identify historically available *general* assistance from others including peer colleagues, users, those in advisory or governing roles, or stakeholders and supporters (Friends, foundation, groups using the library's meeting room, area partners, and local groups such as community service groups);
- identify historically available and new EM assistance from umbrella organization, governmental entities, and area first responders; and
- identify existing groups (if the library isn't already involved) who regularly partner to manage area emergency issues and events.

If smaller and solo libraries had been ready:

The smallest libraries—including solo environments—maintain content and structures to prepare them for unique events. In smaller environments, these structures include:

- an emergency plan for resources, services;
- articulated scenarios for preparing, responding, continuity, and recovery;
- emergency/disaster kits;
- a list of commercial and nonprofit environments available and needed to support events and recovery;
- an emergency team (the librarian, representatives from stakeholders, governing and advisory groups, area partners, and the umbrella organization);
- environmental scans of "community";
- a decision-making document that outlines what managers have control over and what they don't have control over; and
- an information path identifying infrastructure content needed for preparing, responding, continuity, and recovery.

Maintaining this content assists in reducing the fear and uncertainty that comes with events, business continuity, and recovery. And, although there are many ways to design scenarios, a valuable set of scenarios—with careful credentialing—provides diverse buildouts of service possibilities to address a variety of needs and stages of events and recovery with varying worker support. But what is credentialing, and how does it differ from other vetting processes?

## Credentialing

Although the term *credentialing* is primarily used in the health sciences field, the process of credentialing can and should be applied to any situation where individuals need to identify and verify critical information and in an emergency-management situation—usually in a long-term or ongoing process.

Although there are a variety of ways to credential information, organizations, or individuals, two primary ways are: (1) the identification of information, the location of the source of the information, and then an assessment of the information and the source to see if they are credible, valid, respected, and so on; (2) the reverse process—critical information is needed and those needing it choose an organization or individual who typically provides valid, respected, recommended information, expertise, and so on, and then the organization's or individual's credentials (education, training, experience, licensure, rankings, successes, etc.) are verified and the individual and/or organization is identified as the primary source for content as needed, throughout the event. In the case of a disaster or—in this case—a pandemic, the organization or individual is "announced" as the primary source. This organization or individual is studied as to how their information is distributed, the timelines, underlying research, and so on, throughout the event.

And, although this might appear to be an obvious step to be taken—with the advent of fake news, vast media outlets and sources of content on the web, and literally hundreds of people speaking out, speaking up, and claiming expertise and credit—a critical step for the organization is to be systematic about whose directions, advice, and recommendations will be used. But in emergency and disaster situations, isn't every organization required to use only certain sources? Yes and no. Also, what do the two processes look like for credentialing, and how do they differ?

### Yes and No—Who's Out There Already, Aren't These Things in Place, and How Do I Update? Create? Choose What Works for Me?

Yes: Most library umbrella organizations are part of a larger community in EM that might exist in one or more county, city, state, regional, and federal entities (to name a few) who—by nature of who they are or who they employ—are considered the experts in any number of areas. That being said, libraries often have their experts identified for them, and these may be multiple sources at once as well as multiple sources that change during the stages of the event.

No: Although many libraries may have sources identified and required *for* them regarding spaces, staffing, serving users, and providing support for the event itself, libraries will have to choose additional sources that are unique and specific for them given their services, spaces, and resources such as print/paper, media/plastic surfaces, use of shared technology, equipment, and those services driven by numbers of users such as study areas, programming, games, and so on.

Choosing additional or even primary resources must be grounded in critically reviewing what is available. This assessment or "credentialing" is an important step to take not only for these documents but also in choosing relevant, related, or recommended approaches.

### Why Credential?

It is important to credential *and* to use a specific replicable process for credentialing due to a number of issues, including that when people—workers or users—are involved methodical, well-thought-out, and careful actions must be used and documented given the seriousness of health and pandemic issues. Why? In addition to the importance of consulting experts when making critical decisions that affect people's health and well-being:

- Library workers—just as everyone is now—are exposed to dozens of opinions and ideas on health, staying safe in general, and staying safe in the workspace. To avoid politicizing situations, workers bringing in a variety of ideas—general and specific—and people refuting what the organization has chosen, those in authority must choose a systematic way of making decisions and communicating those decisions to provide continuity and structure to the workplace.
- Establishing a rubric for why a source, opinion, or recommendation is chosen in the institution's process not only adds validity to decision making but also provides a documented path for those who bring in other ideas to vet *their* ideas and often discover why their idea won't work or isn't true/accurate.
- While workers, managers, and leaders should have a strong sense of trust for decision makers and

decision making as well as decisions made by their own managers and leaders and others in the organization, there are areas of expertise—health and pandemic related—that are *not* part of people's current set of competencies. So if the trust *is* there but not in the expertise, or even if the trust *isn't* there, processes for vetting and making these decisions provide that level of trust critical to managing during these difficult times.

So credentialing—a well-known aspect of information literacy in education in identifying validity of sources and authors—should be one of the first approaches for those striving to manage and lead during pandemics. Two credentialing examples are outlined below.

## Example Process 1

The library has just gone through a renovation and a number of new subject-, topic-, or discipline-specific spaces had been created to better serve unique users. The pandemic, however, has prompted the library to reduce hours overall and also to completely close several of the smaller rooms where materials (available by subject/specialized content and typically used by constituents through browsing techniques) are housed/shelved due to space constraints and the variety of formats of materials. One of the spaces—genealogy/local history—is a favorite among researchers and several local community groups, and the library has been seriously criticized for closing the new space. The director—knowing that the decision would not be a popular one—has her data/evidence ready for the meeting with the administration where this decision will be discussed and—more than likely—debated. Her evidence and process include the following:

- The director chose the decision of the genealogy/local history (G/LH) librarian who presented to the director in a meeting prior to the meeting with the administration; the decision was based on:
  ◦ a report with recommendations on the virus' "life" on materials and resources—over twenty years old/after twenty years of use; and
  ◦ his plan on identifying resources that were newer that could be advertised as accessible as well as pulled by request and used by researchers for reduced periods of time in socially distanced research areas of the library that were cordoned off.
- During the meeting, the director approved the information found and asked the G/LH librarian to identify the credentials of the author/authors and publication date of the report, the list of people/sources that created the alternate service plan (including the

two users/members who participated in the library's alternate-service discussions), and where the G/LH librarian and the reference assistant had found the measurements and allotted use times for use of resources in the library. The director then took the report, the author's credentials, the names of the library users who were part of the decision-making process, and the administration's recommendations for distancing and use time.
- In the meeting with the administration, the director provided information about the timeline for updating their decisions based on the report addendums—scheduled to come out monthly, then every two weeks, and then weekly as the pandemic numbers were studied. In the meeting with the administration, the director clarified the administration's plans for updating their stance based on CDC and FEMA information distribution on social distancing and materials usage time.

## Example Process 2

The library has just gone through a renovation, and a number of new subject spaces had been created to better serve unique users. The pandemic, however, has prompted the library to reduce hours overall and also to completely close several of the smaller rooms where materials (available by subject/specialized content) are housed/shelved due to space constraints and the variety of formats of materials. One of the spaces—genealogy/local history—is a favorite among researchers and several local community groups, and the library has been seriously criticized for closing the new space. The director—knowing that the decision would not be a popular one—has her data/evidence ready for the meeting with the administration where this decision will be discussed and—more than likely—debated. Her evidence and process include the following:

- The director called the state library, which had statewide recognition and two experts in genealogy and local history. In an online meeting, the director—with her G/LH specialist/clerk, her reference assistant, and two frequent users of the G/LH collection—posed the question of access and use to the state library experts. After answering questions (based on their research and a semiannual report they prepare) regarding the age of the materials and usage patterns from the community, the director and the G/LH specialist made decisions on access and use, sent meeting minutes to the state library for verification of correct recommendations, requested and received a copy of the report from a web download, and made decisions limiting access and usage times as well as closing the space but making newer materials available. The director took the agency credentials from the website and summarized the decision and criticism they received and:

- included the credentials of the agency experts;
- included the expertise/names, and so on, of the collection users; and
- prepared a report and presentation for her administration.

- The director then took the decisions made, agency reputation information in general and for this unique subject area, the agency expert's credentials, the names and credentials of the library users who were part of the decision-making process, and the administration's recommendations (it turns out) for distancing and use time from both the Centers for Disease Control and from their county's FEMA office.

- In the meeting with the administration, the director provided information about the agency's timeline for updating their recommendations on their website and clarified the administration's plans for updating their stance based on CDC and FEMA information distribution.

## How Do We Credential Content?

Librarians find themselves with so much content that it is hard to narrow down what will work for their environment. And while librarians have processes for and regularly assess author expertise and research/datasets and reputable agencies, they do not have—for the most part—the in-depth knowledge of emergency-management literature. In addition, there is significant emergency-management literature, and—obviously—this has expanded significantly for pandemics and post-pandemic situations since the beginning of 2020. The literature of the library and information profession has also expanded—in regard to EM and libraries—since 9/11, with obviously the biggest increases regarding user and worker health beginning in February of 2020. Also, general societal content has grown exponentially with information, knowledge, research, and recommendations about pandemics and post-pandemic content now available to all, unlike—for example—tourism recommendations from a decade ago covering the bedbug crises and outbreaks—broad, but certainly short-lived. That being said, categorizing and credentialing emergency-management literature identifies the following more-defined areas for managers to study and use:

- *Emergency Management—General:* The bigger picture provides an overview in general, state, and city/local emergency and nonprofit management including community preparedness for public health; preparedness with planning and partnerships among health organizations; competencies (skills focus, leadership, communication, etc.); job descriptions of current public health positions (e.g., contact tracers and EM media directors); basic content for education and training of health program participants; planning for recovery; and information technology such as apps to assist in detection and awareness, tracking and recordkeeping, and internet infrastructure support in maintaining remote work, as well as prevention, training, and recovery

- *Disaster Management—General Event:* the narrower focus on the one area or location or level of seriousness of the event with a focus on the effect of a specific disaster on vulnerable local populations; citizen response and assistance as well as a focus on the whole-person-as-worker during contagion surges in their area; and communication processes including warning and recovery communication (community, public health, safety apps)

- *Disasters—Infrastructure Failures:* from man-made events and events occurring due to poor organizational planning or nature, causing both short-term and long-term emergency situations such as power outages—natural and man-made—and structural safety

- *Emergency/Public Management:* including public policy, legislation, federal, state, and local agency roles and responsibilities; risk; insurance; relief/funding; regulation; management of fire/burning events; national, state, and local security including threats, consequences, and planning; public-health legislation; pandemic-related or other terrorism and global conflict and warfare regarding biological hazards; toxic agents and infectious disease; and communication and media issues in emergency/public management

- *Emergency/Public Management—Response:* roles and responsibilities; guidelines; delivery of services; state and local initiatives; community and higher education programs (credit and continuing education, and layperson training and education resources)

- *Societal Issues:* business continuity and recovery; legal issues; sociological and psychological issues (perception, beliefs, values, stress response, adaptation, uncertainty, demoralization, and traumatic neurosis and fear); mental health and wellness; the economy; economic issues; and political issues

- *Research:* (measurement, evaluation, and analysis) disaster/event research, data collection and analysis, aggregated data (dashboards, interactive federal datasets, and program evaluation)

Finally, this depth and breadth of pandemic content illustrates the need for managers to read and learn broadly because—due to the seriousness of the pandemic—the general public, users, workers, and so on, are all *also* reading about changes—whether temporary or permanent—that need to happen to make their spaces safe. Managers and leaders need to have as many if not more tools and information to make decisions. Narrowing down EM and related content, therefore, creates a manageable set of documents, organizations, and—if possible—experts to focus on.

# 2

# Facilities

## *Services, Support, and Storage Spaces*

I MANAGE ELEVEN LIBRARIES and a technical services department. Of the eleven facilities, I am currently expanding one library (a low-end remodel), and another library—originally planned as a new space within a historic renovation—has now been moved and shrunk in physical space by 70 percent. So—by some people's standards—I manage *many* libraries—but given most academic library standards and certainly most that serve approximately 27,000 students, faculty, staff members, and some of the local community members (approximately 40,000 seats filled), these spaces are smaller to medium-sized. The library system overall (in-person and digitally and spread out over eight counties) is very busy and very successful each year.

So how do I know the library is successful? First of all, it isn't just me; I have twelve management positions (two of these are vacant and the twelfth is the manager of technical services), and along with consistently high scores (positively ranked) in the standard accreditation assessment every five to six years, during the past two decades, we have scored in the top or "best" three to four services each time the college offers its internal customer survey, and repeatedly (and surprisingly, in my opinion) score very highly in the alumni survey. We also have great scores on standardized or "commercial" surveys (CCSSE, Noel-Levitz) and from our in-house surveys (even though CCSSE and Noel-Levitz do not offer many library-related questions), and we also scored well in the CCSSE survey on information literacy.

Prior to our COVID closing date—mid-March 2020—the majority of the libraries were heavily used with much in-person traffic, and both public spaces and worker workspaces were located very close together in each library location. Public and worker worktables, chairs, shelving, offices, and so on—at every location—have primarily shared-surface worker environments (with some

forty-four-plus-year-old upholstered study carrels and chairs). These conditions are clearly the perfect storm for transmitting infectious diseases, and many—if not most—libraries experience the same space issues and, therefore, the same risks. I should add that half of the spaces are newer and half are older *and* the college has always adhered to construction and space guidelines, but let's just say that we make the most of every inch of our spaces.

Of course, sizes and spaces of libraries are often not designed as they are because of choices that librarians make. Why? Facilities everywhere—in all types and sizes of libraries—vary dramatically. Whether or not the library is an academic, public, school, or special library—and no matter the needs of the community of library users served by the environment—most spaces don't meet these needs, for many different reasons including a lack of money to begin the project; the project running out of money; competing needs of planners, administrators, or higher-level decision makers winning out; library space not generating funding and other spaces needing to make up for that; and the lack of understanding of what library spaces can and should provide by administrators and architects.

So, although "tethered technology"—which always restricts space flexibility—is dwindling due to the expanding use of laptop and portable and personal devices, library spaces were still too small and resources were too close together before COVID and certainly for post-COVID full or partial services opening. And given how many spaces started out too small, what *are* libraries now experiencing when looking at opening all areas of library services back up—whether all or once or gradually?

- Libraries—in the vast majority of community and institutional environments—are typically too small. And yes, although the majority of bond elections for public libraries (for example) passed in 2020, that figure represents bond elections in only a few libraries in 42 percent of the states in the country, in a very limited number of areas. So, annually, we *do* see stunning, newer, larger libraries across the globe built in public, academic, and some school settings as well as in governments (state and national libraries); those are still not the majority of over 115,000 library spaces in the United States alone.

- Different types of libraries have varied missions and should have different focuses for design and delivery of services. This means that guidelines for creating safer spaces—post-pandemic—have to be very broad and have to be current. Sadly, there are few standards, and very few are required, so many libraries have to make it up as they go along.
- Many administrators—often lacking in technological expertise—do not understand today's users' needs for either digitally or in-person spaces—so when faced with requests for renovating old or providing new services but (more than likely) in drastically different ways, final funding decisions are often dramatically off the mark.
- Many architects—most likely not having built many libraries or related facilities—have not had experience in creating these unique spaces either by themselves or within or contiguous to other spaces. In addition, many architects are looking for projects where they can include unique, one-of-a-kind, cutting-edge, or "heroic" features (a word used by an architect to me once), and these often do *not* work well across all types of buildings or in libraries at all.
- Many projects—already beginning and ending without consulting library workers—continue to move ahead without consulting workers on the additional or new "safer spaces" data and research needed for library retrofitting, renovation, or new building projects that entities such as OCLC's Project REALM are creating during the pandemic.
- Projects seldom take library workers into account, so libraries—already short-staffed—must push architects to attempt to have appropriate and safe space management possible with the number of workers in the library.
- Many architectural visions do not conform to the critical changes needed in library spaces (e.g., fewer pieces of furniture than planned, the types of furniture chosen, the cluster or sticky space reconfiguration for safety, and portable PPE around public services desks or barriers between public study and research workstation spaces).
- Library workers do *not* take formal coursework (credits, continuing education, workshops, formal education, etc.) in facilities management much less architecture so they are unaware of their needs; therefore:
  ◦ library administrators and managers are lacking in facilities, building, or renovation knowledge—which is completely understandable;
  ◦ library workers—lacking the knowledge or user information—do not communicate their *needs* nor do they know *how* to communicate their needs;
  ◦ library workers are less proactive than is needed for ongoing upkeep, maintaining contemporary spaces, remodeling, renovating, or building new; and
  ◦ library workers are afraid of—as they don't have enough space to begin with—sharing spaces with other adjacent or related services; therefore they appear—as well they might be—resistant to change.
- Although some librarians and some architects are aware of archival, historical materials' storage, or closed-stack needs, no one—literally, no one—understands the general storage needs of the library.
- The majority of today's workshops are offered for librarians by vendors or consultants—whether through associations or not—and these events are designed to create awareness and not build competencies. Clearly architects and interior-environment experts have a great deal of education, and one workshop does create awareness but does not offer even a firm knowledge base.
- Many architectural or consultant processes include taking clients to newly built, grand edifices, whether they are libraries or not. And while these outings *do* serve to motivate and energize groups into seeing what the possibilities are, seldom do attendees get to hear:
  ◦ what works in specific types of library areas (context);
  ◦ what is right *and* what is wrong about the space;
  ◦ how to ask for specific needs;
  ◦ budget issues; and
  ◦ staffing comparisons.
- Finally, architectural projects for a number of years have attempted to take business office space trends as well as building and design trends in general and lay them on top of library design—both in public and behind-the-scenes worker spaces. And although these are technically office spaces, library office spaces are significantly smaller, there are dramatically different types of work taking place, and typical office worker scheduling does not apply to library scheduling. In addition, frontline workspaces—

circulation and reference desks—are distinctly different from other frontline spaces in department stores, reception desks in offices, hospitals intake and service desks, typical K–12 school office administrator areas, general nonprofits, churches, and governmental buildings. In fact, given the volume and use patterns, the intellectual vs. services vs. rote activities of different levels and types of staff, the organization is unique, and many pre-COVID trends were ill-suited to library spaces overall. To be specific, there are a number of trends that have now been rolled back and deemed—also by architects—unlikely to return when spaces become more normalized as well as in the long run of design and functioning of environments. These include concepts with different names, but the same focus.

○ Hot-desking, or touch-down spaces—also called "hoteling"—are seen as short-term workspaces indicative of corporate office environments. A designation as an unassigned, shared workstation in an office space, this idea was considered an "innovation" in recent years, but is now recognized as a risky venture. Designed to de-densify (a term used both for public and worker spaces) and keep costs down, reduce the need for physical size of offices through double-scheduling staff and not assigning specific workspaces, the idea—not that great to begin with—was sold to organizations as a generational approach to networking, natural teaming, a boon to creativity, and—of course—a big cost saver. It is, however, fraught with problems in that workers never know who they are going to be sharing a space with, they have to regiment their use of workspace and their schedules, and the concepts of team *building*, creativity, and spontaneous productivity are not possible. In addition, the recent literature has been very clear on the critical need for a focus on inclusion, teamwork, equity, wellness, and bringing some element of self back to the workspace again. Almost like wandering around a coffee shop looking for a place to sit down, workspaces end up with no areas able to be personalized and no concern for special needs (whether the needs come from personal or project elements), and the concept greatly increases the likelihood that workers will feel as if they have no real "place" at work. Other aspects of concern for the individual—also a critical part of building a work culture—are nonexistent as workers struggle to concentrate and are forced to try to work creatively within specific constraints within a space that has no concern for the myriad of ways people learn.

○ Frontline interaction (service desks) is considered to be an important element in customer service today. A long-standing part of service organizations, service desks are not the reception desk for pointing and moving people around or the checkout desk where an item is identified and logged in or out nor a sign-in desk where users "take a number"; rather, frontline workers are asked to engage users, provide a service, and connect them with additional services and resources they need. In libraries, there are actually two types of desks—best described as one for brief interactions and one for more intellectual interactions with longer user/client/patron engagement for learning technology, solving a research problem, or discovering the critical piece of information needed to make the project work—all in all a longer-term delivery of services. In pre-COVID design, architects included these spaces on request, but they tended to be too small, similar to locations for brief encounters, and ultimately all "one-stop" with all staff (no matter the service, staffing level, or pay grade) using the space and ultimately creating a more frustrating time for customers as they were handed from person to person, all shoehorned in one space. These spaces—now post-COVID, must be bigger and must provide for social distancing among those staffing them and from client to library worker. No longer encouraged to "step out from behind the desk" for the foreseeable future, desks will be used by only one worker and one user with PPE between them, and they will have to schedule in for longer encounters at makeshift areas. Simply fixed by—at the very least—providing two desks, this trend was seldom heralded by users and never by professional staff.

What is fascinating to me—as a library dean, administrator, and veteran of *many* unusual, emergency events creating issues causing great impact—is that the pandemic has lasted long enough to come "full circle" for higher education, cities, and counties as well as K–12 school settings and special library environments. What does this mean? I have observed a number of cycles to planning or—more accurately—dealing with chaos that comes from emergency situations. The pandemic, however, created the following situations:

- the need for an initial handling of facilities issues, service delivery, and support;
- a secondary realization that there had to be significant but immediate investment in technology—

often long requested, but not fulfilled—for users or workers to provide them with the need to work remotely;

- a need to address the design of service support by instituting alternative deliveries; and
- the late-in-the-game realization that people are social animals and that technology—no matter how "active" or interactive—does not substitute for the in-person assistance, programming, or working in shared spaces, in-person public service desks and workers, or support space workplaces for individuals or groups.

Furthermore, given the lack of space, poor design, and overcrowded spaces in libraries prior to COVID, we now have a situation, unaddressed realization, and great concern that reopening with care, guidelines, and recommendations—met or unmet, adhered to or ignored—would *not* be enough given sizes and footprints or designs of spaces and types of furniture.

So what does this create? A perfect storm of enormous post-COVID problems for facilities as well as workers, services, and resources. Recommendations for spaces vary as to size and whether or not libraries have been open all along, partially closed, and so on, and are included in not only lists but also charts to address the stages of the pandemic—which varied in almost every geographic area.

So—knowing what we have to work with, that there isn't a quick end, and that other public-health crises are projected to return—how do we move forward?

Moving forward—although libraries typically find themselves "making do" with whatever space is given to them—today's and tomorrow's spaces need to be flexibly designed to protect not only users but also workers, while accommodating maximum use of space and safe distancing to address public-health concerns on a grand pandemic scale as well as everyone's annual cough, cold, and flu seasons. These concerns need to take a careful look at not only short-term changes in spaces but also long-term decision making, planning renovations and remodels, and new construction.

Note: I fully understand that it is ridiculous and actually disrespectful for someone to make cavalier suggestions for librarians such as "buy all new furniture" or "reupholster your cloth furniture" or "replace all of your desktops with laptops." So consider this an apology up front. But, with that in mind, the following space and social distancing charts are designed to offer short-term, longer-term, and more strategic suggestions so that managers can begin to rethink current spaces, identify what goes and what stays, build budgets for the future, revise wish lists, seek private dollars, and—where possible—

apply for federal relief dollars (projected through 2022, and watch for the IMLS federal funding program definitions through state libraries) and seek outside funding and (possibly) revise library needs and content for estate planning, gifts, and donations.

In addition, libraries should begin to work with architects, construction/builders, and maintenance groups, Friends groups, foundations and philanthropic professionals, wills and estates experts/estate planning groups, and collaborators such as state libraries, regional networks, and partnerships for discussions on the changes that have to take place and how to articulate funding needs for their members and audiences.

## Pandemic and Post-Pandemic Spaces

Specific recommendations and data are listed in charts regarding physical spaces, functions, services, and resources offered as well as where and when. But librarians also need to seek advice and best practices beyond their own profession and beyond one type or size of library. It should be noted, therefore, that the following recommendations were found through research into higher education, health science environments, public and county sectors (public administration), and the travel industry, the hotel/motel tourism industry, and the food industry. The following general statements include recommendations for both workers and users, and for physical spaces.

### Users

- Users numbers should be reduced throughout the library with some spaces closed due to their size—obviously throughout the pandemic and in compliance with guidelines and regulations—but also when they cease—primarily with library workers in mind but also given the size of spaces to begin with, the number of shared workstations, and the fact that many libraries have poor to almost no ventilation.
- PPE—an odd mixture of costs from free to very expensive, then unavailable to available and reasonable—should remain available for workers and users who seek them but don't have any when they visit the library (e.g., single-use masks).

### Workers and Users/Constituents

- Libraries require workers and users to wear masks and also require limited-time appointments, and then regulations for masks taper off by space, numbers of users, and vaccination percentage by age and area of the country and public health statistics.

Throughout, workers have felt consistently safer when they are wearing masks, and users are as well. Although libraries typically cannot require masks of users unless the umbrella entity or governing authorities do [exclusive of 501(c)(3) organizations], employees can continue to wear them. And because people who continue to wear masks are supposed to include those people who don't have their vaccinations yet, workers may want to wear buttons or some identifying pin/ribbon that they have been vaccinated but are wearing masks to increase safety factors for them and their users.

- Any assistance with users is managed at a distance, and while numbers expand and reduce, library queues, reference, and research assistance will have to be carefully staged to avoid voices being heard from confidential requests, checkout questions, and so on. (See table 2.3.)
- Standard, approved PPE and related practices are required for all users/workers (e.g., gloves for services for cleaning to protect against infections for shared space cleaning, but also chemicals, possible contact tracing at entry, marked usable spaces, spaces with no 3' or 6' distancing and Plexi-glass maintained).
- Although many institutions are making cleaning materials available for users and workers to use themselves, care must be taken and managers must be aware of toxicity of products by themselves or when mixed with others (umbrella institution, library products, user-purchased/brought [signs posted] vs. worker owned).

## Spaces

- Cleaning materials are made publicly available (packets with care to avoid chemical interactions).
- There is scheduled "down time" for technology and surfaces to remain unused as well as cleaning between uses and at the facility opening and closing with posted schedules for user and worker awareness.
- There are and will remain for some time typically reduced hours for in-person (primarily) library services, access, and so on.
- Furniture not being used should be removed from library spaces or, if storage isn't possible, furniture should be made unavailable.
- The library should post both extensive behavioral signage as well as more signage than usual *and* signage that can include "don'ts" and "dos." Wording indicating preferences when mandates are no longer in place should be chosen carefully. For example, when masks are no longer mandated, signs cannot

say that libraries "prefer masks"; rather, they can use wording such as "masks welcomed." If managers are able to use governing bodies as approval boards, boards should be asked to participate to minimize conflict and debate.

- The library should only post or use approved signage and instructions (chosen by the institution or umbrella entity or only with approved content with dates and times with references to guidelines, rules, etc.). In addition, the signage, instructions, customer service, and so on, must be maintained as to accuracy of rules, regulations, and mandates and should note public-health crises, emergency events, or pandemic stages and colors to assure users of compliance.
- If the library is closed for a period of time, HVAC cleaning should be completed prior to library opening. Libraries should consider adding filters mounted on any HVAC intake vents, and air purifier/HEPA filters used in worker areas and—if appropriate—in public spaces.

## Furniture

- Any furniture that is upholstered in any cloth or noncleanable materials should be removed permanently or removed and stored. Cloth such as work clothing covers should be assigned to workers and regularly cleaned.
- Banks of computers need to be divided up into smaller computer clusters with significant feet between each one, with—preferably—PPE partition used.
- If possible, desktops need to be set aside for more flexible tech for users and workers such as laptops, iPads, and so on.
- If desktops are left in the library, keyboards, mice, and other components can be checked out for scheduled users with appropriate timing and cleaning between uses.
- New furniture rented, borrowed, or purchased should have wheels/be easily moved. (Not only are chairs socially distanced, but also some libraries aren't scheduling users and, for example, are "checking out" chairs by removing all from the floor and—literally—checking out the use of the chair with one renewal.)
- Although beanbag chairs—typically made of cloth—should be removed anyway (not easily cleanable, not durable, and invite play or multiple children in close quarters), children's services areas and programs should have children and parents sitting on linoleum squares or rubber mats. Toys, games, stuffed

animals, models, and globes should be removed from public services. The library might consider checking these out for in-library use if cleaning and downtime between uses are possible.

Tables 2.1–2.3 indicate—more specifically—what PPE are recommended for public spaces and activities—representative of all types and sizes of libraries—and what spaces or distances are recommended to aid in striving for safe use for workers and users. Although a "during pandemic" column is included, the reality is that a huge percentage of libraries fluctuated back and forth (depending on the location, umbrella organization, pandemic numbers) between being open and closed. Table 2.1—for stage 1 or during—indicates "varies" where there was typically great variation and then is specific for areas that were handled more consistently. An additional chart outlines workspace PPE and use recommendations. Note: Smaller libraries have a separate chart and list of recommendations at the end of this list.

**TABLE 2.1**
**Pandemic and Post-Pandemic Physical Spaces (Not Including Digital Interactions/Services)**

| Stages | STAGE 1<br>*During Pandemic*<br>*x date–x date* | STAGE 2<br>*Short Term*<br>*x date–x date* | STAGE 3<br>*Long Term*<br>*x date–x date* |
|---|---|---|---|
| Libraries should—using technology (phones, iPads, etc.)—consider recorded messages (phone messages, podcasts) to provide users with short voice messages or media posted online (on YouTube, social media, Facebook, apps, with QR codes, etc.) to explain the stage the library is in and the expectations of users and the services and spaces guidelines. This method—easily updated—eliminates handouts and wordy signage (embedded QR codes on signs) and provides the users with information while taking workers out of the frequent or lengthy updating explanation. | | | |
| Public Service Interactions: **Circulation**—one-on-one | **Varies:** if open any hours, curbside pickup; touchless checkout—lockers; self-check; no use of/no checkout of print/paper | **Varies—Reduced:** curbside pickup; self-check; lockers; PPE at circ. desk (shield, guard, gloves, cleaning or unused between each visit, socially distanced checkout) with quarantined spaces | **Open—Possibly Reduced Hours:** PPE; lockers; PPE at circ. desk (shield, guard, gloves, cleaning or unused between each visit, socially distanced checkout); intermittent quarantine for print/paper |
| Public Service Interactions: **Reference** one-on-one; small group | **Ceased:** possible but if open any hours, very little socially distanced reference with PPE around reference desk; appts.; limited entry; some remote in the library (video stream from offices); mostly closed in-person | **Varies—Reduced Hours or Closed:** PPE (shield, guard, gloves, cleaning between each visit, socially distanced); remote in the library (video stream from offices); appts.; limited entry | **Open—Reduced Hours:** PPE (shield, guard, gloves, cleaning or unused between each visit, socially distanced checkout); appts.; limited entry with overall library visits scheduled |
| **Presentations:** teaching, programs—all ages | **Ceased/On Hiatus:** if open any hours, no events in-person for cultural or entertainment, moved online with generic offered<br><br>**Full Service:** instruction only online; age-level programming only online | **Varies—Reduced Hours or Closed:** PPE (shield, guard, gloves, cleaning or unused between each visit, socially distanced); remote in the library (video stream from offices); appts.; limited entry | **Open—Reduced # of Events and Hours:** requirements for visits to elsewhere, classrooms, etc.; PPE for performers, teachers, presenters; socially distanced for attending; limited entry with overall library visits scheduled; appts for class or group visits may be possible |
| Public **Research** Workstations/Desktops | **Varies:** if open any hours, reduce #; PPE for each; cleaning schedule for users and workers; typically no assistant—if available—at stations | **Varies—Reduced #:** PPE (shield, guard, gloves, cleaning between each visit, socially distanced); remote in the library (video stream from offices); appts.; limited entry | **Open—Reduced # of Spaces:** one user per space; PPE requirements for visits out to classrooms, etc.; PPE for performers, teachers, presenters; socially distanced for attending; limited entry with overall library visits scheduled; appts. for class or group visits may be possible for limited size group |

| Stages | STAGE 1<br>*During Pandemic*<br>*x date–x date* | STAGE 2<br>*Short Term*<br>*x date–x date* | STAGE 3<br>*Long Term*<br>*x date–x date* |
| --- | --- | --- | --- |
| **Study** Spaces: tables, personal tech used | **Varies:** if open any hours, reduce #; PPE for each; cleaning schedule for users and workers | **Varies—Reduced #:** PPE (shield, guard, gloves, cleaning between each visit, socially distanced); appts.; limit one user for 6'/one per study space | **Open—Reduced # of Spaces:** one user per space; socially distanced for attending; limited entry with overall library visits scheduled; appts. for class or group visits may be possible for limited size groups |
| **Study or Events:** tablet chairs, leisure seating, comfortable seats (see note above: sofas and cloth furniture gone), floor seating but on a surface such as tile or linoleum squares, rubber mats, event seating | **Varies—Reduced #:** PPE for space; cleaning schedule for users and workers; floor marked for social distancing | **Varies—Reduced #:** PPE (shield, guard, gloves, cleaning between each visit, socially distanced); appts.; limit one user for 6'/one per study space | **Open—Reduced # of Spaces:** one user per space; socially distanced for attending; limited entry with overall library visits scheduled; appts. for class or group visits may be possible for limited size groups |
| **Shelves:** shelving, browsing, removed from library | **Closed:** if open, worker only; one-way aisles | **Varies:** stacks are closed but if open workers only; one-way aisles; deliver on request to internal or external user; some stacks moved elsewhere and workers provide a touchless retrieval service for students | **Open with Reduced Access:** stacks have one-way aisles or worker access and deliver on request to internal or external user; if users allowed, reduced # per aisle at every 6' if shelving has back panels—if not, every other stack is open for browsing for one; requests and delivery possible; some stacks moved elsewhere and workers provide a touchless retrieval service for students |
| **Productivity:** self-serve (copiers, scanners, staplers, scotch tape, scissors, paper cutters, charging stations), peripherals (camera, external drives, charging cords, USBs, headsets, etc.) | **Closed:** if open any hours, small items removed, printing and scanning not available, floor services such as charging, charging cords, headsets, etc., not available | **Varies with Reduced Access:** small items removed; printing and scanning not available; floor services such as charging, charging cords, headsets, etc., not available; if available reduced # of users at every 6'; cleaning between uses | **Open with Reduced Access:** small items removed; printing and scanning limited to on-demand use or one user at a time; floor services such as charging, charging cords, headsets, etc., not available; if available reduced # of users at every 6'; cleaning between uses |
| **User Resource** Interactions: tech, realia, interactive displays, exhibits | **Closed:** removed or disabled items include tech, realia, and interactive displays and exhibits | **Closed:** removed or disabled items include tech, realia, and interactive displays and exhibits | **Open with Reduced Access:** only non-interactive displays; exhibits if informational in nature |
| **Unprogrammed/Misc.:** access—halls, elevators, stairs; misc. social spaces (stairs, landings); mech. infrastructure | **Closed:** any halls, elevators, and stairs are required and labeled up vs. down; all social spaces closed with any furniture gone; mech. infrastructure for workers open one at a time | **Varies—If Open, Reduced Access:** any halls, elevators, and stairs are required and are labeled up vs. down; all social spaces closed with any furniture gone/spaces marked; mech. infrastructure for workers open one at a time | **Open, Reduced Access:** any halls, elevators, and stairs are required and are labeled up vs. down; all social spaces closed with any furniture gone, spaces marked; mech. infrastructure for workers open one at a time |

| Activities/Functions | STAGE 1<br>*During Pandemic*<br>*x date–x date* | STAGE 2<br>*Short Term*<br>*x date–x date* | STAGE 3<br>*Long Term*<br>*x date–x date* |
|---|---|---|---|
| Libraries should—using technology (phones, iPads, etc.)—consider recorded messages (phone messages, podcasts) to provide users with short voice messages or media posted online (on YouTube, social media, Facebook, apps, with QR codes, etc.) to explain the stage the library is in and the expectations of users and the services and spaces guidelines. This method—easily updated—eliminates handouts and wordy signage (embedded QR codes on signs) and provides the users with information while taking workers out of the frequent or lengthy updating explanation. | | | |
| Checking out materials/ resources (worker masks should vary to allow for see-through masks for users and workers with special needs) | If open—6–10'; PPE around all of the checkout/exchange area (shield, guard, gloves, cleaning between each visit) (touchless as possible) | 3', 6'; PPE around checkout/ exchange area (shield, guard, gloves, cleaning front and top of circulation desk in exchange area between each visit) (touchless as possible) | 3', 6'; PPE around checkout/ exchange area (shield, guard, gloves, cleaning front and top of circulation desk between each visit or systematically) (touchless as possible) |
| Reference, Research, Information, Reader's Advisory (worker masks should vary to allow for see-through masks for users and workers with special needs) | If open—6–10'; PPE around all of the desk exchange area (shield, guard, gloves, cleaning front between each visit) (touchless as possible); block users from setting items on desk/small side desk available or cart; no exchanges of handouts or paper | If open—reduced hours of workers staffing the reference desk, 6–10'; PPE around all of the desk exchange area (shield, guard, gloves, cleaning front between each visit) (touchless as possible); block users from setting items on desk/small side desk available or cart; no exchanges of handouts or paper | Open—reduced hours of workers staffing the reference desk, 6–10'; PPE around all of the desk exchange area (shield, guard, gloves, cleaning front between each visit) (touchless as possible); block users from setting items on desk/small side desk available or cart; no exchanges of handouts or paper |
| Presentations, Programming, Teaching Spaces (worker masks should vary to allow for see-through masks for users and workers with special needs) | Closed; online available in most teaching and some programming and presentation instances | 6' for an event less than two hours in length, 10' for an event two hours or more *or* an event that is in a smaller space—for example, a classroom; PPE around each podium (shield, guard, cleaning between each visit); attendees 6' apart | 3', 6'; PPE for speaker (shield, guard, cleaning around podium between each visit); limited programs; limited length of time of event; limited seating and spaces with attendees apart (3–4' if the 6' rule is no longer needed) |
| Research with institutional tech/ PCs (worker masks should vary to allow for see-through masks for users and workers with special needs, using either a see-through in the mouth mask or the complete face shield if moving among users and work stations) | Closed; no one-on-one assistance; help through technology (chat, FaceTime, Zoom, etc.) | If open, reduced hours of service and it varies; 6'; PPE (shield, guard, cleaning between each visit); reduced hours with help through technology (chat, FaceTime, Zoom, etc.) | Open, reduced hours of service and it varies; 3', 6'; PPE (shield, guard, cleaning between each visit); reduced hours with a retention of online research service through technology (chat, FaceTime, Zoom, etc.) |
| Studying with user materials— individual seating (workers managing the environment should be wearing PPE with a choice of more PPE such as wearing gloves, face shields instead of masks only) | Closed; no one-on-one assistance; if open, seating 6' apart; cleaning between visits; no service delivered to study desk | If open, reduced use with 6'; reduced # and hours of access; any one-on-one assistance at a distance; PPE (shield, guard, cleaning around seating spaces if appropriate); cleaning between visits | If open, reduced use with 3', 6'; reduced # and hours of access; any one-on-one assistance at a distance; PPE (shield, guard); cleaning around seating spaces if appropriate; cleaning or no use between visits |
| Studying in Small User Study Rooms | Closed; quarantining materials; one person in at a time | Closed to studying; if used for workers—one person per room or quarantining materials; recommended to cover glass for less visibility and specific "no use" and "no entry" signage | Closed to studying; if used for workers—one person per room or quarantining materials, recommended to cover glass for less visibility and specific "no use" and "no entry" signage |

| Activities/Functions | STAGE 1 During Pandemic x date–x date | STAGE 2 Short Term x date–x date | STAGE 3 Long Term x date–x date |
|---|---|---|---|
| Meeting Rooms—user groups (possible library programming) | Closed—quarantining materials; one person in at a time or two to three if meeting room is large (larger than 20' × 20') | Closed; if open limited use; 6' for an event less than two hours, 10' for an event two hours or more *or* an event that is in a smaller space; PPE (shield, guard, cleaning between each visit); limited attendees; social distancing; stanchions and marking on floors/in space | Open; limited use by people attending or—if used for quarantine—no more than three depending on space (20' × 20' at a minimum); 3', 6' for an event less than two hours, 10' for an event two hours or more *or* an event that is in a smaller space; PPE (shield, guard, cleaning or no use between each visit); limited attendees; social distancing with stanchions and marking on floors |
| Assistance with Technology—user-owned, institutional | Closed; no one-on-one assistance; help through technology (chat, FaceTime, Zoom, etc.) | If open, reduced hours of service and it varies; 6'; PPE (shield, guard, cleaning between each visit); reduced hours with help through technology (chat, FaceTime, Zoom, etc.) | Open, reduced hours of service and it varies; 3', 6'; PPE (shield, guard, cleaning between each visit); reduced hours with a retention of online research service through technology (chat, FaceTime, Zoom, etc.) |
| Users Interacting—each other, realia, exhibits, displays | None available | If open, none available | Open, remove all realia; any displays or exhibits should be noninteractive only. |
| Shelving/Browsing | Closed—if open, workers only; one-way aisles; if shelves are half-height, closed | Varies—stacks are closed but, if open, workers only; one-way aisles; deliver materials on request to internal or external user; if shelves are half-height, closed with only workers retrieving | Open with Reduced Access—if open and users are allowed around the library, browsing stacks with one-way aisles, any use is 3', 6' apart, if full height and back panel shelving are present; if users are *not* allowed, workers only with one worker per one-way aisle at every 3', 6' if shelving has back panels and is full height; if stacks are half-height, closed to users and workers with only one worker retrieving on request. |
| Productivity—self-serve with institutional tech | Closed | If open, reduced hours and removed from open areas for request/checkout for use at desk (charging devices, charging iPads, laptops, calculators, scissors, stapler, etc.) | If open, reduced hours and removed from open areas for request/check out for use at study tables (charging devices, charging iPads, laptops, calculators, scissors, stapler, etc.) |
| Copying/Printing | Closed | Closed; if open and critical, reduced hours; *not* self-serve/on demand, with limited copies, prints, scans, etc.; queue is 6' apart with stanchions or get a number to be called up or order by text/by appointment | Open, reduced, and *not* self-serve/on demand, with limited copies, prints, scans, etc.; queue is 3', 6' apart with stanchions or get a number to be called up or order by text/by appointment |

**TABLE 2.3**
**Pandemic and Post-Pandemic Work/Office Spaces—Recommended Distances and Distancing**

| Activities/Functions | STAGE 1<br>*During Pandemic*<br>*x date–x date* | STAGE 2<br>*Short Term*<br>*x date–x date* | STAGE 3<br>*Long Term*<br>*x date–x date* |
|---|---|---|---|
| Desks—open areas | Closed—limited workers with limited hours of work, 6', PPE around each space; cleaning after use | Varies—if open, limited workers with limited hours of work; 6'; PPE around each space; cleaning after use; sign-up schedules to use shared equipment if individual tech is not possible | Open—limited workers with limited hours of work; 3', 6'; PPE around each space; cleaning after use; sign-up schedules to use shared equipment if individual tech is not possible |
| Office Carrels | Closed—limited workers with limited hours of work; 6'; PPE around each space/ slightly less if carrels walls are taller; cleaning after use | Varies—if open, limited workers with limited hours of work; 6'; PPE around each space, slightly less if carrels walls are taller; cleaning after use; sign-up schedules to use shared equipment if individual tech is not possible | Open—limited workers with limited hours of work; 3', 6'; PPE around each space, slightly less if carrels walls are taller; cleaning after use; sign-up schedules to use shared equipment if individual tech is not possible |
| Offices—closed with carrels | Closed—limited workers with limited hours of work but, depending on size, two to three workers at one time; 6'; PPE around each space, slightly less if carrels walls are taller; cleaning after use | Varies—if open, limited workers with limited hours of work but, depending on size, two to three workers at one time; 6', PPE around each space, slightly less if carrels walls are taller; cleaning after use; sign-up schedules to use shared equipment if individual tech is not possible | Open—limited workers with limited hours of work but, depending on size, two to three workers at one time; 3', 6'; PPE around each space, slightly less if carrels walls are taller; cleaning after use; sign-up schedules to use shared equipment if individual tech is not possible |
| Closed with carrels | Closed—limited workers with limited hours of work but, depending on size, one to two workers at one time; 6'; PPE around each space, slightly less if carrels walls are taller; cleaning after use | Varies—if open, limited workers with limited hours of work but, depending on size, one to two workers at one time; 6'; PPE around each space, slightly less if carrels walls are taller; cleaning after use; sign-up schedules to use shared equipment if individual tech is not possible | Open—limited workers with limited hours of work but, depending on size, one to two workers at one time; 3', 6'; PPE around each space, slightly less if carrels walls are taller; cleaning after use; sign-up schedules to use shared equipment if individual tech is not possible |
| Technology Workstations— shared (PCs, laptops, iPads, charging stations, printers, scanners) | Closed or greatly reduced service/access hours; some hours of access but no in-person services available; workers with reduced time spent in library and office; no congregating; staggered use of offices; individual cleaning after each use; no in-person meetings; no or scheduled use of tech with cleaning between each session | Open to workers with reduced time spent in office; closed or greatly reduced hours to public; shorter working schedules; no congregating; staggered use of offices; individual cleaning; requirements for meetings (space, attendee numbers); scheduled use of tech with cleaning between each session | Open—shorter working schedules; limited congregating; staggered use of offices; individual cleaning; requirements for meetings (space, attendee numbers); possible scheduled use of tech with cleaning between each session |
| Lockers/Worker Storage— personal | Closed | Varies—one person at a time; cleaned a.m. and p.m. | Open—one person at a time; cleaned a.m. and p.m. |
| Bathrooms—one use | Closed | Varies—one person at a time; cleaned after every use | Open—one person at a time; cleaned after every use |

| Activities/Functions | STAGE 1<br>*During Pandemic*<br>*x date–x date* | STAGE 2<br>*Short Term*<br>*x date–x date* | STAGE 3<br>*Long Term*<br>*x date–x date* |
|---|---|---|---|
| Bathrooms—multiple stalls | Closed | Varies—one person every other stall with no more than two in a bathroom; one person at sink; cleaned after every use | Open—one person every other stall with no more than two in a bathroom; one person at sink; cleaned after every use |
| Lounges—food, drink | Closed | No food or drink prepared on-site; no food brought in unless through accommodation if needed after reduced schedules are possible; drinks with closed lids and straws only; limited time of use for a limited number of people using noncloth seating with post cleaning; no games or resources "out"; no sleeping | No food or drink prepared on-site; food brought in with reduced schedules, never left post use; drinks with closed lids and straws; limited time of use for a limited number of people using noncloth seating with post cleaning; no games or resources "out"; no sleeping |
| Staff Meeting Areas | No meetings/areas closed | Limited number of meetings per work shift; no refreshments; no drinks prepared on-site but can be brought to meeting with lids and straws; no eating in meetings; limited time for meeting for a limited number of attendees using noncloth seating with post cleaning; no handouts; no shared tech | No refreshments; no drinks prepared on-site but can be brought to meeting with lids and straws; no eating in meetings; limited time for meeting for a limited number of attendees using noncloth seating with post cleaning; no handouts; no shared tech |

Anyone who has visited a number of different libraries in this or other countries understands—much as I discussed at the beginning of this chapter—that library spaces are often very small and try to—within reason—deliver the same services and resources with the same expertise, in small spaces. This (of course) means the choices for some libraries intensify as managers realize they have to take a hard look at the future of service, spaces, and furniture, and it may also mean that unique care or recommended behaviors or PPE may have to stay in place for longer periods of time.

In addition, typically older library structures, no matter how big or the size of the library building overall, are often designed with departments and services in separate rooms (e.g., special materials or age-level resources and services) that qualify as much smaller spaces. The breadth, by type and size of library—as well as all worker areas—include the following:

- small departments within larger higher education environments (lounges, self-services, specialized resources, unique collections, temperature controlled, tutoring labs, computer labs, archives, classrooms for librarians/information literacy, classroom faculty spaces);

- small departments within larger public library environments (youth services, children's activities, maker spaces/innovation spaces, lounges, genealogy, computer labs, specialized resources, unique collections, temperature controlled);

- small public and academic libraries co-located inside other buildings of the institution, community;

- entities that share some common support areas (common meeting rooms, shared small group, innovation or study rooms, shared lounges, shared technology hubs or information commons, entry foyers, bathrooms, kitchens, patio/outdoor areas, computer labs);

- special libraries within other environments (law firms, hospitals, agencies, companies, associations, etc.); and

- school libraries within all levels and sizes of schools—public and private—as they are often smaller spaces, central spaces with no walls (literally), or areas within school libraries with their own or shared spaces (study rooms, lounges, technology hubs or information commons, entry foyers, bathrooms, patio/outdoor areas, computer labs, self-services, tutoring labs, computer labs, maker spaces/innovation spaces, lounges).

While managers may say, "Of course we know—we live with this!" it helps to cost out areas—for no other reason and at the very least—to order signage and to remind ourselves of longer timelines needed for some areas such as relocations of services or closures.

### *Post*-Post Pandemic (with a Focus on Facilities)

*Is* there a return to normal after the pandemic? Like all good researchers, let's look at history and precedent—and if one looks at 1918 post-pandemic, the answer is "no" or "not for many years" or "not really." But what does that mean for us?

Beginning in 1918, the pandemic killed millions of people and "lasted" until the early 1920s. That means in 2020 language, this situation could easily last until 2022 or 2023. So what is the good news and what is the bad news and what does that mean for managers? In addition, it is almost impossible—when talking about the "normal"—to separate out facilities from other issues since so many precautions and care issues revolve around "space" and "distancing" so all areas are integrated when looking at both good and bad news.

### Good News

- In any public-health situation or transmittable disease situations, herd immunity is both a natural and vaccine-related issue, and with COVID-19 or the more serious viruses, herd immunity happens one virus at a time and only comes or most likely comes with vaccines based on the percentage of the population vaccinated, typically of certain ages. Clearly a virus can run its course, but typically only in its first form, and—more realistically—the vaccine must first be broadly applied and given time to create immunity with most of the population participating in variation by variation.
- Although controversial throughout, precautions taken—like face masks—are expected to become more commonplace and accepted in society. And while personal choice and masks became politically polarizing, the reality is—given leadership and political influences—less than 100 percent of the adult population—for example—will get vaccinated.

- Almost automatically and sometimes unknowingly, people continue to socially distance on their own and fewer people (certainly not everyone) feel comfortable in very crowded environments *without* taking care to wear a face covering, keep their distance from those obviously sick, and be aware of cleaning spaces.
- Cleaning is more commonplace as to frequency, product type, and consistency—both personal handwashing and face cleaning continues as also more consistent and more thorough. (People carry cleaning packets and hand sanitizers with them in great numbers.)
- People learn to touch their face less than they used to—also unknowingly as well as capturing sneezes and coughing.
- It's a different world than in the early 1920s or during the 1918 pandemic; that is, technology assists us in distancing ourselves, transportation is different, and work life is different. It is easier to—for example—continue to work remotely and—obviously—a greater percentage of people can continue to be successful remotely than before.

### Bad News (and You Knew the Big "But" Was Coming)

- It *is* a different world than in the early 1920s, but that is bad news as well. Although technology assists us in distancing ourselves and delivering information, it may not be the correct information—either accidently or deliberately—and society has to work harder to communicate clearly and educate others on information that is skewed incorrectly for—among other things—political gain.
- Transportation *is* different, but it is faster, and more people transported is *not* good news, as the virus can spread significantly more quickly and globally.
- Work life *is* different, and it is easier to—for example—continue to work remotely, but managing people remotely is hard work for both the workers and management. In addition, people are social animals, and bringing people to the "marketplace" for synergy and collaboration happens remotely but *not* as successfully as in person.
- Technology could easily (as it has in the past) define classes of haves and have-nots, but in greater numbers than those based on "those who can afford the newest" or "at all." That is, those who can will easily form a new class of "haves" who—like generations before them—"can afford to work remotely," so have-nots are frontline, where many (though not all) lower-paid, less-credentialed jobs are happening.

- Workers can easily be disenfranchised by institutions that require their return as the jobs available to them are only in-person jobs.
- The virus mutates—as we have been told all along and as 1918 science and every other pandemic have shown us. So although there is evidence that herd immunity and vaccines assist in preventing even mutating viruses, it stays present and morphs into how we see it today—cold and flu season necessitating the continued search for vaccines.
- The big issues—such as we have seen—are political issues and—with such an incredibly political beginning—odds are politicizing of the virus remains.
- As the uninsured population and job market grow, those increasing numbers of people in this category who have no insurance are most vulnerable to new strains of the virus.

What does this mean for managers and for their workers? Their users and their spaces?

## Workers/Users

- It is difficult—at best—as well as inappropriate to require "behaviors and actions," some of which people count as personal, for workers.
- Managers must work with attorneys, worker unions, and other work groups, as well as workers themselves, to outline safety practices and to remember to keep safety—rather than profits—in the forefront.
- Managers must track and pursue information on the "pandemic" laws, suspended or new, such as those allowing organizations to require contact tracing for workers and users. Even though these activities can be perceived as "medical tests," their continuance needs to be possible for workplace use.
- Consequences for workers not following new guidelines, practices, policies, and requirements need to be formalized and—as in other situations—created with legal issues explored.
- Consequences for users not following new guidelines, practices, policies, and requirements need to be formalized and—as in other situations—created with legal issues explored.

## Spaces

- Environments must be reviewed (even if it pains managers to do so) for percentage of users allowed in and for what length of time. It is unlikely that foundational laws for "occupancy" will be changed, but—for some time—percentage of space that can be occupied will be naturally limited less by man-

dates and more by location of seating, fewer tables, or fewer chairs at tables. As it expands, the reality is that as occupancy percentage shifts (they began at 25 percent, went to 50 percent, went back to 25 percent, and then—in some cases—went to 75 percent or 100 percent), even at 75 percent of occupancy, managers will find that they:
  ○ can assist fewer users during a day;
  ○ will not be able to allow as many users rotating in as quickly on uncleaned hardwired desktops;
  ○ must replace desktops with laptops (very gradually unless funding is available);
  ○ must continue e-resource/hybrid collection building (difficult to sustain unless operations funding is available); and
  ○ create ongoing programming but for fewer attendees, with a goal of maintaining the core of many libraries: connecting users to information, literature, and reading through author visits, story times, book clubs, and instruction.

Given the good and bad news, what specific proactive steps can be taken to move ahead for facilities, spaces, and furniture decisions?

It should be said that although there are recommended steps to take in each chapter on topics such as human resources, services, and so on, because facilities and in-person services are under scrutiny in this chapter and the underpinning of so many of the library's activities, some content is repeated. In addition, although the norm for the number of hours of contact for events to take place in "same spaces" such as teaching, stories, presentations, and so on, is two hours throughout this content, libraries may want to limit time to one hour or less. Although this deprives users of a significant block of time, it means that fewer users get what they need. To combat this, libraries can provide some public desktops for two hours, some for one hour, and some for thirty minutes or pre-prepare for users seeking two hours with recommended search strategies or resource links emailed in advance when users schedule appointments.

- As stated before—furniture should be upholstered in washable or pretreated materials. (Note: All upholstery—but especially fabric that is advertised as "sanitized" or "germ-resistant"—should be carefully researched prior to consideration for purchase or use.)
- Libraries should consider providing fewer pieces of furniture (chairs, etc.) to assist in having fewer people in the library at any one time.
- Furniture must be "flexible" and should be able to be easily moved (e.g., chairs with wheels, handles, etc.).

- Libraries should have fewer "installations" of hardwired technology, and although chapter 10 includes recommendations on public printing as a service, the printing issues with hardware drive the printing service. If libraries cannot provide a contactless printing service (and few can), scheduled printing for printers removed from direct public access might be used if printing companies or kiosks are not able to be purchased/under subscription.
- Study or work carrels should not be purchased in large, attached units and—if they are—they should be flexible and able to be relocated without deconstruction.
- Floorplans must have furniture positioned farther apart than previously. Users moving flexible furniture should be asked (via signage) to return furniture to previous arrangements, or these roles and responsibilities should be added into worker position descriptions. Floor markings can assist in outlining where furniture can and can't go as well as signage that indicates (for example) "No more than one study table and four chairs are available for this space" or "When your scheduled time is up, please return your furniture to the floorplan design posted on the back of the door of the room."
- Individual seating should exceed group seating—if possible—but these individual seats should be flexible (wheels, handles) to allow groups to gather, but naturally further apart.
- During stages of the pandemic identified at designated levels, workers will work fewer hours in spaces. While in the library, they will move around throughout the day choosing (1) public space for their work, (2) remote work spaces, (3) to work elsewhere in the facility, or (4) use (alone) smaller rooms typically used by students.
- Smaller areas—for example, study rooms, small enclosed or cordoned off departments, and work areas—must be changed in scope and have fewer users in spaces at one time, frequent cleaning, signage for social distancing, and fewer hours in shifts for library workers in these spaces.
- Facility cleaning must be increased and standardized.
- Workers must have cleaning rituals—within reason—built into their work practices.
- Workers must have continuous training in:
  ○ cleaning—worker area and worker expectations;
  ○ cleaning—public service spaces;
  ○ teamwork (e.g., working together successfully while ensuring respect for differing ideas on safety, etc.); and
  ○ social distancing with users and other workers.

- Circulation desks need to maintain some PPE barriers—distancing, fewer in line, restructuring queuing at desks, cleaning, and options for workers to continue to wear masks or when necessary.
- Reference desks—previously on the road to morphing into more contact and relationship-building spaces—need to reconsider reverting back, if only temporarily, for protection and distances by using existing PPE, careful hardwired placement, queuing using stanchions, and positioning desks with chairs but with substantially less access. One concern is that ongoing debates on a standup desk vs. a sit-down desk are continuing because of the dichotomy of choices; that is—a standup desk means less time exposed to users but also means people can move closer to those on duty.
- Libraries should identify the best way for them to have furniture return to original—post-pandemic plans including signage, a campaign for involving others in "righting" furniture, and a re-education program.
- Limiting users overall or to certain spaces or for lengths of time is achieved through signups and appointments for assistance, using spaces, using technology, and so on.
- Post-pandemic budgets include free-to-users PPE to minimize conflict and concern when users forget what is required, recommended, or welcomed.
- Although a number of individuals refuse to comply (e.g., get vaccinated, use PPE, stay distanced), narratives for dealing with conflict should be maintained.
- Library administrators should work with local or institutional police or security forces to determine recommended language for libraries to seek assistance in dealing with users who do not comply or comply but are combative or inappropriate to each other or to library workers.
- Libraries should assess their outreach practices, vehicles, and so on, to ensure that both they and their users can practice safe measures while using outreach materials or during outreach events. (Vehicles may be more difficult to use for boarding, and events might instead be planned exclusively for outside.)

Again, paying attention to spacing of furniture and technology as well as altering frontline schedules are key elements in providing protection for workers and improving their comfort levels. Fewer hours of long public service desk shifts—while masks are required and after—allows for workers with shorter frontline schedules to have fewer hours of exposure to users as well as opportunities to clean and rest from using and working with

PPE. Giving workers choices provides a positive process for managing through restrictive situations.

## HVAC

Finally, one issue that cuts across all types and sizes of libraries and is a critical element for library workers and their users is—to put it bluntly—air. And one can discuss "air" in many categories including ventilation, heating, working outside, air-conditioning, access to external air exchange, purification, and filtering—to name just a few—but it remains to be an important issue.

Oddly enough, however, halfway through the pandemic, little research seems to prove that—for example—HVAC systems carry or transmit the virus. This realization, however, expressed in pandemic recovery training events by scientists and researchers as well as from science-based presentations from vendors, provides information about what *is* important to know as we prepare our environments for the short returns and long hauls of setting up our spaces for the future.

Problems abound in this area regarding recovery literature, as many recommendations go beyond the usual "How can we clean or actually sanitize?" and instead include unrealistic solutions. These recommendations, voiced by consultants and experts suggesting broad changes as well as specific location-only changes, may be providing ideas for better-funded environments, but many are ideas libraries simply can't afford or afford immediately. So, before pandemic concerns and recovery related to air can be suggested, there are a number of situations that must be noted:

1. Regularly opening windows or getting different screens for windows or having windows thoroughly cleaned is helpful, but the majority of libraries today—whether newer or remodeled facilities—do not have windows at all and if they do, they are not windows that can be opened.

2. Regulating temperatures as to on and off and colder vs. hotter is not always possible. In a growing number of locations—and especially in more recent remodels or newer constructions—libraries located within other facilities or libraries where umbrella organizations choose to "modernize" or automate to regulate air cannot control their own temperature and use related to heating and cooling. In addition, many air regulation systems do have units for local control but these units are locked to avoid negative maintenance contracts abused through constant changes by workers or users.

3. Choice of air systems, filtering, and so on, while a good idea, often has to conform to green standards in today's libraries; therefore, products used in heating and cooling might be required to be certified or maintained in order to maintain a green ranking. (It is very possible, however, that the energy efficiency gained through achieving levels of green standards can already meet clean air suggestions and should be explored.)

4. Varying air flows in spaces is not often possible as smaller rooms in libraries do not have any air/ventilation (older, historic, or retrofitted facilities) or separate air controls.

5. Purchasing sanitizers or filters of a certain kind is a great idea but not always possible due to cost or—more likely—not possible because the library is restricted to buying off of predetermined lists.

6. Purchasing in bulk or online or a specific product is not always possible as libraries do not always have the latitude to buy separately from their umbrella organization purchasing departments.

So even with all of the caveats, recommendations for changes to air in libraries are relatively simple and include the following:

- Provide as much fresh air as possible to dilute existing air that may contain problem particles.
- Have HVAC units assessed by certified engineers, cleaned prior to opening/going back in, and then increase standard cleaning schedules. Flush the system each morning and every evening after closing—as the engineer recommends given your system and size of building/spaces—but typically for two hours.
- Investigate if your system can exchange air more quickly or more times than it currently does (is two to three times per hour possible?) to—as stated earlier—dilute existing air.
- If building new or remodeling an existing library or an environment built for another tenant, consider replacing air systems with Dedicated Outside Air Systems. These increase ventilation by using 100 percent outside air. HVAC systems designed for limited percentages of outside air intake might be compromised.
- Increase filter efficiency (considered more effective than more frequent exchange of air).
- If you have windows, explore creating air ventilation more often through these windows with specific technology/equipment instead of just opening windows.
- Use wall-mounted or HEPA filters along with fans—for example—as fans in and of themselves don't circulate the air as needed. (Sound mitigation may

be needed for larger units with more circulation or exchanges of air.)

- Purchase standalone air filters for heavy-use spaces.
- In the absence of funding or the availability of much technological change, use overhead fans or table fans that are higher than floor fans. Use an expert to identify locations where fans can blow but not spread air from one user or one worker to another—that is, find fans that draw air upward.
- Engineers recommend—to slow virus growth—a level of humidity in spaces that is 40 to 60 percent relative humidity with 70–75 degrees Fahrenheit temperature.
- Consider placing high-energy filters in systems or the standalone ones over intakes or exchanges in public areas. (MERV)-13 grade filters are recommended—if the library's system can maintain this grade. If the system cannot handle the recommended grade, make sure they are inspected and changed/cleaned more often.
- Buy from reputable dealers (obviously) by reading research reports and industry reviews as well as by looking for certified testing designations from the American Society of Heating, Refrigerating and Air-Conditioning Engineers or from the (older) American Society for Testing and Materials. Also, although ionization is used and touted in many non-U.S. settings, it has not been proved as a process that has success in killing the virus. Subscribe to expert resources for readiness and good emergency-management practices from:
  - Centers for Disease Control (CDC) (current levels of danger, frequency of spread, employer suggestions for workplace safety, building ventilation, etc.);
  - Environmental Protection Agency (EPA) (public-space indoor air, ventilation, air cleaners, filters, viruses, and how they spread);
  - American Society of Heating, Refrigerating and Air Conditioning Engineers (ASHRAE) (certified products, standards, product impact, use);
  - American Industrial Hygiene Association (AIHA) (cleaning standard); and
  - U.S. Department of Labor OSHA Newsletters (public health recommendations for workplaces, public settings, and general worker safety).

## Smaller Libraries and Solo Librarian Environments

Many of the libraries in the United States are small environments with small physical spaces and few workers. While the sizes of physical facilities and the number of service points should typically dictate the number of workers in the library, that isn't always the case. *And al-*though smaller environments are integrated throughout this chapter, the following information includes overall recommendations for physical spaces and a chart that includes thirteen library services and how they would be handled in two pandemic stages: during the pandemic (short term) and during the pandemic (longer term).

Overall recommendations for the smallest of library spaces (again, some content in this section is similar to some of the information provided in context in charts):

- Libraries seeking expanded spaces for user computer use, research, or programming might provide distancing among tables/chairs/public service desks by using outdoor areas (finished or unfinished), meeting rooms, or unused indoor or outdoor spaces in contiguous, nearby entities.
- The availability of library resources can continue during the worst of pandemic stages with outdoor or curbside services. If these services are piloted, advertising and labeling should take care to be accurate. That is, "touchless" during pandemics is a complicated approach—but doable—when transmitting materials; however, touchless is dictated by a series of steps that should be followed to ensure safety.
- Using external (near to the library) containers such as lockboxes, cages, or lockers provides extended timing using password or combination locks or third parties.
- Commercial entities/vendors such as car services or community services that continue to deliver (food, groceries, medical, etc.) can expand resource delivery. While some services pick up materials, others have lockers throughout the community that can be temporarily used and can also represent 24/7 services when lockers or containers outside the library are not possible.
- Remote or device-driven services are suggested, using—if the library does not have a video or web-based service or software package—online, free, live, synchronous access. If print/paper resources are not accessible or are accessible but not safe, a librarian can identify e-resources to substitute. Advertising should clarify this temporary approach and should reflect careful assessment or vetting processes for choosing online content.
- Reduced hours of service are recommended to avoid creating services that the worker cannot sustain during the alternative service project. If it is not possible to choose a block of time, a librarian can provide the service but by appointment only.

- As in larger settings, if the library is open for any area or for any length of time, staggered open hours of use are recommended with periods of time between hours open. In smaller spaces where workers are limited and cleaning is not possible, the librarian can increase the length of time between uses, or work with an outside group (much like the community "Junior League" service approach of "done in a day") to provide cleaning of resources between uses.
- Smaller libraries with fewer workers need to consider—if any open hours are chosen—greatly limiting available areas for use, with an eye to excluding interactive areas such as office productivity areas, restroom access, and tech availability. In addition, the library should review their circulation policies with longer checkout times, items going out that didn't circulate before, and suspending fines and fees. In addition, limits on items checked out can be lifted to reduce the timing of people returning to the library even though fines and fees may no longer be maintained.

### Frontline Space Usage in Small Libraries

The actions suggested in table 2.4 can be characterized by the fact that far fewer spaces are open at all, and if they are open, they have greatly reduced hours for interactions. In addition, the focus on services includes primarily those areas where users do not "interact" with resources to minimize contact, cleaning, and so on.

TABLE 2.4
Pandemic and Post-Pandemic Public Spaces—Smaller Environments

| Activities/Functions | STAGE 1 *During Pandemic* *x date–x date* | STAGE 2 *Short Term* *x date–x date* | STAGE 3 *Long Term* *x date–x date* |
|---|---|---|---|
| Libraries should—using technology (phones, iPads, etc.)—consider recorded messages (phone messages, podcasts) to provide users with short voice messages or media posted online (on YouTube, social media, Facebook, apps, with QR codes, etc.) to explain the stage the library is in and the expectations of users and the services and spaces guidelines. This method—easily updated—eliminates handouts and wordy signage (embedded QR codes on signs) and provides the users with information while taking workers out of the frequent or lengthy updating explanation. | | | |
| Checking out materials, resources and Reference, Reader's Advisory, Information (any and all must use PPE for presenter area with users and presenter required to wear PPE) | Closed to in-person; if outdoor area is available, temporary 6' distancing by appointment for no in-person assistance but economic assistance such as use of job-search files, scholarship, pandemic relief packets of information to give away, resume materials, etc., and printing delivery to a locker/on demand *or* curbside pickup; touchless checkout—lockers; self-check; no checkout of print/paper | Closed to in-person; continued use of outdoor area if available, temporary 6' distancing with PPE by appointment for no in-person assistance but newspapers, reference materials, homework help, tech content, and economic assistance such as use of research materials, scholarship info, assignments and papers, job-search files, resume materials, and use of small tech for productivity, etc., and printing delivery to a locker/on demand *or* curbside pickup; touchless checkout—lockers; self-check; no checkout of print/paper, self-check if possible<br><br>(PPE: shield, guard, gloves, cleaning between each visit, socially distanced checkout, and intermittently quarantined spaces) | Open with reduced hours of service and *very* limited use with PPE and 3', 6' environment and continued use of outdoor area if available; temporary 3', 6' distancing with PPE by appointment; by appointment in-person assistance and some use of materials such as newspapers, reference materials, homework help, tech content, and economic assistance such as use of research materials, scholarship info, assignments and papers, job-search files, resume materials, and use of small tech for productivity, etc., and printing delivery to a locker/on demand *or* curbside pickup; touchless checkout—lockers; self-check; no checkout of print/paper; self-check if possible<br><br>(PPE: shield, guard, gloves, cleaning between each visit, socially distanced checkout, and intermittently quarantined spaces) |

*(continued)*

TABLE 2.4   *(continued)*

| Activities/Functions | STAGE 1<br>*During Pandemic*<br>*x date–x date* | STAGE 2<br>*Short Term*<br>*x date–x date* | STAGE 3<br>*Long Term*<br>*x date–x date* |
|---|---|---|---|
| Presentations, Programming, Teaching Spaces (any and all must use PPE for presenter area with users and presenter required to wear PPE) | Closed, online only | If open, no in-person except for appointments that can be held outside or only/ single use of library | Open with reduced hours for general work and spaces; open only—for example—two days a week in a.m. and p.m. for teaching, presentations, etc., single use of library; if a scheduled event, no more than one to two hours, limited to 3', 6' apart social distancing |
| Research with institutional tech/PCs and no in-person assistance | Closed | Closed; outside area can be booked and tech checked out or personal tech can be used | If open, reduced hours, 3', 6' apart, and PPE inside; outside area can be booked and tech checked out or personal tech can be used |
| Studying with user materials— individual seating and no in-person assistance | Closed | Closed; outside area can be booked for studying by appointment only less than two hours; areas cleaned pre- and post-use and self-cleaning materials available | If open, reduced hours, 3', 6' apart and PPE inside; outside area can be booked and tech checked out or personal tech can be used; appointment only less than two hours; areas cleaned pre- and post-use and self-cleaning materials available |
| Studying in small user study rooms | Closed to users; workers can use if PPE and 6' and for quarantining materials | Closed to users; workers can use if PPE and 6' and for quarantining materials | Closed to users; workers can use if PPE and 3', 6' and for quarantining materials |
| Meeting Rooms (not used for meetings, programs, or teaching due to size typically and enclosed) | Closed to users; workers can use if PPE and 6' and for quarantining materials | Closed to users; workers can use if PPE and 6' and for quarantining materials | Closed to users; workers can use if PPE and 3', 6' and for quarantining materials |
| Assistance with technology— user-owned, institutional | Closed | Closed, online assistance only | If open, reduced hours, 3', 6' apart and PPE inside; outside area can be booked and tech checked out or personal tech can be used with assistance by worker; appointment only less than two hours; areas cleaned pre- and post-use and self-cleaning materials available |
| Users Interacting—each other, realia, exhibits, displays | Closed | Closed | If open, reduced hours and no interaction; view exhibits and displays only; no handouts/ giveaways |
| Shelving/Browsing | Closed | Closed | If open, reduced hours; no browsing, but workers can retrieve for use outside or touchless checkout |
| Productivity—self-serve with institutional tech | Closed | Closed—can be checked out and distributed through locker or checked out and used outside with request/ checkout for use at desk (charging devices, charging iPads, laptops, calculators, scissors, stapler, etc.) | If open, can be checked out and distributed through locker or checked out and used outside with request/checkout for use at desk (charging devices, charging iPads, laptops, calculators, scissors, stapler, etc.) |

| Activities/Functions | **STAGE 1**<br>*During Pandemic*<br>*x date–x date* | **STAGE 2**<br>*Short Term*<br>*x date–x date* | **STAGE 3**<br>*Long Term*<br>*x date–x date* |
|---|---|---|---|
| Copying/Printing | Closed | Closed; if open and critical, reduced hours, and use outside, so *not* self-serve/on demand, with limited copies, prints, scans, etc.; queue is 6' apart with stanchions or get a number to be called up or order by text/by appointment | Open with reduced hours, and if open and critical, reduced hours, and use outside so *not* self-serve/on demand, with limited copies, prints, scans, etc.; queue is 3', 6' apart with stanchions or get a number to be called up or order by text/by appointment |

# 3

# Collections and Resources

ALTHOUGH LIBRARIANS have long heard the refrain that (print/paper) books are going away, and therefore we don't need libraries, most know that this isn't the case. Interestingly though, over this past year, many decision makers, legislators, and leaders have been convinced (or at least more convinced!) of the importance of what we *do* offer. In fact, libraries have been in the spotlight—whether their physical facilities are open or closed—providing invaluable services and resources to offer classic as well as current print materials, technology, information, realia, and expert assistance with research and information. They have provided home schooling resources, the latest consumer information users can trust, instructions on how to build that deck, access—for tens of thousands of people—to high-speed internet and the opportunity to borrow that e-device so the 850 books they want can go along with them on their trip, and—if open—places to study, complete business paperwork, focus on taxes, and sign in to online learning. But there are bigger reasons why libraries are needed:

- Not all books or print/paper materials are or ever will be available digitally.
- Information, research, and resources are *not* easy to find and—if found—are not easy to use or access.
- People need assistance in getting the right answer or getting on the path so they can make the best choice, whether they are buying a car, repairing their HVAC, or writing that paper on Maya Angelou. It's not enough—for many and sometimes most needing help—to hand someone a Bluebook and have them locate their car or showing them the medical reference materials and having them find the specific side effects needed.
- Not every e-device can or will access or download every resource.

- Not everything in print/paper has been or will be digitized.
- Many content creators (publishers, vendors, agencies, researchers, etc.) use a publishing or accessibility model that embargos content from immediate availability—especially in research, scientific, or educational environments.
- Some readers learn best with the written word/in print/paper, others learn with visuals, and some are more successful with auditory ways of learning. People read and learn at very different levels and have (or don't have) success with many different modes and methods of reading, learning, and life-long learning.
- Many people only enjoy the print/paper information format. Others may read something online and then want to print out content they wish to keep.
- Many people use one format for reading or learning for work while preferring another for leisure.
- Some users have all of the latest technology they need at both home and work to access, read, understand, select, store, and maintain content, while others do not have the newest hardware or software and do not have jobs where technology is available to them to use other than for work (or at all).
- Some users have the hardware they need to read content online, but do not have all the needed, fastest, or most appropriate connections.
- Some users use technology every day for eight or more hours at a time at work and do not want to use technology for leisure, recreation, or DIY, to name just a few areas.
- E-titles are significantly higher in cost than print/paper (for libraries but typically not for general users) with some prices doubling or even 2.5 times higher for an e-title vs. the same title in print/paper.

There have been many global events and major changes over the last seventy-five years that have greatly affected how libraries "do business," including technology (hardware and software), technology connectivity (networks, wireless), and—with the broadest definition of content delivery platforms—the internet. These changes have caused, led, and even forced libraries to change as they embraced and often were early adopters for not only their use but also for their design and delivery of resources to support and deliver their expertise, services, and resources, for community and constituent use of existing as well as new and cutting-edge elements.

The pandemic has been no exception. At the start of the pandemic, libraries realized they needed to ensure critical points of access to collections (if they didn't have them already)—while restricting or limiting access to and use of in-person and common-use areas—but it hasn't been easy or possible to introduce and sustain pandemic-driven collection and resource activities. Why?

- While a significant number of resources needed to be made available online and accessible remotely, many were cost prohibitive for initial purchase or subscription or sustained funding.
- Many existing resource and service operating agreements and contracts did not allow for remote access and in some cases allowed for remote use, but only for a predetermined limited or targeted number or group of users, and increased users (obviously) increases costs.
- Although vendors created COVID-19 assistance packages, bundles, or offerings that were free or reduced in cost, it was and is reasonable to expect that "deals" were not going to be available in perpetuity and libraries—looking ahead to nonpandemic times—could not afford to commit to online collection prices beyond initial free periods.
- Accessible materials—to ensure adherence to contracts and agreements—needed to be behind authentication software, and as stated above, while "balloon" payment product amounts could not be promised, future costs of authentication were not possible either.
- Email, free video conferencing, texting, synchronous chatting, and the telephone—needed to connect users to information and research assistance and access to collections—did provide some access points and venues initially, but many connectivity vendors would not provide ongoing access or access as robust or at the price points needed to support remote users for access, assistance, and resources.

- Infrastructure software was and is now needed to provide the necessary level of sophistication for online programs, "web conferencing," or synchronous chatting that—for example—allows webpages and library-collection content to be "pushed" to users.

So—with the realization that libraries were important or even more important than before and with the challenges of counting who is using what and from whom—libraries are reviewing their policies, considering shifting formats of resources, and exploring collection access and acquisitions processes to face a possible different future and balance of resources. And although this chapter is not a "how to" for collection development overall, several definitions and comments are needed for a broad overview for discussing what is changing.

## Managing Today's and Tomorrow's Collections

*Collection management* is the very broad term most commonly used to describe the area of the profession that includes not only the development of collections (e.g., scanning the who, what, when, and where of users and potential users for need/use; selecting; and acquiring) but also management issues, including evidence-based collection building, justifying the choice and balance format, budgeting, committing to purchased and subscription materials; the role of OER, collection-parameter identification (e.g., subject headings, classification for categorizing, labeling, housing, shelving, and storing), deselection/weeding, gift materials, preservation and conservation, emergency and disaster management for collection items and collection spaces, usage such as copyright, challenges to inclusion and exclusion, intellectual freedom issues (choice of labeling, restrictions, etc.), as well as counting, measurement, and assessment and then justification and accountability for collection processes and content. The additional or parallel management decisions include loaning technology for users unable to initially purchase or maintain technology, including equipment and connectivity.

As always, collection-management processes and practices need to be articulated in a collection-management program policy, and ancillary and infrastructure documents such as guidelines and standards, related policies, and connections (including constituent contacts or position descriptions and assignments for those who handle the acquisitions, bibliographic, content selection, and management processes) must be included. These aspects of a written policy are necessary to provide constituents with rationale for expending public dollars for the public or for the library's community, which—of course—varies by type of library.

And, although all collection-development activities have long been and should always be conducted according to a collection-development or collection-management policy, recent events have driven the need to revisit policy and procedures—in all areas—but especially relating to the balance of formats, allowing for the variety of different models of vendor contracts, the types of formats made available, parameters for use of resources, evidence gathered to support decision making for titles and authors, the use of newer resources such as OER, emergency-management timelines, purchases and subscriptions, the use of standing orders, and—as always—access vs. ownership.

These changing issues, due to the dramatic increase in remote services, however, are not new in the profession. In fact, it is common for librarians to be questioned on the percentage of money spent on resources that are print/paper vs. technology formats, the dollars spent on subscription rather than ownership, as well as dollars spent on any one content area, one user group, or one format. In addition, librarians have had to justify decisions to *not* cover some areas, to only deliver some content in one format, and to expand a format that drives the need for the library to circulate technology or expand wireless access beyond the library's doors or circulate wireless/connectivity.

Not only have recent occurrences spotlighted formats and technology, but the pandemic has also triggered soft money and grants and thus has driven collection decisions for purchases and subscriptions that were COVID-19/pandemic driven due to access or the lack of digital information on a topic. Finally—as all soft dollars and grants do—the need for libraries to count, track, measure, and assess use of materials for specific accountability is necessary for request and awarding of dollars.

Finally, newer titles for collection-management policies are being sought (e.g., "resource access policy") in the professional literature based on today's need to offer broader and more inclusive definitions. In addition, revised procedures are providing new content for collection-management policy appendices such as moving acquisitions steps to remote discussions, changing timelines, and streamlining materials integration and partnership projects. In addition, delivery pathways to using online resources—previously and typically *not* a part of the collection policies or procedures—are growing. In short, libraries are reviewing their collection-management documents with a need to make sure that their documents reflect the myriad of ways they collect, justify, and deliver content.

## What Issues Did the Pandemic Itself Bring to a Head?

In looking at library collections and pandemic issues, there are a number of issues that began and typically end during public-health emergencies such as a pandemic. Specifically, these include:

- updating library user profiles (with expectations that post-pandemic library user needs have changed);
- the depth and breadth of digital coverage;
- changes seen in the support of both formal and informal learning;
- the need to recognize and—within reason—address the issues related to the handling of materials, often done by many people each day *and* as an ongoing issue during all seasons of contagious situations;
- the need for possible updating of policies, practices, and procedures that articulate collection-development decisions behind policies and practices;
- data available outlining expenditure such as the percentage expended on ownership or subscription of e-resources vs. print/paper;
- a possible, strong need for technology/hardware to circulate outside the library;
- the presence of high-speed access to allow as well as increase access needed to view and download materials;
- the use of some aspects of techniques or ways libraries *do* manage choices and selections of materials;
- the decrease in the number of print/paper resources in favor of digital matching and related or appropriate titles or content; and
- the added requirements for subscribing to or purchasing resources that provide significant usage data in a timely fashion.

Aspects of collection management that are often defined as "models" of collection development (many of which are already in practice throughout libraries but prove to be successful models for others) include:

- the growth of access/subscription and stewardship rather than ownership growth;
- altering gift practices (fewer titles taken, materials cleaned when brought in, the resource is shelved and then, if chosen, is added, etc.);
- differently supporting existing or new user populations;
- maintaining fewer print volumes on-site overall:
  ○ weeding/deselection of outdated,
  ○ fewer volumes,

- fewer titles based on available matching or similar/acceptable data online/free (e.g., reference materials, aggregated governmental, and global statistics),
- cooperative acquisitions practices:
    - not every branch has to own an item/internal sharing, and
    - partnerships and collaborations for external sharing among types of libraries within a region where loading agreements are reached,
- organizational remote storage,
- cooperative remote storage among organizations, and
- special collections (ceasing, changing, choosing, preserving, conserving, supporting);
- reducing periodical purchases in print/paper and instead subscribing to digital sets (e.g., genres, popularity [bestsellers], author series, media adaptations);
- gap analysis and identification of needed resources in areas such as EDI (all areas), STEM (all areas), LGBTQ, health and wellness, "fake" news;
- scanning users and community/potential uses for format decisions such as technology access possible by checking out e-devices, wireless access hotspots;
- preservation and conservation and the effects of cleaning on resources;
- collection building for OER (because of, e.g., cost— of course—but also increase in interest given the need for digital resources in support of education);
- identification and importance of scholarly materials (access and availability of scholarly materials); and
- assessing the hosting possibilities of resources to either reduce or manage extensive platforms.

Additionally, several selection techniques (often referred to as "models" and *not* inclusive) are providing a standard for an organization for comparing and contrasting selection:

- Collaborative: expanding and formalizing the process of working with partners in organizations (K–12, higher education) to share in the final decision making for building collections
- Just-in-case: purchasing or making available one or more types of resources—based on data—that are *expected* or *projected* to be needed and used (popular fiction, bestsellers, nonfiction bestsellers, and nonfiction "other")
- Just-in-time: purchasing after requests/specific identified need for one or more types of resources (popular fiction, bestsellers, nonfiction bestsellers, and nonfiction "other")

- Patron-driven acquisitions: products with designated dollars encumbered where digital resources are offered and "browsed" electronically, and then when patrons locate and download a title, that title is automatically paid for, added to the collection, and charged against the subscription/access fee. (This is not too different from subscription services where print/paper was specifically chosen, items were circulated, and then at the end of the "season," librarians chose to add materials to the collections by paying reduced, separate costs per titles.)
- Approval plans/profile-based purchasing: aggregators for acquisitions seek organization user profiles/ constituent needs and then provide (fee-based) narrower lists of areas of interest. These approval plans (which can be menu driven based on collection-choice characteristics) assess subject and discipline areas and can include or exclude based on formats, costs, learning levels, and a variety of other aspects of collection development. Additional plans are available where other standard fee-based services are built in, such as processing costs so that materials arrive shelf-ready.

In addition to these aspects of collection management that can now be adopted or changed from the library's typical or usual approach, more and different content needs to be in the collection-management policy documents in the appendices. These items for the appendices include:

- umbrella organization vision, mission and value statements, outcomes, and so on;
- the library's foundational documents that guide the library overall and in their collection building such as the vision, mission, and value statements that should be reviewed when umbrella organizations review their content, or at least every two years or after a major event (a disaster/emergency event, etc.) and, if needed, revised (although typically not considered a disaster or emergency event, a significant budget cut or a change in the leadership of the organization should trigger a review as well);
- content from OCLC in general but also content from the OCLC's *Realm Project: Reopening Archives, Libraries and Museums*—the profession's research center on preservation, conservator issues, public-health emergencies such as pandemic conditions, and all of the effects these events might have on resources and services;
- any new metrics that began during the pandemic and continue post-pandemic such as usage stats

on new or temporary resources, use of technology, online assistance with collections, use of online collection pathfinders, access through library connections, and so on;

- CDC and other federal agency guidelines related to transmission through resources, resource storage, and use of collections;
- new practices—whether temporary or permanent—as reference points for future questions or issues that may arise (e.g., circulation of print/paper, use of equipment, suspension or start of any collection-related fines and fees);
- changes in position descriptions of those in collection management; and
- paradigm shifts to characterize temporary and/or permanent collection-development practices, policies, and so on.

## What Are the Typical Sections of a Collection-Management Policy?

Although sample and best practices or model policies are available for all sizes and types of libraries, every library typically has unique sections or content that supports only their library and their library's practices.

Examples of this outline prior to the pandemic are numerous; however, after the pandemic, there are many possible areas where policies need to be reviewed and—more than likely—revised. And, even though many post-pandemic changes will not be permanent, these changes will last significantly longer than previously thought because of the spread of the virus and virus variants as well as different communities' approaches to handling the pandemic and pandemic recovery. Pre-pandemic and post-pandemic examples include those illustrated in table 3.1.

**TABLE 3.1**
**Temporary Changes, Permanent Changes**

Publication Date: _____
Review Date/Revised Date: _____
Process Owner: _____

| Department/Area/ Function | As Is | Pandemic Changes, Temporary: all PPE required no matter what the government spaces dictate; contact tracing required at the door | Pandemic Changes, Post-Pandemic: all PPE required no matter what the government spaces dictate; tracing required at the door |
|---|---|---|---|
| **Collections** | | | |
| Browsing shelving; disinfecting project continues | | No browsing by users | Possible browsing designed row-by-row with one-way aisles; usage/capacity designated by government or less |
| Resources/Materials—print/ paper: disinfecting project continues | | Inaccessible | Accessible intermittently with quarantines on handling/use (see chapter 2) |
| Resources/Materials—media: disinfecting project continues | X | Inaccessible to in-person; requests taken by e-processes; materials pulled and circulated by outside lockers | Accessible intermittently with quarantines (longer than for print/paper; see chapter 2) |
| Realia: disinfecting project continues, but not all realia can be cleaned—items that can't be are not accessible | | Inaccessible; disinfecting project begins | Inaccessible until a significant amount of time with herd immunity; disinfecting project continues, but not all realia can be cleaned |
| Other—archival, genealogy, rare materials, manuscripts, maps, sheet music, local oral histories, area journals/ diaries, etc. | | When room is open or when materials are accessible, they are—as much as possible—contactless: 1. genealogy: cleaned once when accessed; quarantined after viewing; staff sets up and refiles 2. local oral histories: staff sets up and refiles tech with gloves 3. area journals and diaries: cleaned once when accessed; quarantined after viewing; staff sets up and refiles | When users access, materials are wiped when accessed; staff and users wear gloves; users have masks made available to them |
| **Furniture** | | | |
| Public Seating—inside: disinfecting project continues | | Inaccessible | Reduced numbers of tables and chairs; limits per hour and # using |

*(continued)*

TABLE 3.1 *(continued)*

| Department/Area/ Function | As Is | Pandemic Changes, Temporary: all PPE required no matter what the government spaces dictate; contact tracing required at the door | Pandemic Changes, Post-Pandemic: all PPE required no matter what the government spaces dictate; tracing required at the door |
|---|---|---|---|
| Public Seating—outside/ patio: disinfecting project continues | X | Socially distanced; registration at capacity designated by government | Socially distanced; registration at capacity designated by government |
| Workspace, Library Worker Office, Staff Bathrooms, Seating: disinfecting project continues | | Accessible intermittently; hot desks ceased; disinfecting project continues | Accessible intermittently with rotating use of limited timelines; hot desks ceased; disinfecting project continues |
| Others such as play area furniture, leisure seating, outside recreational items, etc. | | | |

**Spaces**

| | | | |
|---|---|---|---|
| Open Seating/Study: disinfecting project continues | | Closed; inaccessible | Reduced numbers of tables and chairs; limits per hour and registration at capacity designated by government |
| Small Group Rooms: disinfecting project continues | | Closed; inaccessible | Inaccessible until a significant amount of time with herd immunity; space used to accommodate library workers' hot desks prior to closing |
| Individual Spaces (tablet chairs, study carrels): disinfecting project continues | | Closed; inaccessible | Reduced numbers of tables and chairs; limits per hour and # using; when herd immunity is growing, these numbers of chairs will be introduced back in systematically; registration at capacity designated by government or less |
| Other such as museum areas, display/exhibit spaces, meeting rooms, public gardens, unique storage, lockers, water fountains, small construction (little libraries) area, work spaces, balconies, porches, etc. | | | |
| Public Bathrooms | | Closed | Closed |

**Public Service Workstations**

| | | | |
|---|---|---|---|
| Circulation Desk | X | Queue established with social distancing; PPE installed | Queue established with social distancing; PPE installed |
| Reference "Desks" | | Closed in-person; appointments only for virtual assistance; email; chat reference still available during library hours of service and until midnight at announced times; drop-in live assistance available during library hours of service | Social distancing; PPE installed; appointments only |
| Tech Assistance | | Closed in-person; appointments only/virtual live assistance only; available during library hours of service | Social distancing; PPE installed; appointments only/virtual and in-person |
| Other such as small business research assistance | | | |

**Student Technology/Public Workstations**

| | | | |
|---|---|---|---|
| Desktop PCs | | Closed in-person; inaccessible | Integrated back into user access through first thirty days post-pandemic; by sixty days, tech checked out using locker pickup—no inside use |

| Department/Area/ Function | As Is | Pandemic Changes, Temporary: all PPE required no matter what the government spaces dictate; contact tracing required at the door | Pandemic Changes, Post-Pandemic: all PPE required no matter what the government spaces dictate; tracing required at the door |
| --- | --- | --- | --- |
| Laptops | | Inaccessible | Integrated back into user access through first thirty days post-pandemic; by sixty days, tech checked out—no internal use; cleaning protocols are not as successful on charging devices |
| Personal Devices | X | Wireless on; outside use in PPE; socially distanced patio areas | Integrated back into user access through first thirty days post-pandemic; by sixty days, tech checked out—no internal use |
| Power/Charging | X | Wireless on; outside use in PPE; socially distanced patio areas; hot plugs unlocked/available for personal devices | Integrated back into user access to circulating units through first thirty days post-pandemic; by sixty days, tech checked out—no inside use, as cleaning protocols will not be successful on charging devices |
| Other such as simulation training | | | |
| **Teaching/Presentation Spaces** | | | |
| Computer Lab | | Inaccessible to the users; if approved, librarians will teach remotely through the lab | Integrated back into user access through first thirty days post-pandemic; registration at capacity designated by government |
| Information Literacy Teaching Spaces | | Inaccessible to the users; if approved, librarians will teach remotely through the lab | Integrated back into user access through first thirty days post-pandemic; by sixty days, tech checked out—no internal use but some appointments taken |
| Age-Level Activities | | Inaccessible to the users; if approved, librarians will teach remotely through the lab | Integrated back into user access through first thirty days post-pandemic; by sixty days, tech checked out—no internal use but some appointments taken |
| Other such as recording studios, film studios | | | |
| **Innovation Spaces (Discovery Activities, One-Button Studios, Maker Spaces)** | | | |
| Maker Room | | Inaccessible; not offered in-person; virtual presentations only and broadcast from spaces | Inaccessible; not offered; postponed |
| One-Button Studio | | Inaccessible; not offered in-person; virtual presentations only and broadcast from spaces | Inaccessible; not offered; postponed |
| Discovery Center | | Inaccessible; not offered; postponed | Inaccessible; not offered; postponed |
| Other entrepreneurial spaces for small businesses (app design, Etsy owners) | | | |
| **Partners (Tutoring, Supplemental Instruction, etc.)** | | | |
| Workshops: small-group and one-on-one tutoring | | Not offered; postponed; inaccessible; virtual use with registrations only | Slowly integrated back into socially distanced, public meeting room use |
| Other such as clubs meeting there; sponsoring special collections; government groups offering services (IRS, job fairs); nonprofit assistance (food stamps, job-seeking skills) | | | |

## How Do Smaller Libraries Manage Collections?

Although smaller libraries with smaller collections and budgets have to provide the same structure and accountability as large libraries, clearly keeping significant collection-management plans up to date is challenging. Typically, however, smaller libraries use more standard collection-management and -development plans identified as best practices available to them, and within those, forms for (for example) procedures and recordkeeping and assistance such as vendor/jobber aggregators and purchasing recommendations/plans/lists. Other smaller library collection-management issues include:

- fewer dollars for expenditures so paired-down numbers of both volumes and titles;
- fewer dollars for digital format and thus a need for partnerships;
- a need to create "wish lists" to structure gift giving, donations, and wills and estates to ensure that gifts and donations practices are under the control of the professional;
- choice of purchasing plans where processing materials is wrapped into prices so print/paper resources arrive shelf-ready or almost ready to shelve;
- weeding taking place more frequently to keep the collection—more than likely in a small space—fresh and relevant; and
- taking great care (for solo or smaller libraries and librarians) to identify the data needed for the decision makers in the umbrella structure—given limited time and opportunity—to be able to choose to spend time on what has an impact and what is relevant to those in control of dollars.

It should be said that it is *not* easier to spend money in a smaller setting or with reduced dollars. In fact, it is often harder to choose from among titles when dollars limit not only added copies but also a range of titles.

## If We Had Been Ready

Collections are so different throughout the library profession as well as the structures and funding that govern them, and it is almost impossible to discuss them as one or articulate one recommended process. So—rather than do that—libraries make sure that they have a set of guidelines that provide an accountable structure for spending public money, and—with the communities' trust—they spend the money responsibly. This structure includes extensive accountability with justification on how public dollars are spent.

Libraries have up-to-date collection-management policies with evaluations of products and processes (relating to the collection) every one to two years.

Collection content is dynamic and reflects constant changes in society, the publishing industry, the community, the profession, and the world of knowledge, information, and research.

Processes for collection data gathering and assessment are in place, and local, regional, and statewide data are readily available.

Libraries have local and statewide consortia and cooperative networks in place to aid in supporting the use of remote collections to capitalize on available dollars.

Library collections are valued (both literally and figuratively) as well as the expertise that supports the collection choices and connection of resources to users.

Libraries have extensive marketing of collections to focus on not just the collection but also the connection of the resources to the users as well as to make use of the available data on expertise and collection value.

*Note:* Pandemic relief funding came from the federal government in several packages and was designed to focus on collection expansion to digital resources and access and for equipment and software. Although libraries are used to applying for, using, tracking, and justifying soft funding or grant money, pandemic funding comes with a variety of tracking issues, including the following:

- Invoices for dollars spent during the pandemic must be dated as expended during the specific pandemic year. Specific start and stop timelines for expenditures are determined by grant/funding language and should be immediately referenced so that managers can work with vendors to get invoiced within grant parameters.
- Expenditures are spread out over a variety of timelines or annual expenditure timelines.
- Some funding must be spent within the grant guidelines, while some isn't restricted. Managers should review expenditure dates carefully.
- Dollars cannot be retroactively spent or requested for items—for example—that were heavily used during the pandemic but were—for example—paid for in the year previous to the pandemic.
- Although grant parameters for justification may be more general than managers are used to, umbrella organizations—in most if not all cases—can set additional parameters, such as target populations, only capital and no operating, and so on.
- Post-pandemic changes in collection processes may well include moving funding around to maintain funding for collection or collection-support materials.

- Post-pandemic ongoing funding estimates are not available until vendors choose post-pandemic timing for late, reduced, or bundled pricing, piggybacking cost on consortia contracts in existence and/or cost of access based on an organization's community population or user/student population, and so on.

Finally, few are aware of the human element of collection management. Organizations should review their collection-management policy to ensure that librarian roles and responsibilities are clear and that the support use of data analytics is clear for evidence for decision making, as well as to provide data that people don't know they need (percent spent on disciplines or by subject areas or by age-level group, the ratio of formats, the range of digital collections, the balance of classic and new, the assessment of not only breadth but also depth of subject areas, the percent of volumes to titles, and so on); these analytics are available for providing the rich profile of how collections are built deliberately—by experts—to support all information and research as well as educational, cultural, recreational, informational, and lifelong learning.

# 4

# Assessment and Accountability

THERE ARE MANY WAYS to assess services, resources, and use in libraries. And although *impact* and *success* with content or services are not as easy to assess for accountability or justification to everyone's satisfaction, this content identifies ways that librarians practice assessment is general and how general assessment translates to emergency situations as well as ways for assessing unique aspects within the pandemic and post-pandemic environments. Specifically, these approaches outline assessment tools and techniques a library can use to gather perceptions, opinions, facts, and ideas from those directly involved in or close to frontline library activities as well as approaches that review overall practices used before, during, and after the pandemic for data gathering and the questions to determine the types and kinds of data assessed. In addition, besides assessment of library-worker, system, and operations performance, it is imperative that libraries also assess and provide feedback on:

- how *umbrella organization* activities, choices, approaches, guidelines, and so on, worked for libraries;
- how *oversight groups* supported, helped, or hindered;
- how *partner organization* activities, choices, approaches, guidelines, and so on, worked for libraries; and
- how *external systems* that included libraries helped (or hindered).

## Techniques and Exercises: The Big Picture

It is important—when looking at either assessment techniques or data from techniques—that those asking the questions look at the big picture, that is, from day one or even before and on. This seems easy, but it is actually difficult to focus on "how did we get here" as much as "where we are now" or "where we ended up." The questions in table 4.1 are basic "end of" or "post" pandemic questions designed to review performance, but the most effective use of the chart is a process with individuals and groups—such as departments or teams or even partners or users—completing the columns (initially) independent of each other and any discussion. Completing the basic information as well as comparisons of data gathered will provide a 360-degree look of how—from a variety of perspectives—the organization performed and where it "is" in recovery and going forward.

Going forward based on assessment can be accomplished in many ways:

- Any group discussion data is best accomplished using outside facilitators or discussion leaders brought in to provide an equitable approach to completing assessment activities through the establishment of safe spaces.
- Once results are gathered and the decision is made of how to share the information, managers have to decide how the data is discussed:
  ○ An overview of opinions and data is gathered and any results are "published," and then departments or units work together up the chain of command to present ways of changing and moving forward in their specific areas, and so on.
  ○ An overview of opinions and data is gathered and any results are "published," and then departments or units meet together with managers and departments for data presentation, discussion, and solution discussion.
  ○ An overview of opinions and data is gathered and results are grouped, and then departments or units meet together with managers and departments

**TABLE 4.1**
**The Big Picture**

Publication Date:_____
Review Date/Revised Date: _____
Process Owner:_____

| Questions | Location/Service/ Area/Function *(narrowly defined areas are better for finding fail points and a solution)* | Process Owner/Decision Maker/Service Provider | Success on 1–7 Scale and Why (1 = did *not* work very well; 7 = worked very well) |
|---|---|---|---|
| 1. Did you/your library appoint specific COVID/pandemic coordinators? A team? If not, what is your pandemic oversight for library decisions? | • Each manager took a role? <br>• Senior librarian has full role? <br>• A pandemic coordinator and an advisory group/one from each department? <br>• We began with x, then halfway in, we changed to x. | • Managers already in place? <br>• Assistant managers elevated to management? <br>• Nonmanagers elevated to acting management? <br>• Co-managers or leaders? <br>• Other? | Rating: 5; we appointed people new to management and leadership. They did *very* well, but the survey they completed revealed they could have used more mentoring thru the process as well as a mechanism for immediate feedback in communication. |
| 2. Did you/your library appoint specific COVID/pandemic leaders? A leadership team? If not, what is your pandemic oversight for library decisions? | • Each one appointed took a role? <br>• Senior librarian has full role? <br>• A pandemic coordinator and an advisory group of one from each department? | • Leaders already in place? <br>• Nonleaders elevated to acting leaders? <br>• Other? | Rating: 7; each one appointed was rated very successful in an organizational survey. Open comments revealed those in the roles were good at delivering administrative information and finding answers when they did not know them. |
| 3. How would you summarize and rank the service model activities during the pandemic? | • Circulation—e-checkout and curb/touchless only <br>• Reference—all synchronous drop-in <br>• Age level—online programming with curb/touchless <br>• Special collections—access to print/paper closed; online reference/research scheduled appointments available | • Circ manager and pandemic coordinator <br>• Ref manager <br>• Youth manager and pandemic coordinator <br>• Special collections manager | Rating: 7; perfectly planned and executed well; no complaints; no illness <br><br>Rating: 6; good, didn't start soon enough <br><br>Rating: 5; did well but content delivered had notes returned indicating the content requested was not in the resources chosen. <br><br>Rating: 6; criticized, but not for being closed but had to be; handled conflict very well. |
| 4. No matter how your services are currently being offered (none; all or business as usual with PPE/safety rules; hybrid, some closed, some moved to virtual, some open, etc.), what three service changes have you made for the pandemic? | Shorter hours at public service desks <br><br>More appointments for those needing longer time with workers <br><br>Live synchronous instead of asynchronous | Circ and ref <br><br>Ref <br><br>Hours parallel to hours pre-pandemic | Rating: 5; circ needed more tech training (hardware and software) <br><br>Rating: 7; red/no training needed <br><br>Rating: 6; needed more tech training <br><br>Rating: 7; excellent |
| 5. Whatever operations/ business model you have during the pandemic, how are you keeping your workers motivated? | More choices <br><br>Flexible hours <br><br>New skills <br><br>One to three new web projects heretofore not allowed to do | All workers <br><br><br><br><br><br>Only applies to circ workers | Rating: 7 <br><br>Rating: 7 <br><br>Rating: 7 <br><br>Rating: 7; loved it, we need to continue post-pandemic |

| Questions | Location/Service/Area/Function (narrowly defined areas are better for finding fail points and a solution) | Process Owner/Decision Maker/Service Provider | Success on 1–7 Scale and Why (1 = did not work very well; 7 = worked very well) |
|---|---|---|---|
| 6. What are upper-level management and worker challenges? | Too much work for size of administration | Managers and leaders (both new and temporary) | Very difficult to "rank," but I think we could have done more. |
| 7. Identify three middle-level management challenges. | Too much work for manager for size of workforce in the circulation department<br><br>Need some training beforehand<br><br>Needed remote mentors; too much to expect existing managers to do | Managers (new and temporary) | Rating: 5, 6; very difficult to "rank," but I think we could have done more with more workers and external assistance as well as temporary funding. |
| 8. Identify three challenges for library workers. | Shift happened too quickly, but we couldn't help that.<br><br>We did not have enough online projects for them.<br><br>Networking with colleagues—each manager did this, and we could have created a wrangler to assist. | All levels | Rating: 5; very difficult to "rank," and we need to find a way to be prepared for more shifts and shorter hours.<br><br>Rating: 2; this has to change in general; huge miss for more than thirty days!<br><br>Rating: 2; add to communication plan |
| 9. Identify three problems/failures/mistakes. | Upper-level administration failures<br>• communication<br>• rationale<br>• no/little planning | Most levels | Rating: 3 (for organization), 6 (for how the library handled it); very little we could do |
| 10. What safety practices are in place for library workers? | Redesign service areas<br><br>Redesign worker areas<br><br>Full PPE/shorter schedules | All levels | Rating: 7<br><br>Rating: 7<br><br>Rating: 7 |
| 11. What safety practices are in place for users? | Redesign service areas<br><br>Redesign user self-service areas, no group work possible (study tables, browsing, media checkout, printing)<br><br>PPE required | All levels, all locations, all users | Rating: 6<br><br>Rating: 6<br><br>Rating: 6 |
| 12. No matter the service model, what resources are unavailable, and what services are halted due to the pandemic? | Small-group areas for users and workers<br><br>No shared work spaces<br><br>Special collections remain closed | All | Rating: 7; easy to close<br><br>Rating: 6; hard to implement<br><br>Rating: 7; easy to close |
| 13. Do library workers have access to what they need for success in pandemic roles? | It took a while to get there (two weeks), but we did. | All | Rating: 5 (at beginning), 7 (at end) |

*(continued)*

**TABLE 4.1** *(continued)*

| Questions | Location/Service/ Area/Function *(narrowly defined areas are better for finding fail points and a solution)* | Process Owner/Decision Maker/Service Provider | Success on 1–7 Scale and Why (1 = did *not* work very well; 7 = worked very well) |
|---|---|---|---|
| 14. Given changes made for the pandemic, is anything *not* returning to a pre-pandemic model? | We will reduce shared space.<br><br>We will increase cleaning overall and especially public service desks and shared spaces. | Workers, for sure, and most user spaces that we can control<br><br>Built into roles and responsibilities | Rating: 7 (for workers), 5 (for users)<br><br>Rating: 7 |

for data discussion and solution recommendations for looking forward.

- Aggregated data are presented by middle managers who assessed choices and directions and present categorized solutions, then distribute for departments to report back.
- Data are presented to a mixed-level worker group for either vetting suggestions or creating their own suggestions and recommendations.
- Data are presented to an independent third party who assesses content and designs recommendations and then consults in new directions.

No matter the approach decided on, however, instructions to individuals and groups should include an initial embargoing of shared information and opinion, a "compare and contrast" view of the evidence based vs. sheer opinion (both are valuable). Other aspects of data include: frequency of use of comments and concepts, the "word cloud" of chosen perceptions, opinions, comments by aggregation but mapped back to worker category (if managers want this information), any prioritized or forced-choice content, and other narrowing aspects such as ideas by location of respondent, ideas by level of respondent in the organization, comparing and contrasting internal and external and overall "grading" of the organization or department or location performance. To allow for assessing specific wording chosen, and so on, instructions should include "in your own words" (etc.), but more importantly, column entry answers should not be suggested or use of ideas through "for example" aren't provided—rather, trigger phrases, comments to start discussions, or statements and questions to assist people in framing their own responses should be used. And aggregated data is most helpful when consistent approaches are taken such as "using the same questions in categories," "using the same instructions," or similar or identical trigger words or phrases.

General recommendations to be included in instructions for successful use of this process include five issues:

1. No names should be used or personal information included. For initial, fair, and equitable assessments, request that names and titles *not* be included in positive or negative information. Answers, however, should be tailored enough so managers can identify specific categories of need, fail points, and mistakes and then make changes as needed including immediately, if necessary. Specificity should also lead—if any identifying questions are required—to egregious issues being addressed should they be identified or reported at this point in time. Tailored approaches for identification might include seeking:
   a. categories of workers such as "frontline staff" or "workers staffing the phones"; and
   b. general locations such as "frontline staff in circulation" or "workers staffing the phones in reference," "in [*designated school building*]" or "in [*designated library branch*]" (if they aren't too narrow).
2. Timing is critical in looking back, as often (and especially in emergency situations) the end does not justify the means. Timelines should be used either specifically or in general as "frontline staff in circulation during weekdays" or "workers staffing the contact-tracing doors at [*designated time*] on Saturdays." Timelines within the event can also be used, that is, "within the first month of the pandemic" or "immediately after we closed" or "in x month when we were open and everyone else was still closed."
3. If major or difficult issues may be targeted, the membership of those weighing in—in a focus group—might be limited to "no one in [*designated office*]" or "no one above third-level leaders."
4. Assessment processes should begin either during the emergency or immediately after, and clearly since there may not be an "end" to the pandemic as such, a specific measure of time can be chosen such as "at the beginning of the semester," "after the first of the year," or "when the county opens up again." When those dates are chosen, assessment should

begin quickly—not only to be able to correct mistakes quickly but also to identify positive elements of and impediments to moving forward.

5. Although both individuals and groups can be assessed and the data used in the reporting, the smaller the institution or elements of the institution and the fewer the employees or categories of employees, the less frequent that elements identification should be optional or not included at all. Considering anonymity, individual completion should always offer a

more safe space for reporting issues, problems, and elements such as ranking performance.

SWOTs are commonly done to offer the bigger picture of the organization or "all of the services" as a whole, for example. Their data provides for overviews or snapshots of services or areas (see table 4.2). Both SWOTs and SOARs, however, work well for the pandemic work because of the length of time and the fact that all departments—whether open or not—were involved.

**TABLE 4.2**
**SWOT Managers and Administrators**

Publication Date: _____
Review Date/Revised Date: _____
Process Owner: _____

| Strengths | Weaknesses |
|---|---|
| • Imagine yourself in an emergency situation—for example, an outbreak and need to close. In your specific role on the public service floor, what do you feel—based on your recent performance—that you did/do well?<br>• What unique resources do we think we can draw on to make sure we handle events/activities successfully?<br>• What do you identify as strengths of our overall management/ administrative team in handling emergency situations? | • As an individual, what could you improve in handling the event (with closure, with service model changes)?<br>• In thinking back over the resources we have for this situation, where do you think we had fewer resources than needed?<br>• List three things that the public service team might find as weaknesses in our handling of the situation. |
| **Opportunities** | **Threats** |
| • What opportunities are open to you in learning how to manage/ handle a long-term or emergency situation with altered services and closure in the future?<br>• What examples did you see in behaviors of others you want to ask about or learn about?<br>• How can you use/share your strengths to provide opportunities for other administrators or managers? | • If certain things in the pandemic/closure are not handled properly, they could be identified as threats. Name three.<br>• How are other departments/services handling the pandemic/ closures?<br>• What threats do your weaknesses expose you to in achieving a level of success in a future event? |

*Note:* Every level of an organization should complete *some* process; in a larger library, even though a worker might not be a manager, they might be a coordinator or in a position to coordinate activities, or at the very least a worker who had to follow service directions, and so on, to little avail. In addition, all survey questions should be worded to provide a structure for an individual who is the only person in the department to complete the SWOT in confidence. (See table 4.3.)

### Data Gathered: Supporting Data

Although "Big Picture" assessments with individual and facilitated surveys, focus groups, departments, divisions, SWOTs, or SOARS provide the necessary overview of opinion, perception, and facts, the pictures "painted" can be characterized by data, and librarians are not strangers to counting, measuring, assessing, and evaluating. Historically, libraries not only counted almost everything but also formed networks, membership initia-

tives, and consortia and identified who they were by the number of units in categories or by size (of collection, of staff members, and of facility—to name just a few areas). External groups gathered counts as well—by using sizes, numbers of materials, number of staff or workers (by levels), and square footage to categorize opportunities such as grants and state and federal funding.

Counting usage—also a critical part of a manager's work—includes counting how many people (individuals and types of individuals) walked in the door, signed up to use the library, or attended programs. These counts—primarily flat or basic data—were then supplemented with multi-leveled counts, combining data to determine who is using the library in what way and for what reason. Other management areas to measure what libraries "do" and "why" has and still does include very diverse data gathering and assessment, including the broader look at the community of the library for "Who is out there?" "What might they need?" and "What can we provide them?" along with the narrower when they visit us (in-person or now digitally): "Which materials are used

**TABLE 4.3**
**SWOT for Middle-Level Coordinators and Solo Worker in a Department**

Publication Date: _____
Review Date/Revised Date: _____
Process Owner: _____

**Strengths**
- Rethinking your role in the pandemic/event and your decisions regarding public services, what do you feel you do well?
- What unique resources are available to draw on to make sure difficult situations like this are handled successfully (e.g., knowledge of the community, prior partnerships with county FEMA, network of peers)?
- List three strengths exhibited in handling this emergency event.

**Weaknesses**
- In thinking of yourself only—as an individual—what could you have improved in handling the situation? In the first two weeks? Six months in?
- In thinking back over the resources available for this situation, where did we have fewer resources than needed?
- Identify another service in the library, and list three things you observed as weaknesses in their handling of the situation that affected our library?

**Opportunities**
- What opportunities are open to you in learning how to manage/handle a similar emergency situation in the future?
- What examples did you see in behaviors of others you want to ask about or learn about in order to emulate them?
- What strengths do you feel you can share to provide opportunities for others in the library?

**Threats**
- If certain things in the pandemic are not handled properly, they could be identified as threats. Name three (e.g., PR announcements, outreach, etc.).
- Did you see other departments/services handling similar situations as you did? Why do you think that was?
- What threats do weaknesses expose you to in achieving a level of success in a future emergency event (e.g., poor PR for what services were offered could hurt chances for budget requests this coming year; not collecting data creates a void of accountability)?

by whom, and why?" Additional data sought include: "When were programs well attended?" "By whom?" and "What did they do while they were here?" along with "What brought them in?" and "Did they return?"

Over the years, libraries have sought ways to count electronically to gather even more valuable information and supplemented goals statements with outcomes with data estimates gathered and assessed to see if the desired library outcomes are met. Data—now used to also denote digital entry and usage—have been coupled with evaluation tools and aggregation, measurement, and assessment practices for planning. Pre-pandemic, libraries' robust practices provided baseline data or data for comparison to most if not all usage areas. During the pandemic, however, huge areas of data became irrelevant to determine how libraries were meeting needs as use was restricted—if open or closed—resources were limited or even excluded from many services, and all that appeared to be "left" were digital data and measuring expertise—the hardest part of any measurement and evaluation. So, while the majority of goals and outcomes were shelved during the pandemic, on the spot, librarians had to decide what they were going to measure and why.

Although most libraries—shortly after the event began—had to plan to strike out on their own, decision making for numbers during the pandemic had to be prioritized as to "what could cease" or "why did those on vacation . . ." So, while libraries waited for umbrella groups to decide what overarching numbers were on hold and what had to be continued, most library managers:

- reviewed their own forms and tools to see what data would be effective and what might not be used;
- assessed their own organizations to see what accountability was needed by determining available data and which data most directly affected ongoing budgets and next year's funding levels;
- tried to determine which numbers had the most impact on decision makers;
- reviewed their goals and outcomes to determine the data needed for goal and outcome fulfillment;
- tried to determine what data was not able to be gathered;
- queried their own organization (and others as needed or possible) about which numbers would be put on hold;
- identified which data was not possible but still needed and explored alternate or substitute data gathering or data that could be delayed, put on hold, or postponed and how they might characterize what would be revised or rewritten for the pandemic library; and
- tracked local, state, regional, and federal data reportage decisions as to delays, and so on.

What most managers are not aware of is that there are many post-pandemic assessment and evaluation decisions to be made and questions to ask about justification—including using assessment data from this past year *and* going forward. In this process, libraries should identify which data were successful during the pandemic to determine if those successful practices can be used in all or part for the long term and assess looking at all previously gathered data and if it still needs or requires gathering. Library managers want answers to and need to know the following:

- Which data—during the pandemic—was perceived as the most successful data for telling the library's story and meeting user needs during emergency times?
- What different, new pandemic data play the biggest part in describing what the library contributes to its constituents, its community, or the umbrella organization?
- Besides returning to the previous goals and outcomes *and* continuing possible pandemic ones, will the library be tasked with adding any new post-pandemic assessment? For general business? To fulfill requirements or any restrictions on any grant dollars received? On any private money received? On any dollars spent in different account codes?
- Should pandemic recordkeeping tools and forms be retained for use by the umbrella organization? (It *is* recommended that all forms used be retained—if not for ongoing use, but for retention if they need to be used again, in case reoccurrences, similar public-health emergencies, or natural causes force the library to close for a significant amount of time, influenza outbreaks when there is concern for early intervention, etc.)
- Are there any issues or accountability data needed by the umbrella organization? Partners? State agencies? Regional groups? Memberships? Federal programs? More simply put: Who did what, when, and for how long?
- Do profiles of constituents with new or different needs require any unique tracking or recordkeeping post-pandemic, or can all recordkeeping be added as "another set of users" on existing techniques or forms?

**Assessment Tool Audit**

One purpose of information and data gathering (big picture, general, and specific data) is to determine:

- What data are kept and will continue to be, going forward?
- What tools and forms are in place to continue to gather the same data? and
- Will new data or new categories be added to existing forms or tools? Will new tools or forms be needed?

And more unusual data questions include the following:

- Are there any different data (but on the same services) needed?
- Is there new terminology needed to articulate the same data? and
- Do partners, consortia, or external entities need new or different data?

See table 4.4 for a list of assessment tools.

**TABLE 4.4**
**Assessment Tools**

Publication Date: _____
Review Date/Revised Date: _____
Process Owner: _____

| Area/Function, Where Is Data Used and What For? | Assessment Pre-Pandemic Tracking/Forms/Templates | Assessment Tracking/Forms/Templates during Pandemic (post-pandemic is italicized) |
|---|---|---|
| Services—General<br>• Budget justification<br>• Strategic planning<br>• State agency report<br>• Federal report<br>• Annual report<br>• Friends' budget requests | • In-person (count/front door)<br>• SenSource (dept.)<br>• Digital top-level page hit (web counter)<br>• Full digital download (web counter)<br>• Zoom attendance<br>• Anecdotal patron feedback and stories | • *In-person (count/front door)*<br>• *SenSource (dept.)*<br>• Curbside<br>• Seat reservation system plus usage hours<br>• *Digital top-level page hit (web counter)*<br>• *Full digital download (counter/platform)*<br>• COVID page<br>• Zoom attendance<br>• *Anecdotal patron feedback and stories* |
| Services—General Reference<br>• Budget justification<br>• Federal report<br>• Annual report<br>• Staffing/schedules | • In-person (at desk with software)<br>• SenSource (reference dept.)<br>• Online reference guides<br>• Zoom for ref/asynchronous<br>• Social media reference delivery<br>• Chat, phone, text | • *In-person (at desk with software)*<br>• *SenSource (reference dept.)*<br>• *Online reference guides*<br>• *Zoom for ref/asynchronous*<br>• *Zoom for ref/synchronous*<br>• *Social media reference delivery*<br>• *Chat, phone, text* |

*(continued)*

**TABLE 4.4**  *(continued)*

| Area/Function, Where Is Data Used and What For? | Assessment Pre-Pandemic Tracking/Forms/Templates | Assessment Tracking/Forms/Templates during Pandemic (post-pandemic is italicized) |
|---|---|---|
| Services—Research/Appointments<br>• Strategic planning<br>• State agency report<br>• Annual report | • Online reference guides<br>• Zoom for ref/asynchronous<br>• Zoom for ref/synchronous<br>• Social media ref delivery<br>• Chat, phone | • *Online reference guides*<br>• *Zoom for ref/asynchronous*<br>• *Zoom for ref/synchronous*<br>• *Social media ref delivery*<br>• *Chat, phone*<br>• *In-person pre-scheduled* |
| Services—Age Level, Youth<br>• Budget justification<br>• Strategic planning<br>• State agency report<br>• Annual report<br>• Friends' budget requests | • In-person youth services desk (at desk with software)<br>• SenSource (youth serv. dept.)<br>• Online youth pages<br>• Zoom for ref/asynchronous<br>• Chat, phone<br>• In-person pre-scheduled<br>• Anecdotal patron feedback and stories | • *In-person youth services desk (at desk with software)*<br>• *SenSource (youth serv. dept.)*<br>• *Online youth pages*<br>• *Zoom for ref/asynchronous*<br>• *Chat, phone*<br>• *In-person pre-scheduled*<br>• *Anecdotal patron feedback and stories* |
| Services—Age Level, Seniors<br>• Budget justification<br>• Strategic planning<br>• State agency report<br>• Annual report | • In-person seniors' coordinator office<br>• Online seniors' pages<br>• Seniors blog<br>• Zoom for ref/asynchronous<br>• Zoom for ref/synchronous<br>• Outreach data—phone, mail out, material sets/drop-off<br>• Chat, phone<br>• In-person pre-scheduled | • *In-person seniors' coordinator office*<br>• *Online seniors' pages*<br>• *Seniors blog*<br>• *Zoom for ref/asynchronous*<br>• *Zoom for ref/synchronous*<br>• *Outreach data—phone, mail out, material sets/drop-off*<br>• Wellness calls<br>• *Chat, phone*<br>• *In-person pre-scheduled* |
| Services—Special Pops<br>• Budget justification<br>• Strategic planning<br>• Annual report<br>• Friends' budget requests | • In-person special pops coordinator office<br>• Online information guides<br>• Zoom for ref/asynchronous<br>• Outreach data—facilities, home, school, material sets/drop-off<br>• In-person pre-scheduled<br>• Anecdotal patron feedback and stories | • *Online information guides*<br>• *Zoom for ref/asynchronous*<br>• *Special pops caregiver blog*<br>• *Outreach data—facilities, home, school, material sets/drop-off*<br>• *In-person pre-scheduled*<br>• *Anecdotal patron feedback and stories* |
| Services—Instruction/IL<br>• Strategic planning<br>• State agency report<br>• Annual report<br>• Student success content | Tracking forms for:<br>• Preparation<br>• Hours teaching<br>• Class content<br>• Students in class<br>• Contact post presentation<br>• Pedagogy<br>• Online platform | *Tracking forms for:*<br>• *Preparation*<br>• *Hours teaching*<br>• *Class content*<br>• *Students in class*<br>• *Contact post presentation*<br>• *Pedagogy* |
| Services—Facility—Small Rooms<br>• Strategic planning | Service includes:<br>• Reservations scheduled<br>• Reservations kept<br>• Technology booked<br>• Size of groups<br>• Times and days of week | Closed during pandemics with post-pandemic return to:<br>• *Reservations scheduled*<br>• *Reservations kept*<br>• *Technology booked*<br>• *Size of groups*<br>• *Times and days of week* |
| Services—Facility—Meeting Room<br>• Budget justification<br>• Strategic planning<br>• Annual report<br>• Friends' budget requests | Service includes:<br>• Reservations scheduled<br>• Program/event topic<br>• Reservations kept<br>• Technology booked<br>• Size of groups<br>• Times and days of week | Closed during pandemics with post-pandemic return to:<br>• *Reservations scheduled*<br>• *Program/event topic*<br>• *Reservations kept*<br>• *Technology booked*<br>• *Size of groups*<br>• *Times and days of week* |

| Area/Function, Where Is Data Used and What For? | Assessment Pre-Pandemic Tracking/Forms/Templates | Assessment Tracking/Forms/Templates during Pandemic (post-pandemic is italicized) |
|---|---|---|
| Services—Programs<br>• Budget justification<br>• Annual report<br>• Friends' budget requests | Programs include:<br>• Topic/program with speaker<br>• Audience profile<br>• Advertising/marketing done<br>• Technology booked<br>• Size of groups (reserved vs. attendance)<br>• Times and days of week<br>• Meeting room vs. online venue<br>• Platform | Closed in-person during pandemics, so virtual only with:<br>• *Topic/program with speaker*<br>• *Audience profile*<br>• *Advertising/marketing done*<br>• *Technology booked*<br>• *Size of groups (reserved vs. attendance)*<br>• *Times and days of week*<br>• *Meeting room vs. online venue*<br>• *Platform* |
| Services—Facilities Discovery/Innovation<br>• Budget justification<br>• Strategic planning<br>• Annual report<br>• Friends' budget requests | Maker and DIY<br>• Topic/program with speaker<br>• Audience profile<br>• Advertising/marketing done<br>• Technology booked<br>• Size of groups (reserved vs. attendance)<br>• Times and days of week<br>• Meeting room vs. online venue<br>• Platform | Closed in-person during pandemics, so virtual only with Maker and DIY<br>• *Topic/program with speaker*<br>• *Audience profile*<br>• *Advertising/marketing done*<br>• *Technology booked*<br>• *Size of groups (reserved vs. attendance)*<br>• *Times and days of week*<br>• *Meeting room vs. online venue*<br>• *Platform* |
| Services—Outreach<br>• Budget justification<br>• Strategic planning<br>• Annual report | Service<br>• Age level<br>• Transport<br>• Resources delivered<br>• Audience profile<br>• Advertising/marketing done<br>• Times and days of week | Service<br>• *Age level*<br>• *Transport*<br>• *Resources delivered*<br>• *Audience profile*<br>• *Advertising/marketing done*<br>• *Times and days of week* |
| Resources—Print/Paper<br>• Budget justification<br>• Strategic planning<br>• Annual report | Service/Resource<br>• Circulated<br>• Age level<br>• Resources delivered<br>• Audience profile<br>• Times and days of week | Service/Resource<br>• *Circulated*<br>• *Age level*<br>• *Resources delivered*<br>• *Audience profile*<br>• *Times and days of week* |
| Resources—Digital<br>• Budget justification<br>• Strategic planning | Service/Resource<br>• Circulated stats<br>• Specs<br>• Audience profile<br>• Times and days of week | Service/Resource<br>• *Circulated stats*<br>• *Specs*<br>• *Audience profile*<br>• *Times and days of week* |

## Just How Flexible Are We?

Given the fact that libraries often have to change direction or strategies, upgrade and learn new technology, plan projects, as well as adopt and adapt practices, and so on, it is no wonder that libraries of all types and sizes should get an "A" for flexibility. The pandemic, however, redefined the meaning of *flexibility* and highlighted the need to be flexible and to change almost "everything" for not only library workers but also constituents in a matter of weeks. So why are we spending so much time on flexibility?

Almost every list of recommended future paths and practices for the future for managers and leaders have *flexibility* on them—facility design, staffing patterns, competencies to match roles and responsibilities, cross-departmental projects, mentoring opportunities for leadership both midcareer and mid-organizational level, floor plans, types and styles of furniture, management styles, leadership styles, communication plans—you name it, and flexibility is recommended and at the top of the list. But it is not easy, fast, or automatic to just suddenly be flexible. However, there are easier ways to get there or at least start to get there along with longer, harder ways. The first step is to assess the presence of flexibility in the organization now. That begins by asking and answering a series of questions about the organization overall or the "big picture."

## Flexibility for Big-Picture Delivery of Services and Resources

This expanded need for and role of flexibility requires librarians to look at the organization overall and to review all aspects of services and resources, access to, design of, and use of the facility; a review of frontline schedules and staffing patterns; a "re-think" of the library's community; as well as a review of most if not all of the competencies expected of and possessed by library workers. This large look at the presence and level of flexibility must be assessed to determine the best way to decide, post-pandemic: How flexible were we? Were changes made the right ones? Are changers here to stay? What returns did we see, and—in the future—how do we retain flexibility as a process?

Determining the answers to these questions requires a look into the levels and types of flexibility including steps that are important but time-consuming, and so these reviews should not be approached lightly. And—because it is important to determine successes and failures quickly—there are both shortcuts and faster ways to assess the presence and integration of flexibility.

## Shortcuts to Assessment Given Flexibility of the Organization

In the absence of time or if the organization is smaller or a solo library setting, the following shortcuts can introduce flexibility and create a variety of possibilities.

- The post-pandemic near-future (one to two years) can be divided into stages, and just as the pandemic often had dramatic changes within each pandemic stage, the post-pandemic return may have stages with recommended return practices that change within stages. Managers can define post-stages in a few ways such as *timing* (the first six months back or the first year back); by the *organization's community structure of services* (such as the fall, spring, or summer); by the *support services* provided to the umbrella organization (the fall quarter, the spring semester, summer school, the summer reading club); by a year-round K–12 schedule, and so on. In summary, organizations should pick their own definitions for time periods or stages of the pandemic. This is especially true because there were more differences than similarities among types and sizes of libraries given the variety of umbrella organizations, levels of seriousness across the country, and—in some places—the ping-pong approach many communities had to take as they moved both forward

and backward throughout the process. In addition, and sadly, the politics of the different areas proved to be predictors in how the levels were identified and managed, so while there were more risks with some areas, there were fewer risks with others.

- The library may be directed to parallel their stages against the stages of the local county emergency-management services, and so on, but could and should still prepare multiple scenarios of what might and might not work for business continuity.
- While post-pandemic communication makes it clear that elements and activities for returning to normal can vary, all content needs to reference the fact that the library's control varies as to what it has and doesn't have—such as, "Whether it is good practice or necessary at the library or not, these service practices are in place until the governing authority (public entities, boards, etc.) indicates an 'all clear' post-pandemic return."

Multiple shortcut scenarios can be created then distributed to others for input or prioritization, with "others" being boards, peers, frontline library workers, stakeholders, and so on. Following input on all or part of the scenarios and a prioritization, managers should send out the scenarios that will be in place and list what is possible to change and what is not and why.

## Faster Ways to Assessment Given Flexibility of the Organization

Conduct one or more focus group(s) with staff who have been invited or chosen to represent a department in discussion. Focus discussion questions (using SWOT trigger questions) on what was changed only to assess if those changes and how the library arrived at those changes were successful. For example:

Our first focus group—"Stage 1 Post-Pandemic—Reopen with Reduced Service Hours"—next Wednesday from 9:00 to 11:00 now has twelve people representing circulation, reference, youth services, instruction, stack maintenance, and middle management and coordinators. Using the questions distributed recently, we will be focusing on and discussing our pandemic circulation practices, specifically no fines or fees, no limits on materials, extended loan periods, and a "floating collection" approach to locating materials. Following the focus group, notes will be circulated (no names will be recorded) to participants, who will then share them with their departments. Then two or three scenarios will be distributed on how these activities may be (or may not be) integrated into post-pandemic library services.

Add broad questions on flexibility to the "Big Picture" chart (see table 4.1, above). For example, as a follow-up to question #14 ("Given changes made for the pandemic, is anything *not* returning to a pre-pandemic model?"), add the following question: "Given the loan policy and other circulation changes during the pandemic, should the library continue any of the following: no fines or fees, no limits on materials checked out on one card, extended loan periods, or a 'floating collection' approach?"

Add specific trigger questions to the SWOT discussions tasking participants to consider flexibility. For example, add "no fines or fees, no limits on materials, extended loan periods, and a 'floating collection' approach" to the examples under each of the four SWOT areas to determine support or not—as well as levels of positive or negative opinions for each—by comparing the answers for the four different directions from which the pandemic changes could be viewed.

Focus on SWOTs:

- Conduct a SWOT *just* on what was changed and the process for changing it. For example, have a SWOT session just on post-pandemic circulation practices.
- Conduct a SWOT just on flexibility. For example, in order to accomplish this, the organization should choose a broad, representative group and provide a small educational presentation on the definition of *flexibility* as well as examples of the past year (or another event or flexibility in another library or in a workplace or service setting) and then provide the general four-part structure, using the same examples for each.

Slower ways to assess flexibility could be used in tandem with or after the shorter assessments in order to reach everyone involved or provide a more in-depth view. Slower ways include:

- broader distribution of surveys to larger populations;
- ad hoc groups formed to investigate a single incident where—for example—the organization or an assessment or a critic or information (from a shorter process that revealed problems) has determined that things were *not* flexible; and
- in-depth trainings (lengths of time, pre-learning, retreats, identifying benchmarks and best practices for study and comparison).

Imagine that a consultant's review has charged the organization with a lack of flexibility. While any of the above assessments are valuable, the transition from pandemic to post-pandemic will be faster than imagined, and because flexibility is so important, the assessment of flexibility—at the very least—should be built into management's "Big Picture" review.

## Flexibility for Frontline Library Workers Providing New or Changed Services and Resources

Although the major assessment of the library's post-pandemic flexibility are typically those questions asked of the bigger issues or policy changes, the pandemic necessitated another level of flexibility needed—frontline flexibility. These frontline changes are significant, however, because they represent those very specific roles and responsibilities of primarily frontline library workers. They are related—of course—though, to most if not all of the bigger issues or general policy changes, and they must be assessed for their popularity, design, appropriateness, and success as well, and the assessment must include in-depth input from frontline library workers.

This input can take place relatively rapidly through a subgroup survey of frontline staff as well as their direct managers; a focus group discussion; asking frontline staff and managers to prioritize lists of changes as to popularity, success, and so on, and then an individual, department, or team comparison; and, nearing the end of the stage, a slightly longer assessment of flexibility process might be the establishment of a frontline team or subgroup—chosen by the staff themselves—where temporary changes are identified and discussed through a longer survey or staff interviews or through a SWOT.

Although any or all changes in the organization's services are critical to assess, the frontline areas must come near the top of the list—if not the top—to assess for flexibility primarily because, unique to some emergencies, the effect of the event on services and resources is significant with typically more changes for frontline employees. In addition, given the organizational human resources structures, managers must determine the practices going forward given issues such as timelines for any temporary changes to union contracts, additional hazard pay, policies placed in hiatus or abeyance, and compensation guidelines for changing work roles and responsibility parameters expiring.

Specific frontline changes under review, those needing the most flexibility, and those most often implemented—as possible—during one or more pandemic stages include:

- work schedules on public service desks (whether virtual or in-person):
  ○ schedules with hours outside of normal workday hours;
  ○ adaption to new managers;
  ○ performance on new software;

- different clothing or PPE while on duty or in some spaces;
- required clothing or PPE while on duty or in some spaces;
- balancing workday breaks, meals;
- less lead time for permissions to change schedules;
- new/ongoing responsibilities such as cleaning, monitoring, and so on;
- need for new customer service training; and
- shifts change in length (longer or shorter);
- locations:
  - rotating in to alternative *open* library locations;
  - long-term new workloads, recordkeeping, and so on;
  - working remotely (from home, from other closed libraries); and
  - hybrid work with 49 percent of day at a remote location and 51 percent in the workplace;
- performance:
  - primary vs. secondary roles (position descriptions, individual and departmental worker goals changed, and now new or altered work projects);
  - expanded competencies and skillsets assigned (with training) during the pandemic such as cross-departmental work teams; and
  - committees, teams, and so on, using *online* work venues for a significant part of a team project;
- communication:
  - fewer staff meetings due to more systematic but daily communication (online, in-person, staff meetings to touch base with reports and posting updates on departmental online blogs); and
  - more online meetings rather than in-person meetings for staff, regularly scheduled worker meetings, point-of-use and group training, and so on.

## Why Is an Immediate Assessment of Flexibility Needed?

Post-pandemic assessment of flexibility and changes made at any level of staff and at any level of importance of service is critical to success in going forward—but not easy. Choosing how to assess, timing for assessment, and what to assess, including *who* should assess, is a broad process in which results often end up exploring and exposing aspects of organizational culture, communication strengths and weaknesses, negativity toward and a lack of commitment to or interest in change, work structures and practices that do and don't work, outdated approaches to management of people or resources, and—at its most

successful—the identification of good and bad risk-taking and experimental mindsets in the organization.

If the following issues rise to the top, organizations should review the presence or lack of needed flexibility to underpin successful post-pandemic planning:

- if change was hard (and continues to be hard) at the onset of the pandemic and throughout;
- if the organization chooses to make fewer changes than possibly needed or recommended;
- if assessments and evaluative content were consistently negative;
- if pandemic assessments and evaluation identified activities, changes, and so on, as less than successful in many or most areas;
- if only a few people in the organization (or not enough) make the decision to change;
- if lower-level managers or non-managers ended up making a significant number of change decisions;
- if worker morale (determined by organizational culture assessments) during and moving to post-pandemic is not positive (taking into account the difficult internal and external, local, statewide, or global situations overall); and
- if overall, the organization gets "low marks" in the post-pandemic structured review.

## Becoming Flexible

Once it is apparent that the organization has challenges with change and flexibility and therefore does not approach or implement change successfully, unfortunately, there is no magic wand or single event that managers or leaders may attend to *become* flexible. Understanding what it means to be flexible, learning to value flexibility, identifying what *must* be flexible, and making a commitment to flexibility, however, can be as simple as a professional development or as difficult as management and/or leadership changing roles in the organization or even exiting the organization, but whatever the decision, not only can lack of flexibility be identified but also the evidence or presence of flexibility can be assessed to denote a presence, a willingness to take an action, the use of experimentation, or the ability to change. And, while there was no magic number of problems identified that proves there is little or *no* flexibility, there is no magic number of how *many* of the activities in the following list should be *present* for the library to be thought of as "flexible." Obviously, it *is* safe to say definitely that more than one of the following activities, approaches, or programs should be identified in the organization, with special attention paid to the last half of the list.

## Evidence of Flexibility

1. *Is someone tasked with trending?* Organizations who regularly review, report on, and measure themselves against trends; cutting-edge activities, ideas, and products; and "what's next" content signal a willingness to be flexible and—when presented with possible changes—excel at making those changes.

2. *Where possible, are workers cross-trained? And if they are not trained, do they have interdepartmental knowledge?* The more workers know about and are trained to assist in other departments and for service roles and responsibilities, and the more that teams in the organization work together across departments and levels of positions, the more flexible an organization is and the easier it is to make changes. (*Note:* This suggestion is not designed to indicate in any way that levels of positions can be done by "anyone" in the organization or that positions and roles and responsibilities with required education and experience can be opened up to other workers. Instead, the organization should identify those roles that *can* be expanded to others and the competencies and training needed to expand and perform them successfully.)

3. *Does the organization provide administrative support for "new"?* Managers and leaders who suggest or support pilots, experimentation, and innovation—and find rewards as well as create environments where failure at such activities is not punished—are more flexible administrators.

4. *Are workers/employees able to bring forward ideas for innovation and change?* If managers are not flexible themselves, they can create pathways and support structures that allow workers to be flexible and provide rewards for those who bring ideas and projects forward.

5. *Is risk taking possible? Encouraged? Rewarded?* Although libraries are typically not thought of as flexible or as organizations associated with a great deal of risk, like managers and leaders of any business, administrators taking risks is common and should be encouraged. Risks being encouraged, rewarded if successful, and not punished if not successful are signs of a flexible organization with more flexible administrators.

6. *Does the library maintain dynamic planning?* Operational, short-term, long-term, and strategic plans are *not* effective if—once completed—they are shelved. Instead, a flexible plan that includes (and executes) systematic and consistent reviews of the organization's direction indicates a flexibility and a willingness to change. A plan that integrates an ongoing critical review of the direction in which the organization is going provides workers an environment where thinking about "doing things differently" is not foreign to anyone on the team. An ongoing review of plans creates not only a more flexible administration but also a more flexible team.

7. *Is change—in and of itself—recognized? Possible?* Studying, understanding, and implementing practices that welcome change allows an organization to employ techniques to successfully change—no matter the timing, timeline, or specific change needed or required. Techniques that assist in the flexibility that change brings include: scenario design, worker surveys, and focus groups—in general and for specific ideas—advisory councils designed for input, and broad representation of workers on workgroups.

8. *Are workers training in change?* Library workers who have been educated and trained in what change *is*, as well as *how* to change, have a higher comfort level with "new" and "different" and prove to be more flexible. In addition, education and training in "change" serves to reduce fears and build trust in an organization's leadership and management, who—because of the curriculum they have sponsored—have indicated a commitment to a process for change instead of—for example—making unilateral changes.

9. *Are there processes present for problem identification?* Organizations who integrate a process for determining and solving problems indicate an openness to feedback, criticism, and change and thus are more flexible.

10. *Does the organization employ tools and techniques to ensure flexibility?* Tools and techniques that integrate change and drive flexibility are found in management styles, assessment guides, organizational analysis models, planning, group think (techniques to gather input and opinion), and research methods. Employing these throughout all levels of the organization provides avenues for change and flexibility for administrators as well as for all library workers.

## The Biggest Assessment: Additions to the Big Picture

Although reviewing and assessing the organization's "Big Picture" questions is very valuable, not matter how far into the event they are, library administrators should continue to assess different components of the event such as the emergency response team and the emergency response plan. Gathering this additional information should take place throughout the event and through the use of different techniques to determine if there is synergy in the answers, if there is any unanimity in library worker group or individual responses, and if there are improvements after problems are identified, changes are made, and initial practices are revised.

Because it is very difficult to determine when a pandemic ends or when the organization can shift into post-pandemic, the administration—in tandem with the emergency response team—should conduct at least a basic assessment, such as a SWOT or a SOAR, six months into the event. *Note:* Basic assessments are characterized as one-shot assessments, with a variety of workers and other participants, conducted in one to two days, and facilitated by an external participant. (See table 4.5.)

**TABLE 4.5**
**SWOT: Emergency Management Plan (EMP) and Emergency Response Team (ERT) Questions**

Publication Date: _____
Review Date/Revised Date: _____
Process Owner: _____

**Strengths**
- What do you do well?
- What unique resources can you draw on?
- What do others see as your strengths?

**Trigger Questions**
1. Identify two strengths of the ERT membership representatives from the library workers.
2. Identify two strengths of the ERT membership representatives from the emergency-management county offices.
3. What problems were identified by the first ERT meeting?

**Weaknesses**
- What could you improve?
- Where do you have fewer resources than peer organizations?
- What are partners established pre-, during, and post-pandemic likely to see as weaknesses?

**Trigger Questions**
1. Was the EMP easy to follow?
2. Was the contact list up to date?
3. Did the EMP provide appropriate information for the pandemic as an event?
4. Are administrator roles clearly articulated?
5. Are library worker roles clearly articulated?
6. Was the sample timeline easy to adapt to the pandemic?

**Opportunities**
- What opportunities are open to you?
- What trends could you take advantage of?
- How can you turn your strengths into opportunities?

**Trigger Questions**
1. List three opportunities that might come out of the ERT.
2. With respect for the tragic nature of pandemic consequences, are there *any* opportunities that might come out of the emergency event?

**Threats**
- What threats could harm you?
- What is your competition doing?
- What threats do your weaknesses expose you to?

**Trigger Questions**
1. List three threats to the library that can come out of the emergency-event partnerships such as the ERT.
2. What participants in the ERT should have been involved but weren't?
3. What problems are associated with the timeline?

## Justification

While it might seem obvious why justification is needed or what goes into justification, emergency events can easily bring about different or new justification. Also, many other aspects of justification exist; for example, you may find that you will need to justify your existence. The list of reasons to justify includes (but certainly isn't limited to):

- what you provide matters;
- why you and your information is valuable to your constituents;
- how what you do or what you provide to constituents or entities saves money;
- why you need the same level of funding;
- why you need more funding;
- why you need new money (in areas not designated before);

- why you want to move money among accounts;
- how common perceptions are actually misconceptions, such as:
  - why we need to buy online resources ("because everything online is free"), and
  - why e-books are not $10.00 each for the library (as they are to the mayor, etc.);
- how you arrived at the request for funding during or after the pandemic; and
- why you choose to subscribe to (or purchase) one resource over another.

More very specific post-pandemic justifications include:

- why you might want to spend more money on remote/digital materials this coming year;
- why you now need tech hardware and connectivity to check out or circulate to users;

- why your wireless connection needs to be upgraded;
- why you need to buy different furniture with cabling, and so on, going forward;
- why your website needs an overhaul;
- why you need to subscribe to more than the free version for online meetings; and
- why social distancing for your library might cost money.

While the listing of "why" is important, it *is* the best way to determine what kind of data is needed to "make the case." In fact, documenting "why" allows managers to begin at the end and work their way back. For example, you might know your website needs an overhaul but others don't know it, nor do they have knowledge of how it might be done or what needs to change. Beginning at the end allows you to explore the data you do have already, determine who you need to convince or justify, and match the data you have to the argument, and if doesn't convince others who don't have your knowledge base, then you determine what data you *do* need or how you need to assess the situation in order to make your case. In deciding what data is necessary, managers should review best practices, identify commercial products as well as meaningful justifications for choosing them, gather miscellaneous data you have about the website, and identify gaps you need to fill with new or different information.

Generic data that libraries track to justify are helpful and include:

- statistics of the library for relevant years;
- statistics of functions, services, and so on;
- percentage and dollar increases and decreases in the recent years (three, four, or five years as a sample number or placed in the context of a significant budget year for the library or the budget entity);
- applicable professional standards;
- applicable professional formulas;
- vendor/commercial information;
- lists of cost from professional agencies and journals;
- relevant census or entity "population" data;
- articles/information that relates, justifies, or explains requests;
- consultant recommendations;
- portfolio of formal and informal dialogue;
- general user or constituent complaints;
- specific user or constituent complaints;
- survey data (institutional, snapshot, day/national/statewide);
- output measures information/outcomes information;
- formal/informal client requests/sessions or assessments (focus groups, official complaints, etc.);
- reports—monthly, annual, special;

- paper trail of memos (information, repairs, costs, etc.);
- working and measurable outcomes, goals/objectives/strategies of the organization; and
- shelf life of product with amount of time spent fixing or on repairs vs. time and money spent on a new product.

Approaches to use can include:

- narrowing timelines or inserting probes for context or discussion such as pandemic timing only or specific constituent information only/focus groups;
- dividing justification information into primary and secondary sources;
- assessing decision-maker styles to determine which sources carry most weight; and
- anecdotal information specific to users/constituents during the relevant, recent, and meaningful time (pandemic timing).

When assessing and justifying, the hope is that you assess, group the content, catch people's attention, and make the library's case or justify the decisions managers are wishing to make. So, while the focus should always begin with the assessment data and the justification based on the data, one of the most important steps is seen as "catching people's attention." Just a few techniques for doing so include:

- visuals such as design of data or justification, use of color, images, pictures and media, expert information or testimonials;
- unusual information that decision makers are not familiar with but are likely to be convinced by;
- social networking information/data gathered (newer, relevant);
- unique data that people haven't seen before or haven't seen used in this manner;
- meaningful or relevant contrasts and comparisons;
- compelling data (length of time, depth of information);
- pathos (meaningful storytelling);
- unique, more successful approach to gathering the information presented; and
- the "will of the people" (overwhelming numbers, significant data overall or significant information, opinion from target populations).

### Smaller and Solo Library Environments

No matter the size of library, if the manager is not conducting significant assessment—during and post-pandemic events—they are at risk due to the lack of accountability for not only public money but also their performance. Data gathering must be present and be ongoing for general services and resources but also for planning for upcoming public-health issues and other events. In addition, smaller and solo libraries need to gather perceptions, opinions, facts, and ideas about library web content and any library activities.

That being said, although not all sizes and types of libraries can or should assess using the techniques in this chapter, the tables indicate where solo and small libraries can specifically use all or parts of them. The techniques that can be used in these libraries to provide specific data in general can also be used for emergencies—specifically pandemic emergency times. In addition, in larger libraries, these techniques can be used for consistent, general data to build significant baseline data for not only the longer looks at performance but also comparison data with comparable institutions. Other specific assessments valuable for smaller libraries can also be used for larger systems that have smaller, individual campus libraries, branch libraries, or libraries in schools.

It goes without saying that the fewer staff there are, the less likely it is that time is available and the expertise is possible to create significant and in-depth assessment. When looking at the scale of what is needed, managers of smaller spaces might focus on no more than two to three areas of need for both assessment and justification and then concentrate on testimonials from those who might have an impact on the decision makers, choose self-directed assessment for constituents, consider invited focus groups rather than general attendance sessions, piggyback on other area assessment, seek to be a case study for an available educational process by either an individual or a class, or seek to be a community project for nonprofit support assistance.

## If We Had Been Ready

Because you are ready, you have updated data entry and recordkeeping templates, processes in place for using the templates, and a prioritized list of where the information is used by data piece and data set and by template. The library's assessment processes have:

- automatic data aggregation on spreadsheets and through software;
- data-aggregation timelines;
- a set of library "stories" indicating value, impact;
- current, relevant images from throughout the year with user permissions for reprinting and publishing;
- matches of metrics to services and resources; and
- constituent input.

And the library's justification content includes articulated content and previous processes such as:

- identified vendor content;
- previous successful assessment and justification scenarios;
- multiple approaches to making the case;
- a clearinghouse of constituents who can provide support during unique events;
- a clearinghouse of constituents who have provided testimonials in support of the library in general as well as budget aspects;
- stakeholders who assist in draft content review who are aware of timelines and are prepared to assess for realistic justifications;
- annual data set within the framework of the library's goals and values; and
- outcomes matched to assessment and justification content.

Finally, although the phrases used to articulate the library include "the heart of the community," and so on, the reality is that decision makers need to make hard decisions. In addition, decision makers need to justify their choices to others, and if library management doesn't provide them with the why, it is likely that the organization that does provide them with the best data and "why" will get the funding they need.

# 5

# Human Resources, Critical Training, and Education

LIBRARIES OF ALL TYPES and sizes and their person-nel—for the most part—have been in upheaval in what are typically organizations with little dramatic change in any given year. A simple return to "normal" is highly unlikely throughout all libraries given that not only have libraries themselves changed but also their entire infrastructure has changed as well as society, in both a local and global sense. Things are likely to keep changing and these changes are met with some trepidation in this rapidly moving and technology-driven world.

But what should managers address first in organizations? Most would agree that an organization's *people* are the most important part of a manager's job during and after emergency events and—most certainly—during pandemics. What is especially difficult about this vital area, however, is the fact that all aspects of human resources (HR) are in flux; that is, work roles, responsibilities, policies, practices, procedures, and so on, are changed and must be constantly addressed for both short-term and possibly longer-term and permanent changes. In fact, it is not uncommon for changes made during a pandemic to then have to be addressed again in any of a pandemic's stages and especially during post-pandemic times. In addition, the more serious the pandemic, the more likely it is that aspects of human resources never return to pre-pandemic times, which means that as structures try to recover, the critical infrastructure that guides and governs workers must change and change quickly.

A foundation for recovery and change has to begin with an assessment of all HR content that supports people including the values, strategies, goals, and outcomes; policies, procedures, and practices; roles and responsibilities; worker performance of those roles and responsibilities (individually and in teams); measuring and assessing value, impact, benefit, and worth of expertise; the integration of training, continuing education, and professional development; and organizational climate and culture. To be better able to outline what is changing specifically, it is important to start with basic HR responsibilities and the pre- and post-COVID issues.

Basic pre-COVID management roles and responsibilities include:

- advertising, hiring, and selecting;
- orientation, training, continuing education, and professional development;
- performance expectations;
- communication;
- productivity;
- a good match of learning styles;
- a good match of management styles; and
- laws and legislation.

Basic post-COVID management roles and responsibilities can be found in table 5.1.

One critical aspect of HR is the specific assessment of position roles and responsibilities and identification of job aspects that have changed. Obviously, environments with employee contracts and overarching legal regulations such as union contracts need to be immediately addressed in the organization. And for clarity, managers must be specific as to what workers did do, what they still do, and what completely new and different things—often parts of other people's jobs—they need to do during unique times.

And, although employee performance areas can typically be addressed with general, overall information, in order to ensure that employees understand how general job category changes might affect them, individual one-to-one performance discussions should follow the articulation of revised or new position descriptions to make

**TABLE 5.1**
**Human Resources Functions for Managers and Leaders**

Publication Date: _____
Review Date/Revised Date: _____
Process Owner: _____

| *Pre-COVID* | *Post-COVID ("Needs immediate attention" is characterized by IM immediately following the Post-COVID entries.)* |
|---|---|
| *Advertising, hiring, and selecting* (job ads; job descriptions; institutional/area marketing packets; interview schedule; EEO guidelines; performance/rating sheets for hiring; job evaluation; performance plans; contracts/employment agreements; benefits statements) | All pre-COVID plus new position descriptions to include following safety standards, any new work roles and responsibilities, new competencies required and related language about any new or changed benefits such as remote work/telecommuting *IM* |
| *Orientation, training, continuing education, and professional development* (training plan with "market" analysis; first day, first week, first month checklists; workplace calendar activities and checklists; the match of continuing education, staff development, and professional development to needs, curriculum, and learning style assessment) | All pre-COVID plus safety protocols in orientation, training, and continuing education; awareness of new first day, first week, etc., content re: safety protocols; plans for maintaining current information levels on public health issues; emphasis on well-being activities for workers with a list of how health benefits translate to worker fitness; orientation for back-to-work training *IM* |
| *Performance expectations* (job/position description; employee evaluation; employee goals to match institutional goals; the goals of the employee's department; a manager's list of adult behavior expectations) | All pre-COVID plus updated position descriptions; evaluation content to any performance, roles, and responsibilities changes; new goals; revised/deleted goals and new expectation guidelines related to online work; online behaviors toward others; any new processes such as coming "into" work late; scheduling reporting in; data forms use |
| *Communication* (an outline of how communication in the organization works; statement relating to what management style is; emails; memos; internal communication; external communication) | All pre-COVID plus remote communication issues; reporting in; team communication; knowledge of communication software; protocols for responding to communication; focus on conflict management among workers and between workers and users; guides for signs and signage for office spaces |
| *Productivity* (clear assignment of tasks; good calendars and schedules; employee goals; manager goals; plan for assessing and maintaining morale) | All pre-COVID plus guidelines for new calendar content to document performance; changing employee goals to meet different or new targets; organizational culture planning; work schedule assignments and timelines *IM* |
| *A good match of learning styles* (learning style assessment matched to employee needs and a manager's teaching and learning styles) | All pre-COVID plus new issues regarding preference for technology usage; identifying training needed to match new modes and methods for learning new technology |
| *A good match of management styles* (statement on how manager leads and what management style is) | All pre-COVID plus new issues regarding identifying how current management styles relate to online management changes |
| *A safe workplace environment* (ADA; occupational safety information; ergonomics statements/commitments) | All pre-COVID plus extensive new required CDC protocols and behaviors; application of OSHA guidelines to the workplace; applying workplace guidelines with nonlibrary workspaces *IM* |
| *Laws and legislation* | All pre-COVID plus post-COVID such as organizational, local, regional, state, and federal laws and legislation relating to new practices, safety, HIPAA, and vaccinations *IM* |

sure that workers trust how work is and will be getting done and those in charge.

The paradigm audit/checklist or for classified staff/frontline workers (see table 5.2) is an example of exactly how workers' roles and responsibilities may have changed. Using the paradigm of changes and then a revised position description, managers will find it easier to outline performance expectations.

As all sizes and types of libraries move forward with plans to increase hours for open spaces, reopen some spaces and services, or reopen in general, they must balance worker safety with values and the library's mission and goals for serving constituents. Steps for moving to

the second process (after position descriptions are complete) for HR safety include the following:

1. Establish systems to identify and maintain external decision-maker content that supports the HR infrastructure, such as:
   - umbrella organization/agency guidelines;
   - local, state, and federal laws and legislation that impact plans and policies and not only individual work performance but also public spaces access for workers and users; and
   - the organization's legal counsel or institutional representative regarding relevant and

**TABLE 5.2**
**Classified Staff/Frontline Workers**

Publication Date: _____
Review Date/Revised Date: _____
Process Owner: _____

| Area/Role/Responsibility | *Position Description—Classified Staff/Frontline* | |
| | Classified Staff—Pre-Pandemic | Classified Staff—Post-Pandemic |
| --- | --- | --- |
| Circulation desk work roles and responsibilities | Circulation desk work—shifts directly working with users while staying at circulation; mid-year meeting with manager on goals' progress | Circulation desk work—shorter shifts of public services (two to four hours); frontline work directly working with users; able to choose PPE (masks, gloves); behind PPE; quarterly meetings with manager on goals' progress |
| Circulation workloads | Documented and tracked by circulation staff with managers using software (typically weekly projections on Monday, then compared and entered at end of work week); standardized terminology | Documented and tracked daily by circulation staff with managers using software; standardized terminology |
| Team membership—fall software training | One of two team memberships; several meetings per semester; three projects underway; identifying new software; querying workers on what they feel equipped to do | Three meetings per semester; shorter project timelines; two new projects underway for a total of five projects; revising requests for opinions of training needed—now divided by general online circulation work vs. required training |
| Circulation functions represented by the Circulation Steering Committee | Three in-person meetings annually; general goals for online module training materials; one library-wide project with solo responsibilities such as updating fine-forgiveness data | All virtual; still three meetings; online modules for training materials—more completed, shorter timelines; teamwork only on library-wide projects |
| Safety facilitator for circulation staff working through the Circulation Steering Committee, managers, and risk experts | Roles and responsibilities are by geographic locations—three appointments and meeting three times a year | Roles and responsibilities include one for each library so from three to twelve appointments and two meetings per year (fall and spring) |
| Circulation desk cross-training for projects | Roles and responsibilities are assigned by managers with choices for circulation staff; all staff teams have content/project choices; expertise provided by organizational training; documentation and time spent tracked | Roles and responsibilities are assigned by managers based on size of libraries, user needs, and number of classified staff with choices for circulation staff—managers strive to provide choices but not always possible; expertise provided by organizational training; documentation and time spent tracked |

reasonable interpretations of external plans and policies "over" workers and users with special attention to HIPAA and requirements and confidentiality.

2. Research professional association and institutional policy and procedural templates for safety and security choices/decisions regarding PPE, social distancing, and so on (include references to laws, legislation, and so on, on new or revised policies and procedures).

3. Institute standard opportunities for sharing (meeting agenda slots for presentations, updates, and incident discussions).

4. Assess the availability of worker assistance for health issues such as mental health and anxiety, and establish FAQs to guide employees to a commitment to wellness and self-help.

Once HR safety content and basic processes have been established, orientation, training, and continuing education are critical to making sure the revised or new HR content is implemented accurately. To that end, managers must make sure that training is timely, is appropriate, and supports changed performance. For that to happen, a number of best practices are recommended:

1. Organizations should create timelines for learning, enforcing, and updating new or revised information.

2. Implementation of consistent weekly training times and buddies (for example) for team learning and implementation of practices is recommended while new practices are fully implemented.

3. With the expectation that—although reasonable—there will be conflict in the integration and implementation of new or revised practices and policies,

conflicts and conflict-resolution practices should be part of employee training.

4. With the expectation that—although reasonable—there will be conflict in the interpretation of new or revised practices and policies, marketing and public information specialists—as well as any staff development groups or trainers—should review signage, labels, instructions, and customer service scripts for appropriateness and suggestions in moving forward.

5. When training frontline workers, contextualizing what the learner is hearing is the most effective way to ensure understanding, retention, and application. To that end, managers—especially seeking to train staff in new or revised emergency-management practices—should consider a variety of ways to present information, including:

   • information panels: best practices, multiple approaches, and contexts for providing workers with background to form their own opinions—good for auditory learners;

   • role playing: specific successful examples for immediate use, taking into account varied skillsets of workers and possible conflict-seeking users—good for auditory and tactile learners;

   • demonstrations: how to? And an illustration of how an existing procedure or policy will play out in real time—also for immediate use and hands-on, tactile learners onsite and at point-of-use workstations;

   • simulation exercises/staging events: actual events to observe in progress with a focus on critique of worker actions in safe spaces—for multiple learning styles but certainly for tactile and visual learners; and

   • community professional/first person: like an information professional panel, where the community professional discusses possibilities, support, and relationships and provides historical context—especially good for auditory learners.

So we have done the paperwork. How do we actually keep people safe? Or saf*er*?

It is important to pull together content from other areas for one long look at what public-space experts are doing to communicate to workers that managers have a plan specific to workers and worker safety. And although some steps are more expensive and high tech, some are less expensive and are low tech with simple steps.

• "Wearables" are items workers can wear or that can be issued or checked out to users to determine if people throughout a space are too close to each other. When proximity is a problem, a sensor triggers an alarm and identifies what is happening, and if individuals can't solve the distance issues, staff may step in.

• Automatic opening and closing mechanisms (for doors, etc.) reducing contacts are less expensive and considered a more positive way overall because they don't require the intervention of workers to move people in and out.

• Common areas should be left as is, reduced in hours of use, closed. They can also be reduced in use by days of the week, by times of the day, by certain groups, or for certain activities.

• Modifying spaces includes making simple to complex changes and can be as simple as removing and moving furniture, using blocking PPE, and redesigning service stations, and—as before—these predone heavily marked or signed areas reduce conflict due to reduced interactions with staff and possibly reduced interactions among users.

• Limiting the number, size, frequency, and mode of meetings for workers in libraries or in remote workspaces is—obviously—a primary way to reduce conflicts.

Pandemic changes in HR include a focus on additional worker safety (achieved by the use of digital/virtual means of communication for the foreseeable future); new worker policies (health policy reviews, flexible work locations, work schedule flexibility); and employers offering workers a variety of choices for not only schedules but also PPE.

In addition, based on pandemic changes, HR departments—while using digital/remote hiring processes—need to find new techniques for assessing potential worker tech readiness and the presence or absence of abilities to meet and conquer digital workplace challenges as well as their suitability to productivity and remote work. Other HR needs are creating holistic well-being (including mental health) plans for employees and designing "safe space" opportunities for workers to deal with their shortcomings (e.g., anxiety, depression, fear)—brought on or exacerbated by pandemic practices.

One of the more difficult aspects of new techniques to use and new concerns for workers remains to be the identification and delivery of training for the new techniques and pandemic concerns of remote workers. These difficulties are hard to overcome, as they include identifying instructors who understand the technology and the profession and can teach various skill levels remotely with a clear understanding of roles and responsibilities of workers (and often unique issues to types of libraries). Additional difficulties are also found in identifying instructors who are skilled in assessing worker needs and then providing different levels of mental-health support to individual workers in the broadest range of potential problems.

HR personnel must also provide focus and training on trust—for the organization, for managers and leaders, and for each other. And—as part of trust and as part of the critical need for positive organizational climates—HR must provide managers and leaders with professional development in showing empathy for all workers but especially remote workers during the pandemic, and in training workers to maintain a balance of performance targets and complete projects while also working remote

public-service desks for on-demand information, reference, and research services.

In addition, an excellent trust-building area in organizations is having a clear understanding of decision-making processes in the organization, worker roles in that decision-making process, and any underlying decision-making processes. Often, expanding remote work situations due to emergency events means that there must be completely different approaches to making decisions even though it becomes even more important to include a broad range of workers in these processes.

See table 5.3 for a description of old and new decision-making processes.

**TABLE 5.3**
**Decision Making**

| Old Decision Making | New Decision Making |
|---|---|
| Decisions are made through standard processes, which, given the management style of those primarily responsible for decisions (one or two top-level managers), might include input from opinion, commentary, research, data, and standard practice from other managers and work-group, committee, team, or departmental representatives. | Decisions are made by a variety of individuals, teams, workgroups, etc. Decision-making processes include structures for input, data-driven content, best practice information/data, and—no matter what the management style of those primarily responsible for decisions—input from opinion, commentary, research, data, and standard practice. Significant weight is given to data-driven content, and evaluation is integrated into all decision making. Data gathering is often more difficult to alternate work stations for all or many workers. |
| Input to decision making occurs and is often predicated on management style. It includes not only input from internal individuals but also external input from—for example—surveys and focus groups as well as input in nonstandardized processes from governing bodies, partners, etc. Input includes but is not limited to research, data, standard practice, opinion, commentary, etc. | Input to decision making is significant and required from employees and workers, stakeholders, governing bodies, partners, etc. Input is also gathered from structured groups and processes—either ongoing or ad hoc—that include but are not limited to focus groups brought together to conduct discussions with external facilitators to determine strengths, weaknesses, opportunities, threats, etc. |
| In most organizations, decisions are made by one or two top-level managers in consultation with middle managers (assumed to be asking for input from their staff) and—as needed—with governing or advisory bodies. | Making decisions (if timing permits) or, at the very least, input into making decisions comes from a wider variety of "areas" including more internal and external people/entities (data, commentary, etc.) and more internal and external individuals with specific roles and responsibilities or teams (data, commentary, etc.). |
| Decisions are made for the organization or entity, and decisions primarily affect the organization/entity. | Due to a number of elements (e.g., shared technology, remote world of work, shared facilities, more accountability, etc.), decisions may very well be significantly more far-reaching, and they may affect the organization, the governing entity, stakeholders, partners, vendors, and of course, workers and users, etc. |
| Although documentation of decision making is normal, it is less expected in normal or more typical times, as most decisions are not monumental or far-reaching. | During emergency events, systematic and consistent decision-making practices and data used must be documented to ensure any necessary and required compliance steps are being taken. |
| Although decisions by one or "a few" are often quick to be made (and that's not always a bad thing or incorrect), the fewer the people involved in decision making, the faster the process. | Today managers want thoughtful, collegial decision-making processes, but these often take longer, as they involve more individuals and/or people in the process, and have a wider pool for distribution and—as they are more data driven—take longer to process and vet. Significant parts of the decision-making process, however, during COVID can be faster with data-rich environments, easier distribution to those involved in the decision, and easier dissemination after the decision has been made. |
| Decisions are vetted based on standard evaluation timelines, and successes and failures in decisions made are explored to assist in making necessary changes as needed. | Decisions are vetted more often during emergency events to provide organizations with a systematic way—based on data and as needed—to change direction not only in operations but also for more far-reaching planning and actions. |

## Paradigm Shift

Finally, HR activities for managers is estimated to take up to—during some weeks—70–80 percent of a manager's typical workday; however, during emergency events, these roles and responsibilities can easily take up to 95 percent of a manager's workday. So what are the HR must-dos during the pandemic?

1. Focus on managing change and showing others how to manage change.
2. Take specific steps to ensure that workers understand that trust is a critical part of both management and leadership and keeping their trust is a top priority of management.
3. Guarantee that workers understand their job description as well as how their work relates to their job description and evaluation, and that workers know management performance and behavioral expectations.
4. Ensure that learning opportunities are matched to worker learning styles and learning levels.
5. Be aware that worker development must be part of job descriptions, goals, and objectives, outcomes, and so on, and is budgeted and planned for (continuous learning including on-the-job, general training, and education).
6. Know that clear, consistent, and two-way communication is present and available to workers for input and expressing needs and concerns.
7. Be aware of the role of assessment and accountability in performance and productivity.
8. Understand their safety is important.
9. Ensure that new environments have policies and practices, and that venues have supporting content to ensure equitable treatment (e.g., remote worker policies and agreements, standardized documentation of performance).

## Solo and Smaller Libraries

Finally, this area of management is the most difficult for managers in small environments. This is due to many factors, including the fact that fewer employees may need less attention, so these time-consuming activities are set aside, especially because umbrella organizations don't provide nor require the same kind of HR policies and procedures. And while managers can seek templates for creating the most basic documents, it is often hard to enforce a seemingly bureaucratic structure on two or three people. If solo librarians have to choose, however, position descriptions—kept up to date—are the most important document, with a close second being any kind of evaluative approach to performance. This expanded use of the description can then include the manager sitting down with the position description and asking the employee to self-evaluate their position-description performance, then commenting themselves, and then the two can compare the rankings or comments.

Additional areas of HR in smaller organizations less likely to have this support should include: confidentiality of user information, personnel information, and especially health information as well as basic scheduling forms and checklists for daily, weekly, and monthly to-do lists. This set of papers offers a variety of opportunities for guiding workers toward roles, responsibilities, and productivity and giving feedback needed to reward or improve as needed. More importantly, identifying what *is* getting done assists in communicating what *isn't* getting done, and all documentation should strive for full staffing by identification of needs not being met.

## If We Had Been Ready

If any size organization had been ready, HR forms and descriptions would be up to date, systematic procedures would be chronicled, and the organization would run smoothly in the absence of the manager. While this seems simplistic and unreachable for goals, creating one core set of documents provides managers with the basic content they need to create other documents, choose templates, and build a presence of necessary HR information. Interjecting pandemic issues into this core set means that there is a consistent updating of position-description documents, an overlay of attention to technological factors for all HR information areas.

# 6

# Communication during Emergency Events

ALTHOUGH THE KEY to any successful business environment is good communication, this issue is characterized as a "big tent" issue, as pandemic information typically needs to be immediate, all-encompassing, regimented, and strategic, and include not only carefully orchestrated management communiques but also carefully orchestrated leadership communiques. Also, most pandemic communication is distributed to most, if not all, of those in the organization and surrounding "community" (as defined by the library), those within the umbrella organization including individuals and groups (internal and external), as well as both users *and* nonusers.

This very broad approach does not mean that all pandemic content itself as well as all public relations and marketing and all modes and methods need to be considered and included in their entirety to everyone; instead, it means that the emergency communication plan is revised to be a pandemic communication plan with—probably—not only different but also additional categories with existing individuals and groups, added experts (public health officials, frontline workers, health care specialists, etc.), new definitions of the kinds and types of communiques, timelines, approval processes, standardized terminology, and—whenever possible—approved (by public health or health care officials) templates. And—given the unique situation—a group is formed (an emergency response team or the pandemic task force) who starts with existing plans and then—given the unusual pandemic situation—determines what is missing, what is new, what has changed, and ultimately, who needs to get what, when, and how. So what must managers and leaders consider?

First, does the organization have a communication plan? If no, then managers and leaders—working with the group, team, or task force (or coordinator, facilitator, or team leads, etc.)—should quickly assess what com- munication is already taking place in the organization and how the organization handles emergency emails or communiques or calls that announce changes to routine functions. These routine approaches will need to be changed for a pandemic, given that it is a public-health situation. And even though the organization may have had an outbreak of a regional health scare such as an epidemic, odds are officials have changed, funding has changed, and—of course—the health situation itself has changed, as each situation (virus, etc.) behaves differently (transmission, length of illness, seriousness, age level affected, etc.). Given that, teams, groups, and task forces need to manage this through a series of steps, beginning with knowledge of the virus itself and then the issue of communication. Libraries—in preparation for any public health emergency—should ask themselves the following questions:

How does the organization define their communication? What emergency terminology is used, or what do they "call" things, and given the pandemic, how do the definitions and the language need to change?

Communiques defined as official or primary announcements or statements must be reviewed as to recent samples, to determine the best way to reach audiences that need the information. Related issues are mode and method of distribution of emergency communiques: email, network/internal announcements, website postings, blog postings, and so on. And—of course—the group itself must establish their content recordkeeping considering official minutes from event meetings, data aggregated, and reports. The organization's more formal plans (operational, strategic) should also be reviewed as well as any social media processes (Twitter, Instagram, or Facebook) and departmental or institutional webpages (the umbrella institution's webpage, etc.). In addition, response teams need to assess announcements/ notifications, presentations, and signage to ensure that all modes and methods—as well as content—"match" as to terminology, authority, color, typeface, and logo, branding, or any institutional banner identification.

What wording "works" in the environment regarding emergencies? What critical terminology is new and what has evolved or may evolve during the pandemic should be identified by working with and reviewing wording and modes and methods coming from other response team officials or environments and the emergency management community in general (local hospitals or providers identifying stages or schools choosing labels for class or building location offerings) as well as local, state, and federal agencies updating terminology.

Communicating before, during, and after events requires standard terminology at the very least and, if possible, standard, required terminology, labels, acronyms, and initialisms for pandemic communications. Any terminology used may have to go through an approval process with specific authorities and unique timelines. Throughout the event, managers and leaders should ensure that they use standard terminology as well as terminology tied to possible funding. For example, in the beginning stages of COVID-19, there were conflicting discussions on use of the term *social distancing*, and several organizations declined to use it. Within a month of the beginning of the pandemic, however, the term became the standard use as heralded by—the most important voice—the Centers for Disease Control. Other critical terminology uses include:

- identifying money spent as "recovery" expenditures to assist in eligibility for future grant funding;
- the federal government identifying relief money in stages and requesting and tracking dollars spent, which is then matched to the acronyms of federal dollar availability; and
- requiring certain PPE using language identical to local or state regulations to avoid conflict and challenges (signs should say "users must wear *xxx* approved face mask" rather than "users must wear a facial covering").

Who is responsible—in the organization—for communication now, and who should be identified as responsible for the official communication to both internal and external audiences? Given the pandemic, who continues their role, and how do they intersect with the emergency, pandemic, or response team?

Many organizations are *not* big enough or cannot spare staff to take on an emergency coordination role. If

the team must have specific representation, organizations should consider someone who is familiar with the organization such as advisory or governing board members, stakeholders, someone from the umbrella organization, or a peer within the community who could act as a volunteer representative. *Note:* This action is *not* designed to lower a manager or lessen the impact and decision making the library manager must have; rather, it is designed to be a realistic solution to have more sets of eyes look at critical information and—even more importantly—to have more people looking out for your organization's welfare during difficult times.

If the manager manages and leads alone, they should join the response team and ask a designee to attend as a second seat to ensure the library has the representation they need if the manager can't attend.

What are the communication infrastructures? That is, how are communiques distributed? What are the channels, modes, and methods? Which channels work best with emergency communication? Are there unique pandemic channels? (See chapter 13 for information on the organization branding pandemic communication.)

Beginning to use new modes and methods (new software, untried social media channels) is time-consuming and is typically unwise to do when beginning so critical a project as communicating within a pandemic environment. In the absence of significant or appropriate modes and methods, however, managers should review their last year of emails, calendar entries, and so on, to assess the processes used to see if they were successful. This review should make it possible to create a list of communications that should be helpful. It is also helpful if managers can identify the processes they used during the last emergency situation. For example—if a flood occurred three years ago, what did the library use then? Was it helpful? Did it get the results needed? What positive or negative feedback did the library get?

And, although it isn't ideal for any standard approach, an excellent way to ensure that initial communications "land" where they need to, organizations should identify people with influence within the library's "audience":

- Parks and Recreation might have a popular local TV show, so the host could be asked to relay your communication or have the library's spokesperson appear on the show.
- The university can provide space on their emergency page for library information.
- The principal can let the library piggyback on homework notices on the parents' network email blast.
- The community announcement blog postings can provide space for the library's pandemic updates.

Who are the targeted profiles of individuals and groups? What modes and methods are matched to which individuals and groups? What new or different groups or groupings of people or organizations are added for pandemic information?

Audience/target population: The organization's workers, all staff, and any users and nonusers as well as "community" members need to be identified to be able to match them with need-to-know communiques, timing, and so on. Pandemic identification, however, means some groups need to be further subdivided based on unusual factors due to the pandemic itself (at risk, those using public transportation, those using services and resources for small businesses, internet connections, those needing public assistance, users graduating, etc.).

Given the lack of systematic *anything* during pandemics, what timelines will the organization use for sending out their pandemic information?

The primary use of timelines during pandemics is to update users and nonusers with pandemic information as it relates to your resources and services such as changed hours of the library, different or ceased processes such as fines and fees, any community room use issues for groups, deliveries, or access to resources or facilities. Other timelines libraries want to be aware of—besides public relations guidelines (church publications going out, using county mailouts for library inserts, etc.)—could include deliveries such as mailouts/mail pick-up, deliveries using community groups such as Meals on Wheels, visiting public-health services (if the library has or intends to begin vaccine information or shots), water-services deliveries or access points such as limited wireless becoming 24/7 wireless, and—given the unusual pandemic issues—facilities opening, then closing, then opening again. As much as possible—the library should attempt to follow the umbrella organization or community guidelines to avoid the inevitable confusion of varied organizations having the ability to maintain business continuity and users needing but never having consistent approaches to the variety of businesses, services, areas, and so on, they need.

How is the information to flow? That is, after matching the infrastructure to the target population, the content has to be matched to the timeline. What are the pandemic pathways?

### Flowing in Difficult Times

In this twenty-first-century tech-infrastructure-driven environment, a wide variety of aspects during emergency and pandemic situations can contribute to an extreme slowdown as well as ceasing of critical information chan-

nels. In these situations, organizations still needing to distribute their communication need to turn to signage distributed throughout the community, radio channels, emergency channels, public or free access television channels, or the modes and methods—mentioned earlier—of influencers or other groups with successful infrastructure for getting the word out. The use of emergency apps for phones—where cities, counties, and schools push information *en masse*—should be explored prior to pandemic situations to determine if design of their own lower-cost or free posting is possible.

Obviously—although the very nature of pandemics leads to their far-reaching effects—cloud services and remote uses of content delivery are important to provide opportunities for communication "backups" when local or institutional communication is problematic. These backups can include library systems with the capability of online circulation modules announcements and blast email opportunities as well as commercial or web-based services. Additional "other" venues include K–12 and higher education content-management systems used as delivery mechanisms with remote personalization and—of course—library environments piggybacking on the umbrella institution's processes such as using community transportation scrolling marquees (on roads or buildings), auto-dialing telephone-tree announcements, or city or county billing notices including a library insert or email content addition.

### Flowing Not Only Down and Out, But Also Up

Finally, the flow of communication must *be* a flow—that is, two-way communication—where managers and leaders speak to workers, users, and so on, but also where workers and others can report up to, ask questions of, and provide positive and negative feedback to managers and leaders. To clarify expectations, managers and leaders must revisit any performance or behavioral expectation statements they already have in place to make sure that all workers and other target populations specific to the library know their roles and responsibilities in general and are aware of any that have changed, given the pandemic. Examples can be found in table 6.1.

### The Realities of Pandemic Communication

In the face of emergency events, managers must identify the aspects of *each* emergency event to determine what communication is needed as well as what makes an event unique and, therefore, force managers and leaders to shift to extraordinary communication. That being said, pandemic emergency events are very different from other

**TABLE 6.1**
**Communication Expectations for Emergency Events/Pandemics**

Publication Date: _____
Review Date/Revised Date: _____
Process Owner: _____

| General Expectations for Organizational Communication | Pandemic Expectations for Organizational Communication beginning xx/xx/xxxx |
|---|---|
| Workplace communication should be read before workers take their next shift of duty. | Library workers must read their workplace communiques every day whether they are scheduled to work or not; library workers with two noncontiguous work shifts must read their workplace communication before each shift. |
| Emergency communications must be read immediately. | Emergency communications—identified with the x brand—must be read first and immediately. |
| Questions about any communiques should be sent to immediate supervisors within one hour of receiving the communique needing clarification. | Questions about any communiques should be sent to immediate supervisors and copied to the Emergency Pandemic Team within thirty minutes of receiving any communique needing clarification. |
| | Questions about any communiques should be sent to immediate supervisors, immediately and before starting in-person work shifts. Answers and clarifications are returned to the worker and copied to the Emergency Pandemic Team within thirty minutes of receiving any communique needing answers or clarification. |
| Supervisors and managers will require that their workers indicate that they have read and understood communications; however, different departments/managers may request notifications occur in different ways depending on location, staff schedules, etc. | Supervisors and managers require that all workers indicate receipt of the pandemic communication on the organization's chosen template (e.g., Google doc, etc.). Choice of method must match the event issues—for example, if power is out or web unavailable, appropriate processes, templates, and reportage will be used. |
| Supervisors and managers outline practices in each department for workers' formal and informal sharing of work-related general, topical information. | Workers who want to share general emergency or pandemic information should send it directly to their Pandemic Emergency Team liaison with a copy to their immediate supervisor or manager. |
| Workers are not to share health information about themselves or others with any individuals or groups in the organization. | Workers are not to share health information about themselves or others with any individuals or groups in the organization. |
| Workers are not to share organizational communications with external entity workers, family, or users. If labeled as xxxx, workers are not to share library communications with other internal entities. | Workers are not to share organizational communications with external entity workers, family, or users. If labeled as xxxx, workers are not to share library communications with other internal entities. |
| All communication clarifications or follow-up questions are answered, and the aggregate numbers are kept. | All communication clarifications or follow-up questions are answered and questions (not those who ask) are recorded and used for ongoing dynamic evaluation and improvements as the process is in progress. |
| Media inquiries—from organizational or external outlets—are referred through the organization's standard processes. These processes should be required and identified in each employee's orientation and training. Due to the sensitive nature of external media inquiries, the library should have examples such as: "if someone asks you a question and assures you that your discussion is confidential or that information shared is 'off the record,' the library should reiterate that there is no such thing as confidential or 'off the record.'" Instead the process includes the employee asking questions to managers or departments listed in the process. | Media inquiries (in person, by phone, emails, or texts) from organizational or external outlets are to be referred to the appropriate designated person for immediate handling. |
| Suggestions for media needed or improvements in communications are sent to the appropriate designated person. | Suggestions for media needed or improvements in communications are welcomed and sent to the appropriate designated person for immediate review. |
| Although email signatures, backgrounds, email addresses, buttons, pins, or "writing" on clothing are not typically thought of as communication, they are. Please see the organization's dress code* for public spaces and behind-the-scenes support spaces for information regarding these aspects and the need to avoid or convey nonorganizational information in these ways. | Although email signatures, backgrounds, email addresses, buttons, pins, or "writing" on clothing are not typically thought of as communication, they are. Please see the organization's dress code* for public spaces and behind-the-scenes support spaces for information regarding these aspects and the need to avoid or convey nonorganizational information in these ways. Examples include:<br>• Email addresses used are the college's email addresses only.<br>• Email signatures, backgrounds, headings do not include nonorganizational information nor references to groups or beliefs. |
| *Please use the updated organizational dress code for approved content following Title VII of the Civil Rights Act of 1964 added including: submitting requests for exemptions regarding wearing or not wearing clothing or identification that is against religious beliefs. | *Please use the updated organizational dress code for approved content following Title VII of the Civil Rights Act of 1964 added including: submitting requests for exemptions regarding wearing or not wearing clothing or identification that is against religious beliefs, health requirements, etc. |

emergencies as well as different from each other, including the reach or breadth, depth, physical location, profile of those affected, transmission, and treatments. Due to these and a variety of other issues, pandemic communication is greatly affected. Examples of unique aspects include the following:

Achieving success with *planned* communication—both short term and long term—is almost impossible during pandemics. That being said, long-term or strategic plans should be put on hold, but managers and leaders must assure all workers that organizational values and communication principles and goals are still in place.

Emergency communication timelines are not effective during pandemics, with most issues and many—if not all—aspects of the event changing at breakneck speed. Multiple, forced slowdowns or shutdowns with very little lead time afford little time for communications to be accurate and timely—both factors critical to the success of good communication.

Every pandemic leadership communication should be designed to continue to establish and confirm trust in the administrators and the organization. Because there are typically many divisions within organizations regarding behaviors required during pandemics, trust does not automatically carry over from the general business of the organization. For that reason, from the top down, all communication should be carefully designed to—at the very least—employ trust-building practices and content for any pandemic information distributed.

Managers and leaders need to "credential communication" and must decide on the experts that will be identified as primary to establishing required and recommended behaviors during pandemics. And while one may think they don't need to or there aren't that many choices, significant choices of experts do exist, including federal agencies such as the Centers for Disease Control (CDC) or the local CDC departments located within county or city health departments, a state health department or mandate, a local community authority, or a local community expert. Typically, organizations should identify not one but *two* choices by combining a local spokesperson for a county or state emergency or public health agency—for example—in concert with a federal agency to provide the credentialing needed.

In addition to managers and leaders deciding on the expert or experts to quote, as much attention should be paid to "what *not* to say" and specifically what language *not* to use. Why? Just as general organizational communication is often geared to target populations, the same can be said for pandemic communication. Tables 6.2 and 6.3 provide

**TABLE 6.2**
**Communications: What to Do and Say**

Publication Date: _____
Review Date/Revised Date: _____
Process Owner: _____

| Communiques (what) | Audience/Target Population (who/for whom) | What to Say during Emergency Events (wording, tenor, approach, etc.) |
| --- | --- | --- |
| Communiques typically used to communicate content with standard changes for emergency events. (This content is delivered in many ways, including as separate content or as part of a web environment or emergency event/ pandemic portal.) | Target audiences vary for communications, and content that is restricted from being shared before a recipient group should have that caveat on the communication to clarify and emphasize.<br>• Users<br>• Library workers<br>• Library supporters<br>• Governing entity<br>• Advisory entities<br>• Media/press<br>• Parallel entities<br>• Partners/area Collaborations/memberships<br>• Community-at-large | Comments during emergency events such as pandemics should subscribe to the six elements below.<br>1. Quote agreed-upon experts<br>2. Honor steering committee or advisory group input<br>3. Consider outlining a path for decisions made, but do not identify a decision-maker group incorrectly—rather, identify how the administration *is* making decisions, and then identify a contact for any feedback such as questions, agreements, disagreements<br>4. Acknowledge mistakes and correct quickly<br>5. Provide more behavioral directions<br>6. Celebrate the breadth of the successes in the organization as well as—as appropriate—specific departments, functions, areas, etc. |
| Web Portal | Web content is designed for all, and "front page" event content is used for specific answers to specific questions. The more successful front page minimizes general, vague content and links to the broader world for event content but instead is arranged by user with FAQs with dynamic links. | During emergency events:<br>• Be specific to *your* organization; provide dynamic "what you need to achieve success" content.<br>• Provide visual cues indicating updated content. |

*(continued)*

**TABLE 6.2**   *(continued)*

| Communiques (what) | Audience/Target Population (who/for whom) | What to Say during Emergency Events (wording, tenor, approach, etc.) |
|---|---|---|
| Announcements: Emergency Changes | Change announcements are typically for all involved in the organization and should be used carefully and—if possible—intermittently and should be restricted during events to event-specific changes scheduled for a standard time of day. (Specific days typically aren't enough, as there will be/might be a wide variety of target populations.) | Standardize titles/headings; include the "heading" and if appropriate the headline with progressive distinguishing changes (e.g., Pandemic: day $x$) in the first sentence; be specific as to how the "new" information changes activities, directions, or behaviors |
| Daily Updates | The web portal should provide content for all and should offer an organized information feed (with RSS) for individuals or groups wishing to subscribe to specific updates or frequencies. | When using the organization's standard communications, daily content should be positive, helpful, and low-key and should repeat the organization's dates for public events, any due dates, reminders of hours changes or service changes, etc. |
| | In education settings (K–12, higher education)—for example—the content management system should provide a daily update forum. Organizations offering blogs or having social media (e.g., Facebook, Instagram, etc.) or mirror websites for users to work around firewalls must be sure to replicate or summarize content. | "Inspiring" messages—while obviously right-minded and meant to be positive—are not needed for daily announcements, as they might sound disingenuous when terms used are repetitive or the communique is used too frequently. |
| | Daily content should be systematic with standardized terminology, such as a "check in" or "drop in" with a focus on recommendations, wellness information, etc. In city or county online environments, internal messaging or networks might act as announcement forums as well. | |
| Organizational Plans (in place or in progress) | Administrators should narrow the audience for major planning activities due to the emergency-event changes. Administrators should, however, continue—as much as possible—to follow operational plans during the event as overall guidance for operations or as appropriate or needed to move forward. | New or expanded plans should be presented within the context of existing plans with "up-front" wording for what is new or changed and for how long. Workers need to know if operational, in-depth, or long-standing plans or plans with successes dependent on situational elements not in evidence are going to continue or are being assessed for delays or revisions. If it involves them, workers need information as to "how" they would fit in, go forward, etc. |
| Rumors | Organizational issues often breed rumors among all groups due to the myriad of facts; real, imagined, or self-proclaimed experts; and often-conflicting recommendations from internal, external, and commercial sources. | Those in both management and leadership positions should review all rumors to decide if they need to be addressed or dispelled. If possible, content clarifying rumors can easily be integrated into other communications. If not, and they are determined to be necessary to be addressed, the language should be brief and specific with corrective information that is—if possible—credentialed. |
| Operational Changes (policies, procedures) | Just as with plans, administrators should continue—as much as possible—to follow usual policies and procedures during the emergency events as overall guidance for operations. | Core changes in policies and practices—if needing to be addressed—should be carefully addressed with timelines, rationale, and status of *temporary* or *permanent* as well as the design and delivery of a standard "sign-off" on major changes—even if only temporary. |

| Communiques (what) | Audience/Target Population (who/for whom) | What to Say during Emergency Events (wording, tenor, approach, etc.) |
|---|---|---|
| Individual Emails | Emails handling individual questions and answers should be targeted back to users and user groups unless—using anonymity and having verified content—it becomes a vehicle for major announcements as "breaking news" or "emergency closing." | • Focus on the few issues addressed.<br>• Use positive language and simple sentences, and link to additional information needed rather than including it in the email.<br>• Adopt—if not used already—standard subject lines and formats for all emails.<br>• Follow—as possible—guidelines for technical writing such as "limit coverage to three items for any one communication"—if that many are necessary—and then have a standard ending that clearly repeats needed behaviors, input, changes, or "action items."<br>• Deadlines for completion or feedback should be in communique headings and repeated in the ending as needed. |
| Presentations | Presentation content should be matched to the audience who requested the presentation or the intended audience of the administrator. | The content can focus on what is happening but should focus the most (in the absence of a specific request) on progress in business-as-usual as well as paradigm shifts for pre- and during pandemic activities. Managers can also focus on operations' data successes. |
| Leadership—Team Communiques | Motivational content is typically for all involved in the organization with the content delivered relatively infrequently. | Rotate successes and methodically review the events to make sure all are covered. Language should be positive and—if possible—provide a thank-you or two to specific groups. |
| Signage—Internal and External | Targeted users or workers using the space, service, or area. | All content should be dated; initialed; consistent in terminology, color, font, and universal symbols; and—where possible—offered in more than one language. Signs should focus on dos and what is being allowed. Signage should offer alternatives and be consistently reviewed. |
| Reportage—Internal, External, and Upward | Advisory groups, governing entities, general community, supporters, library workers. | All data in context and with stories, focus on accountability, comparison data with parameters, goal and outcome achievement or not but choices made. |
| Media Press Kits, Press Releases, Social Media | General community, users, supporters, and stakeholders; peripheral responsible groups such as in K–12, parents, and families | Open, positive, honest content with the core message supported by overall mission and goals of the institution. Key elements highlighted, simple directions, testimonials, experts identified. |

a broader look at not only what to say and what not to say but also to whom things should be said or not said.

As stated earlier, although it is always important to identify what to say—making a note of what *not* to say—the critical issues of a pandemic drive the need for managers and leaders to also identify and categorize what not to do and what not to say for communication. And although chapter 11 offers a variety of examples—many of which have to do in some part with communication failures—the topic is important enough (some say the most important aspect) to include at least this content as a basic chapter on communication in pandemics with specificity of communication problems, mistakes, and so on.

Pandemic communication—although primarily unique to the type, location, and seriousness of the specific cause (virus, subgroup, strain, etc.), has a number of communication pieces that are going to be necessary for the organization to include in their list of types or kinds of information needed. These specific content areas can be—obviously—accomplished and distributed in a variety of ways, including one or "a few" communiques (an official memo with follow-up email or a blog posting with follow-up signage with introductory memo) or a combination of signage, emails, calls, webinars, written memos, and announcements (depending on the importance and complexity). The level of complexity and the decision for a set of communiques remain unknown until the situa-

**TABLE 6.3**
**Communications: What Not to Do and Say**

Publication Date: _____
Review Date/Revised Date: _____
Process Owner: _____

| Communiques (what) | Audience/Target Population (who/for whom) | What Not to Say during Emergency Events (wording, tenor, approach, etc.) |
| --- | --- | --- |
| Communiques typically used to communicate content with standard changes for emergency events. (This content is delivered in many ways including as separate content or as part of a web environment or emergency event/ pandemic portal.) | Target audiences vary for communications, and content that is restricted from being shared before a recipient group should have that caveat on the communication to clarify and emphasize.<br>• Users<br>• Library workers<br>• Library supporters<br>• Governing entity<br>• Advisory entities<br>• Media/press<br>• Parallel entities<br>• Partners/area collaborations/memberships<br>• Community-at-large | • Don't interpret health information or publically disagree with experts the organization has chosen to follow; if the administrator or the office or the steering or advisory group, etc., have questions or concerns, follow the organization's emergency procedures for questioning processes.<br>• Don't minimize the seriousness of the situation. Pandemic issues are serious and unique with most if not all audiences unaware of what to do.<br>• Organizations must *not* ignore the critical review and rewriting needed for shutdowns (or shutout*) policies and procedures and should immediately review relevant policies and procedures.<br>* Shutout issues are those where the organization is closed to the user (or any primary or second audiences) but workers may still be inside in some or all areas with some or all hours of service (to be decided). |
| Web Portal | Web content is designed for all, and "front page" event content is used for specific answers to specific questions. The more successful front page minimizes general, vague content and links to the broader world for event content but instead is arranged by user with FAQs with dynamic links. | Don't link to other organizations' content as is without revision, interpretation, or introductory content. If you choose to do what others are doing specifically, note how what they are saying *is* specific to *your* organization and/or your target populations, etc. |
| Announcements: Emergency Changes | Change announcements are typically for all involved in the organization and should be used carefully and—if possible—intermittently and should be restricted during events to event-specific changes scheduled for a standard time of day. (Specific days typically aren't enough, as there will be/might be a wide variety of target populations.) | Don't create clever or useless headings for content. Although they may attract attention, communications need to standardize titles/ headings; include the "headline" in the first sentence; be specific as to how the "new" information changes previous activities, directions, or behaviors; and include—if possible and time is available—the "why" or—if appropriate—the "how." |
| Daily Updates | The web portal should not look exactly the same but should provide content for all and should offer an organized information feed (with RSS) for individuals or groups wishing to subscribe to specific updates or frequencies.<br>In education settings (K–12, higher education)—for example—the content management system should provide a daily update forum. Organizations offering blogs or having social media (e.g., Facebook, Instagram, etc.) or mirror websites for users to work around firewalls must be sure to replicate or summarize content.<br>Daily content (can be less frequently than "daily" but should not be intermittent) should be systematic with standardized terminology, such as a "check in" or "drop in" with a focus on recommendations, wellness information, etc.<br>In city or county online environments, internal messaging or networks (if approved for use) might act as announcement forums as well. | Do not skip a day or days or cease—if you choose to do daily updates—without stating why and estimating the date for the return of daily information. Do not cease production without directing readers to follow-up information. The last posting can suggest where to go for archives and any new postings.<br>If no emergency information is needed, decide on valuable information such as:<br>• Acknowledging specific projects<br>• Compliments for outstanding work<br>• A focus on a succeeding target population member<br>• A brief listing of previous changes, moves forward, etc. |

| Communiques (what) | Audience/Target Population (who/for whom) | What Not to Say during Emergency Events (wording, tenor, approach, etc.) |
|---|---|---|
| Plans | Administrators should narrow the audience for major planning activities due to the emergency event changes. Administrators should, however, continue—as much as possible—to follow operational plans during the event as overall guidance for operations or as appropriate or needed to move forward. | • Don't abandon major projects without announcements of return dates.<br>• Don't launch new services or departments or staff changes without the input needed—if only an email first.<br>• Don't change the planning process without involving the original planners or informing those affected by the existing, new, or changed plans. |
| Rumors | Do not ignore rumors no matter who is affected by or related to the rumor. Emergency event issues and especially serious health-related events (such as pandemic issues) breed rumors due to the myriad of facts; real, imagined, and self-proclaimed experts; and often-conflicting recommendations. | Don't ignore rumors. Although handling of them varies greatly, none should be ignored or go unaddressed—if only to present to the pandemic team or dispel rumors among managers. Administrators, however, should not ignore them. Reporting rumors should not be rewarded but should not be handled punitively for those who come forward to report them. |
| Operational Changes (policies, procedures) | Just as with plans, administrators should continue—as much as possible—to follow usual policies and procedures during the pandemic as overall guidance for operations. | Do not make changes without involving others who need to be informed—if there is no time for standard involvement through the organization's processes. But because so many changes are typically part of pandemic events, managers should not ignore the order in which they are implemented.<br>This process can include an awareness system for communicating changes (e.g., a memo distributed indicating *Circulation Changes #5–11: Fines and Fees Assessments Suspended through 8/2021–Temporary*)<br>Don't leave out timelines, even if it is only possible to say "a post-pandemic review will take place."<br>Don't forget to build in assessment to both temporary and permanent changes in policies and procedures. |
| Individual Emails | Emails handling individual questions and answers should be targeted back to users and user groups unless—using anonymity and having verified content—it becomes a vehicle for major announcements as "breaking news" or "emergency closing." | • Do not answer in general terms. Focus on a single question at one time and answer all questions asked.<br>• Don't use narrative to answer questions. Follow technical writing guidelines (see table 6.1).<br>• Don't load emails with information that isn't vetted, presented clearly, or clear in intent.<br>• Do not overuse breaking news content, or workers *and* users will begin to ignore reused approaches to sharing information. |
| Presentations | Presentation content should *not* be repeated multiple times, as audiences may overlap. (See table 6.1.) | Do not repeat old data. If no new information is available per the event, provide a summary then reflections or opinions or business-continuity data—for example. Do not hesitate to use presentation time as a time to compliment departments, workers, partners, etc. |

*(continued)*

**TABLE 6.3** *(continued)*

| Communiques (what) | Audience/Target Population (who/for whom) | What Not to Say during Emergency Events (wording, tenor, approach, etc.) |
|---|---|---|
| Leadership—Team Communiques | Although motivational content is typically for all involved in the organization with the content delivered—if possible—once or infrequently, administrators as leaders should take care not to mix with management *and* not to provide contrary information. | Language should remain positive and informative—as most leadership language is—and should not use vague content or repeat motivational phrases or wording. Leaders should not be specific as to mentioning some, leaving others out; however, specific groups can be rotated in for focus. Leaders just have to take care and *not* leave people out overall and should literally track who they feature, as during emergency events, some are disconnected from their workplace and seek to see themselves in the organization's successes. |
| Signage—Internal and External | Targeted users or workers using the space or area. | • Mismatched signs should not remain posted, even if they are not part of the event issues. Out-of-date signs should not remain posted beyond their accurate "life." Signs should not be created using one method and updated using another, as readers assume anyone could have done it. <br>• Don't post signs without authorship (even if it is only a committee) and date-posted information. <br>• Don't vary terms for general information and pandemic information (e.g., signs providing information about circulation of materials should not include the word *circulation* for conveying one aspect such as normal circulation guidelines and *checkout* for loaning materials during the pandemic or event). <br>• Signs should not be posted without appropriate approvals and without using the standards adopted for the pandemic (e.g., color, font, size, brand, terminology, authorship, etc.). |
| Reportage—Internal, External, and Upward | Advisory groups; governing entities; general community; supporters; library workers; funders; partners; memberships; vendors (related); federal, state, and local agencies; associations, peers. | • Don't focus on only the good, or successes, but—as possible—provide context, backstory, etc. <br>• Share information and data as needed, and be honest about needs and failures or lessons learned. <br>• Don't leave out the "why" with context and backstory, illustrating accountability. Include plans for correcting—as appropriate—or even "next steps." |
| Media Press Kits, Press Releases, Social Media | Target audiences typically include general community, users, supporters and stakeholders, peripheral responsible groups such as in K–12, parents, and families. (And treat all media "the same" with same or similar information, as target audiences often overlap or share information.) | • Don't avoid conflicting press information, but address it, providing context if there are—in fact—different issues for target groups. <br>• Use clear characterizations of target audiences as users, and don't forget to add meaningful examples. <br>• Don't forget to educate the media—no matter how small the outlet—on your media processes. |

tion itself arises; however, the emergency-management profession and supporting associations provide samples, examples, and templates to use as "Swiss cheese" communication for when the critical issues occur.

Handled by managers and leaders as well as any designated response group, they can be sorted into at least four broad areas: (1) guidelines, rules, and regulations, (2) required health responses, (3) service changes, and (4) employee and customer/user/constituent outreach. These areas—at their core—are typically constantly reoccurring pandemic elements focusing on public health, prevention, care, and protection and behavioral expectations. And although there are many more types and kinds of communication critical in a pandemic, these issues and resulting management and leadership of them are directive with nonoptional behaviors. Obviously—as outlined earlier—those template elements are infrastructure for these areas, and great care must be taken with terminology, timing, references, and credentials. Also—given the rapid changes of issues in general, the number of issues and the lack of control over escalation of issues, as well as the constant changes in guidelines being communicated—choosing simpler paths of preparation and distribution is important as well as the design of a schematic for labeling what is used and created.

Given the need for rapid delivery and often privacy issues with public health, many organizations cannot seek feedback as is typically done on critical information. In addition, some standard processes of feedback on messages are often not possible, so practices where workers signal managers of receipt of information, levels of understanding met, and agreements to comply cannot be used.

### Guidelines, Rules, and Regulations

Throughout pandemics, guidelines, rules, and regulations change based on the progression of the virus, the movement of variants, and production and distribution of a vaccine. And, as the virus changes, grows, and ultimately weakens or is overpowered (herd immunity, vaccine, etc.), the guidelines, rules, and regulations surrounding it are revised, increased, or reduced. As this content is changed, legislated, confirmed, increased, or lengthened, interpretations, safety plans (designed based on official directives), and resulting processes and protocols need to be assessed, integrated, and reintegrated into organizational operations. Each change in directions or protocols is verified and announced to those affected, and—because the content typically builds on previous content—a systematic approach to implementing not only revised or new content but also training and education for those affected must be taken.

The guidelines, rules, and regulation areas require standardization or templates to provide the necessary structure to ensure a consistency to this critical content. Sample content areas presented as guidelines, rules, and regulations include:

- social distancing and de-densifying spaces;
- both cleaning and disinfecting environments;
- products used, restricted, or banned;
- activities ceased or reintegrated;
- attendance and successful completion for worker and user education training and tracking;
- gathering data on medical issues and conditions;
- contact tracing;
- communication regarding pandemic issues, treatment, and exposure;
- changing terminology; and
- new or different metrics as the pandemic progresses.

Also, most human resources (HR) issues during health crises are governed by new or reintroduced rules and regulations as well as any public-health legislative practices in place such as announcing health issues and protection of medical information balanced against public-health measures.

### Required Health Responses

Although health issues are at the heart of all pandemic issues and most communications, those issues that drive requirements for actions, timelines, access, and protection—to name just a few things—need to have very strict processes. In addition, given the seriousness of pandemic situations, there are many other health issues where HR content—either existing or created—comes into play. These issues include not only the health issues outlined in the guidelines, rules, and regulations (prevention, tracking, sanitizing, behaviors, expectations, and vaccinations) but also related issues such as:

- general wellness (during the length of the pandemic) for workers and their families as well as designated people in their home and health spheres;
- mental health issues surrounding isolation, fear, uncertainty;
- values, beliefs of the organization, workers, and treatments;
- general fears of exposure, lack of protection from users;
- general fears of exposure, lack of protection from coworkers;

- managing conflict among workers;
- managing conflict between workers and users;
- conflicts for public-health requirements in general, for medical reasons, or for political or religious beliefs;
- divisiveness for disagreements for handling pandemic situations;
- managing and leading workers with equity in mind (Who works frontline? Who works remotely? Who returns to work and when?);
- managing health issues including sickness, death for workers and people in their spheres;
- managing health issues including sickness, death for workers and users;
- designing and implementing HR policies on tracking remote loads, remote work processes;
- upward communication processes for workers to report on expectations not met by others ("telling" on coworkers as to health status/diagnosis, prevention steps, adherence to policies and practices);
- general fears related to change at work;
- changing roles and responsibilities; and
- ongoing preventive and protection practices of top-level administration—that is, who will assist workers in enforcing COVID required practices and for how long?

### Service Changes

Business-continuity service practices—as well as choices of which services to continue as is, which to continue with changes, or which to cease—vary dramatically from institution to institution during pandemics. Changes or the lack thereof might be governed by umbrella organization directives, institutional directives, or governing or advisory board directives—to name just a few decision makers institutions must work with for pandemic decision making. In addition, it is very typical that—no matter the continuity decisions—there are changes throughout the pandemic, and—obviously—the longer the pandemic, the more likely it is for service changes to occur or to move back and forth along the spectrum of open, not open; accessible, not accessible; or allowable, not allowable.

Given the range and types of changes and given the fact that in many types or kinds and sizes of organizations, libraries may be providing first-responder services and resources as well as continuing to play the critical roles they play in communities, it is essential to get the design and distribution of pandemic information right for the first step and throughout subsequent changes. Also—along with explanatory information for workers and users—*training* workers what to say, how to say it,

and how to address conflicts emerging from services is an important part of communication.

### Employee and Customer/User/Constituent Outreach

Since pandemics and public-health crises are always chaotic at first and often at various stages throughout, a significant amount of time must be spent by those in management *and* those in leadership roles on informing workers and constituents of what is going on. But why is pandemic or public-health information so different from other emergency situations?

### Workers

Because so many pandemic issues mean significant changes—albeit many temporary—for workers, decision makers must carefully choose, articulate, and track changes for library workers. Categories of work often—if not always—change roles and responsibilities, so (if the environment such as HR, unions, etc., allows it) these categories are far more intrusive into spaces external to work (home, other assigned workspaces, other unassigned spaces where people choose to work), and this intrusiveness must be carefully tracked to avoid overstepping HR guidelines, inappropriate activities and interactions, as well as violating local, state, or federal guidelines, rules, or regulations.

Changes of roles and responsibilities often drive revised behavioral as well as performance expectations of managers; examples of changes that can and typically do make significant differences include:

- changes in work locations (remote, frontline service);
- benefits for workers such as organizational guidelines, including use of sick and vacation days, federal law (FMLA, HIPAA), and so on;
- competency attainment required for different work roles and responsibilities with now-required training;
- tracking technology use, location, and access; and
- operational expectations such as accessing and reading organization communication, responding to management queries, attending events (online, in person, etc.), workplace participation, and tracking performance expectation.

An additional issue in pandemic message distribution is a review of workers, users, and/or target population members. And—although this approach is typically part of the library's communication plan—pandemics

**TABLE 6.4**
**Emergency Event Template**

Publication Date: _____
Review Date/Revised Date: _____
Process Owner: _____

Distribution Date: _____
EM Communication (circle one or more focus):

Target Population (list all recipients):


Summary:                                              Keywords:

Implementation Date/Time/Deadline: _____    Distribution/Location(s): _____
Frequency: _____                            Mode/Method (list all used): _____

Point of Origin: Regulator/Agency (include all that apply):

Distribution (match content with mode/method):        Training Needed (by when):

Process Owner (name, title, initials, contact information):

Comments (with initials):

Feedback Required (by when):

*When web URLs are linked, the address should also be spelled out within the message.

typically force decision makers to look at their target populations differently, which actually depends on aspects of the pandemics—that is, identification of users categorized for virus transmission, age, and at-risk individuals; library resources needed by users; added services for specific users; prohibited services given service parameters; users allowed in (e.g., days, times) or restricted from the library based on timing given vulnerability, and so on.

In assessing communication during pandemics, however, managers and leaders must go beyond who needs to use the library and include those who also need to know what the library is doing, who receives budget requests during or after the pandemic, who would be tracking library or user activities, or those needing awareness of the data the library is generating. (See table 6.5.)

There are several unique communication aspects for pandemics, with the most unique and dramatically different areas being among the most difficult discussions managers and leaders have to have: general negative information concerning the pandemic, health status (legal information only), bad news, and worker and user deaths. Additional bad news to communicate includes operational issues such as reduced budgets and pandemic consequences.

Typically—during pandemics—managers have to deliver this kind of negative or bad information often, and an important part of the organization's communication plan is the design of a process for those delivering both negative and positive information. And, although general principles apply for handling the more negative or difficult roles and responsibilities, some specific aspects of delivering this unique communication apply:

- Managers and leaders should take great care not to avoid or delay communicating negative information due to the fact that delay and possible avoidance increase the chances of misinformation and rumors. (This statement is made with the knowledge that some pandemic information is governed by governmental or institutional timelines, and the release of the information is not always within a manager's or leader's control.)
- The communication plan should include recommendations on the choice of the best mode/method of delivering information as well as the timing, such as when in the work day and when in the work week might be the best time. (Other timing includes recommendations that negative information should not be delivered at the close of a business day, the day before a holiday, or at the end of the business week. Doing so offers few opportunities to ask follow-up questions from internal sources as well as seek help from external sources.)

**TABLE 6.5**
**Matching Modes and Methods of Communication to Target Populations**

Publication Date: _____
Review Date/Revised Date: _____
Process Owner: _____

| Target | Communication during Pandemic | Mode/Method (for reaching for information; for reaching and delivering in alternative modes/methods) |
|---|---|---|
| Users—For Any Reason (informational, research, tech, physical facility use, study, recreational, cultural, social services, access to LMS, etc.) | If open any/all hours: • Users scheduled in for specific appointments for services or resources • Potential attendees for upcoming scheduled and advertised events • Typical groups using the services, resources, spaces • Users (as groups or individuals) of specific resources • General users—seeking specific things (tax season coming up) • General users | • Ads in neighborhood/community newsletters • FAQs in organizations' mailings • Interviews for public television morning shows • Online software for presentations for groups scheduled to meet (meeting room users, classrooms, material-designated spaces [special collections, etc.] • Media outlets with free/nonprofit allotments • Organizational media • Partnership media (packets, etc.) • Flyers for pickup at library (external and internal if open) high-use locations; user-group settings/locales • Media streams—public and social media (interviews, text-based announcements) • Posters in high-use area locations • Announcements in organizations (PAs, comments to read with handout or flyer at area meetings of constituents, bulletins/newsletters, posted to group websites, blast emails, mailouts with public mailings) |
| Users—General: Research, Reference | General service information and if open also requirements for use and access with restrictions | • Ads in neighborhood/community newsletters • Interviews for public television morning shows • Online software for reference assistance • Media outlets with free/nonprofit allotments • Organizational media • Media streams—public and social media (interviews, text-based announcements) • Posters in high-use area locations • Announcements in organizations (PAs, comments to read with handout or flyer at area meetings of constituents, bulletins/newsletters, posted to group websites, blast emails, mailouts with public mailings) |
| Users— Higher Ed: Educational Level | • Faculty • First-year experience (FYE) curriculum team • Doctoral students • Student newspaper • AAUP • LMS bulletin board | • Faculty monthly newsletter; adjunct mailouts, new student orientation • Ads in neighborhood newsletters • FAQs in organizations' mailings • Online software for presentations for groups scheduled to meet (meeting room users, classrooms, material-designated spaces [special collections, etc.]) • Organizational media • Media streams—public and social media (interviews, text-based announcements) • Posters in high-use area locations • Announcements (podcasts posted to group websites, blast emails) |
| Users—K–12: Grade Level | • Student groups • Neighborhoods • Parent/family groups • Home schoolers • After-school programs • District mailouts • Partnership groups (charter school infrastructure) • Student newspaper • Area hangouts | • Teacher blast emails by schools • Faculty monthly newsletter; adjunct mailouts, new student orientation • FAQs in organizations' mailings • Organizational media • Media streams—social media (interviews, text-based announcements) • Posters in high-use area locations • Announcements (podcasts posted to group websites, blast emails) |
| Users—Age Level: Lap Sit, Babies | • Student groups • Neighborhoods • Parent/family groups • Home schoolers • After-school programs • Any health-related mailouts from clinics • Caregiver mailouts | • Handouts on door/sign • Mailout piggyback for special events • Area clinics/doc offices • Teacher blast emails by schools • FAQs in organizations' mailings • Organizational media • Media streams—social media (interviews, text-based announcements) |

| Target | Communication during Pandemic | Mode/Method (for reaching for information; for reaching and delivering in alternative modes/methods) |
|---|---|---|
| Decision-Makers, Voters (and Possibly Nonusers) | Readerships for:<br>• Newspaper (print/paper and online) articles on what the library is providing during the pandemic<br>• TV/cable news; interviews; specifically public television<br>• Neighborhood newsletters<br>• Mailouts in public utilities | • Daily newspaper for community overall<br>• Higher-ed newspaper<br>• Newsletters (church, neighborhood)<br>• PTA newsletter<br>• TV/cable: specifically public television |
| Decision-Makers, Press | • Press/media outlet meeting<br>• Press packet (paper/print, USB, podcast of information, webpage created just for media to link to) | • Online software: meeting with extensive links, visuals, and podcasts made accessible for the invitation/interviews<br>• In-person or online editorial board meeting |
| Community Leaders | • Library business-continuity services/resource reports<br>• Content outlining temporary effect of business-continuity reductions or shifts to different service models | • Web content created/targeted emails to vendors/partners<br>• Information packet print/paper for linking |
| Workers, Frontline (includes volunteers as appropriate) | • Service brochure paradigm shift<br>• Organizational chart with labels of who works where, etc.<br>• Paradigm shifts<br>• Announcement of communication plan | • Emails with links to online content<br>• Follow up online meetings<br>• Paradigm shifts of existing position descriptions to new ones<br>• New position descriptions |
| Employees/Workers, Support Services/Backroom (includes volunteers as appropriate) | • Service brochure paradigm shift<br>• Organizational chart with labels of who works where, etc.<br>• Paradigm shifts<br>• Announcement of communication plan | • Emails with links to online content<br>• Follow up online meetings<br>• Paradigm shifts of existing position descriptions to new ones (if needed)<br>• New position descriptions (if needed) |
| Friends | • Business-continuity overview with worker<br>• Draft calendar redistributing Friends activities throughout reduced access times<br>• Scenarios identifying impact of changes with suggestions for moving forward | • Friends newsletter author/editor<br>• Report content emailed to officers<br>• Handouts distributed to officers for possible delivery through emails<br>• New timelines<br>• Copy of the press packet should Friends be asked for interviews<br>• Mailing with decisions Friends may need to make: fundraising events, resuming/stopping library assistance events, resuming/stopping their business meetings, etc. |
| Foundation | • Administrators<br>• Foundation (any member group)<br>• Donor list (FYI)<br>• Donor list (those with scheduled meetings, etc.)<br>• Lists of potential donors<br>• Purchased lists for mailouts | • Foundation newsletter editor<br>• Report content emailed to officers<br>• Handouts distributed to officers for possible delivery through emails<br>• Mailing with decisions foundation officers or principal may need to make: fundraising events, resuming or stopping their business meetings, etc.<br>• Draft calendar redistributing Friends activities throughout reduced access times<br>• Scenarios identifying impact of changes with suggestions for moving forward<br>• Report content emailed/communicated to officers of library supporter groups such as Boards (governing and advisory), Friends, Foundation, Project Advisory, or Strategic Planning groups<br>• Handouts designed for user groups where officers are presenting, distributing, or representing the library<br>• Copy of the press packet should foundation be asked for interviews |

• Be clear and brief in delivering bad information. Be specific about what is being communicated, and don't bury the "headline" or negative information in other information.

• Negative information should not include speculation—only the facts.
• Pandemic bad news should include clarification—if the news is particularly upsetting regarding health—

that requirements of the situation may well include the content and delivery procedures chosen, with (for example) specific references to the limitations imposed by HIPAA.

- When imparting negative news regarding work roles and responsibilities and changes, be specific to worker position descriptions and include cause and effect (if available or appropriate) rather than general information to employees and workers as a whole with vague but possibly diluted effects. That is, sweeping changes can be shared broadly—specific negative content relating to just a few should be told to those few.
- To deal with large-scale issues, managers and leaders can identify initial ways workers can cope if the difficult information affects them individually, in teams, or in other work groups.
- Identify ways for workers to alert their managers if the messages—after delivery—are of particular concern to them and if they need help in dealing with the information.
- Use direct information, and avoid softer language that obscures the truth.
- Avoid the use of any humor in any other content that might have to be in the negative communication.
- In the primary negative message, the message might be best remembered if placed in context as well as repeated—using different but clarifying language—several times.
- Negative information—especially the most serious—cannot be buried in a long list of announcements or shared information but should stand alone.

After a negative message has been delivered, address specific changes and how—if appropriate—worker roles and responsibilities will change/might change. Paradigm shifts of old roles to new roles or old responsibilities to new responsibilities—for example—not only provide a needed context but also build in changes that should be made, making it easier for workers to deal with that change.

Choosing an appropriate mode and/or method to deliver the bad news should be attempted, but—given the issues surrounding the nature of pandemics and public-health situations—it may not be easy to (for example) avoid electronic, asynchronously delivery. There may be no other way to deliver it, however, and managers and leaders should identify why the choice was made at the beginning of the message and—if needed—apologize. Also, some recommend breaking a large group into smaller groups to deliver unpopular information, but the reality is that delivering to a large group contributes to the need for all workers to get the same message at the same time. To avoid members of larger groups feeling uncomfortable seeking clarification or answering questions, however, individuals should consider techniques for gathering questions while guaranteeing confidentiality for participants.

Finally, negative information messaging is a situation where managers should be aware of management content that must be said, but also the fact that leadership approaches must be at the core of the communique. This might include:

- "I know that some may feel discomfort, and we are here to not only deliver this message but to answer your questions and offer follow-up information."
- "We want workers to know that this is a situation we all must face and we can and should do that together."
- "We deal with positive issues as a team, and we are here to say that we will approach negative issues as a team as well."
- "Change affects people in different ways—we will work together to acclimate to this change for each worker."

Although pandemics are situations where as many management and leadership pandemic issues as possible should be discussed and—as much as possible—planned out or, more appropriately, outlined prior to the situation, communication is one area where managers and leaders should go through extensive training (regularly) to be able to move swiftly and accurately through the processes when hit with this untenable situation.

In the absence of time for preparation and training for communication—much less handling negative language—managers and leaders should take the "crash course" approach by adopting best practices outlined in the emergency-management profession and—especially—use templates available in exemplary communication plans.

## Communicating and Signage

General signs and postings, specific signs and postings, and various other critical communications related to signage are covered in chapters 2 and 11 in this book. The bulk of discussion about visual identifiers, however, including print/paper institutional or commercial signs, e-displays (scrolling marquees, television or web displays), and design elements of environments such as directional information on walls, floors, doors, windows, carts, stanchions, or furniture and installations (shelving, technology) should happen in communication. And, although identifying information (signage from any delivery venue) is critical to successfully making it through the event, it is always important to step back to take a long look and discuss the opportunities of identification elements *overall*. And—in this overall discussion—it is important to emphasize the need for ongoing processes and systems for categorizing, then labeling environments and functions with the express purpose of directing constituents, workers, vendors, umbrella organization personnel, vendors, and emergency personnel before, during, and after events, as well as for providing opportunities for business continuity, allowing and denying access, and assisting in repair and recovery.

## Communication Steps in Signage

### Who Is the Sign For?

Although one might argue that the first element of signage/identification is what you want the sign *to do*, the reality is that the first step is to determine who the sign is *for* or the target audience for the message. This target-audience identification is critical for worker and user success—especially during pandemics—and can include: language, color, reading level, location, typeface, size, branding, referral steps, and graphics. While one might imagine that generic or general signs are most sought for everywhere, typically, more exterior signage (e.g., front doors, web "front pages," general phone messages, email bounce backs, and the variety of access contact points such as entry signs) is often generic or designed for "anyone" or more general audiences, while internal signage can be geared toward one or a few target audiences.

There are many audience elements to consider for choosing signage and identification elements, and a number of issues and concerns exist. Just a few examples of these categories are user age, reading level, culture, ethnicity, basic knowledge of the area, types of services and resources, and the user's reason for wanting to enter or use resources or services. Another key target audience element is "relationship to the area," including the following:

Does the worker, vendor, or repair person work for the umbrella organization or for an outside business? *A worker who is an employee of the umbrella institution might need fewer directions, or you might be able to use initials or acronyms "known" in the organization. In addition, they are likely to have a basic knowledge of the space.*

Are children *primary* constituents, such as children who go to the middle school and use the library, or are they community members who come with families or brothers and sisters? *Regular users might have areas more easily identified for them by common names. For example, a sign for children registered in a school might say, "Stay away from the broken window in the story time area! Danger! Broken glass!" while a sign for children not typically in the library might say, "Stay away from the carpet near the window seats! Danger! Broken glass!"*

### What Is the Sign Intended to Do?

After determining target audiences for signage or identification, the next step is determining what signs are supposed to do. Managers need to ask themselves if the signs will be:

- informing—determining status, indicating open or closed (those entering need to know);
- alerting—communicating a problem or change to constituents (those entering need to know what specific thing to look for, what happened, etc.);
- directing—telling people what to do or how to accomplish what they need (those entering need to know what to do to be successful);
- redirecting or wayfinding—indicating very specific ways for constituents to accomplish or be successful (those allowed in should follow step-by-step "paths" to use limited space or find alternate routes); or
- denying access, turning away, or prohibiting activities—what they can't do and why and (possibly) when activities, access, services, and so on, might return to "normal" and/or where they can go instead (those typically entering need to know they now can't do so).

Other issues that might need to be discussed for the organization to successfully direct users and others include the following:

- Does the sign need to *identify consequences* if directions and/or suggestions are not followed?
- Does the sign need to *direct individuals to a specific individual or place* (online or in person)?
- Are constituents encountering signs or identification supposed to move them along or *redirect them along a specific timeline?*

### How Can Signs Be Identifiable (with the Service/ Resource, Expertise, or Organization) to Be More Readily Understood during Emergency Times?

Identification issues—beyond target audiences and the purpose of the sign or identification itself—speak to how the sign is designed as well as how sign elements are chosen to enhance or illustrate the message. These issues are color, wording, typeface, language, size, shape, author, timing, and graphics.

Color issues focus on readability issues such as the color of the background, the color of lettering, and the color of any graphic as well as the contrast that colors create. They are colored differently from standard, typical, or "normal" signage and use colors to attract attention (neon orange, bright red, vibrant yellow) and can morph or change such as glow in the dark. Colors can be deliberately combined for meaning (yellow and black stripes for emergency situation) or meaningful such as school colors. Alerting is especially important, and signs should attract attention, increase retention of information, create a mood, and/or engender a feeling as well as provide takeaways (brochures, bookmarks with URLs or new hours) to take from the container on or near the sign. Signage should also incorporate digital coding such as QR codes for users to access on smartphones, iPads, or other devices.

Managers should be cautious about either designing or buying signage that communicates significantly through color, as some workers, stakeholders, and users may be colorblind. Different cultures and/or ethnic groups as well as genders often indicate they are attracted to some colors over others and prefer certain colors over others. Those preferences can direct managers to choose or combine based on the match of target audience to color preferences, but most importantly to attract attention and communicate expectations and information. Pandemic colors—in the 2019–2022 pandemic—incorporated some color systems from emergency color designations that are a universally recognized spectrum of color to indicate the seriousness of the event. CDC guidelines used these colors to indicate seriousness, while some organizations also used colors to indicate stages of the virus.

Wording for signs and identification should be carefully chosen to match target audiences and/or meet target audience needs. This means—universally—lower reading/grade levels, high school level or below, words with no more than three syllables, avoiding or using colloquialisms (as the situation warrants), using generally accepted terms and phrases, and choosing specific, regulated, or required emergency-management terms. CDC pages as well as public health websites at the local, state, and federal levels used similar wording on signs; and pandemic information early on adopted certain phrases such as *socially distanced* and *PPE*, with a standard referral to COVID-19 with all caps and no periods. Midway through the pandemic the CDC asked that the term *coronavirus* refer to only big-picture discussions, as COVID-19 is one viral strain of the many types of coronavirus.

Politicians and legislators often use slogans or meaningful wording when in charge and then derive other actions—such as relief legislation or sweeping initiatives—using that wording or similar wording. (*Note*: President Biden's COVID-19 slogan was "We can do this," with various images in patriotic colors.)

Different languages can be used for all sign or identification wording or for parts of signs. Choice of language must be careful to reflect a specific language or dialect that is appropriate, respectful, and accepted in the community and must be written as grammatically accurate not only to communicate the situation but also to avoid conflict and offending constituents. Great care was taken in the COVID-19 crisis to use signage in the variety of languages present in North America. This was due—in no small part—to the fact that many people of other cultures and ethnicities—some of whom speak other languages—would not take the vaccine.

"Size," as an indicator in signage, relates to the size of the sign itself (standard, oversized, unusual size to attract attention), the size of lettering, and the size of other sign elements such as graphics and/or illustrations, punctuation, borders, or other designs. Some organizations used the size of signage to indicate virus stages. This became difficult in the COVID-19 pandemic, as the status of the virus moved rapidly among the stages and not always forward—that is, some areas went from stage 3 to 4, then back to 3 again. It is difficult to switch out signs by size when the situation often changed weekly, or—more accurately—every two weeks (in some stages) or the length of time it typically took from transmission to diagnosed serious conditions.

Shapes of signs can be chosen to: distinguish emergency-management signs from other standard or typical organizational signs, identify a sign as different or unusual and thus attract attention, or reflect a specific element of the incident. A shape reflecting a specific element of a situation might include a sign shaped like a house with a roof on it and a line through it to indicate a collapsed roof and therefore a closed-off second floor. Some pandemic signage used signs shaped like the virus itself—a circle with protrusions.

Graphics on signs can provide information through use of standard illustrations or graphics from emergency-management clip art, institutional images (mascots, logos), or humorous graphics to assuage inconvenience of an emergency situation in the hopes of avoiding conflict, and they can also assist in communicating large issues using the theory that "one picture is worth a thousand words." The standard pandemic graphic became the virus itself—referenced earlier. Other effective images included a drawing of a person with a mask.

## Where Should Signage Be Posted?

Placing signs in the appropriate location can be the most critical element of communicating emergency-management status, guidelines in place, issues, and so on. In addition to selecting primary locations, a critical step is selecting secondary locations (front door *and* back or side entrance), and exaggerated placement such as papering an entire front window, using billboards, or projecting on the outside of a building or front door can indicate importance of the issue. Many sign recommendations also include placement at typical eye level, with an identifier to draw attention to the sign nearby but in an unusual area that is in the average line of sight (e.g., a mobile on the ceiling above the door, on the floors in front of customer service desks).

Location issues also include:

- unique aspects of placement on websites such as scrolling marquees, popups, "under" or within the pandemic brand logo or tagline, and/or in a banner headline (all hypertext leading to complete organizational pandemic information);
- placement of neon signs or electronic scrolling marquee signs in libraries (at the circulation desk, an information desk, over the door, at the reference desk);
- placement on outreach organization content (considered proactive) such as on overdue notices, in targeted-population or blast email information, on vans/delivery vehicles, and on signage in other public areas (external to the organization); and
- designing signage and identification for moving patrons from one area to another through labeling floors (e.g., footsteps to follow), labeling ceilings, sidewalks, parking lots, internal and external walls, and/or ceilings.

To aid in successful communication, locations of signs, general floor plans, and specific department, area, or functional sections of floor plans should be designed, duplicated, and labeled as to where emergency-management signs should be placed and mapped to types of events. For example, a pre-prepared floor plan would be labeled for use for water damage, while another plan might be labeled for repair and construction that might—for example—circumvent worker and user travel from a front door to a side door.

An unusual "location" issue is concern for unusual conditions that dictate "interactions" of surfaces and signs needing special adhesive for locations where climate or lack of HVAC controls cause signs to become loose and fall down or blow away. One additional aspect of weather or light is signs fading when placed in sunlight or signs not visible during certain weather conditions or in the evening or at night. While careful placing of signs seems to be a reactive part of emergency management (undiscovered or unrealized conditions cause changes in processes), buildings should be originally designed or retrofitted with grids on all or parts of ceilings to accommodate hung or mounted signs as well as walls that allow for sign hanging or mounting mechanisms and surfaces that allow for easy attachment for signs.

Furthermore, signs should have management initials with a "thank you" or "see you when we open back up" statement, and they should be dated—which places the burden on the organization to keep all content up to date. This labeling can use a combination approach, such as the full year, by the month, or by the week (e.g., "March—Week 1").

Finally, signs need to be designed to follow guidelines presented in the Americans with Disabilities Act (the 2016 ADA with amendments) covering all related issues (size, color, braille, etc.) but especially care using floor-mounted graphics or signage on stands or stanchions.

## Are There Impediments to Communicating through Signage?

Although the previously covered information includes signage issues that may be impediments to the success factors in this communication, three other impediments should be part of the discussion of communicating through signage:

1. Managers should consider pandemic restrictions when deciding not only where but also how to affix signs to external—and even some internal—areas. The reality is signage on doors or internal or external book drops may not be accessible if building access is prohibited, or signs may be too small to be seen any way other than close-up. Because of these kinds of unknowns, at the very least initial pandemic signage has to be reviewed far more often than in other emergency situations: in fact, initial schedules should include a weekly review taking feedback from users (phone, online, reference calls, circulation desk calls, and possibly in person) as well as from on-site staff such as building managers, security or police, and members of the emergency response team (for example).

2. Although the first days of pandemics drive managers to choose steps for handling the situation quickly and sometimes at an expense, managers must be prepared for ongoing costs that may not be easily available.

3. Shared-space situations—very common in all types of libraries—drive initial and ongoing general signage issues; thus it stands to reason that emergency signage would bring a variety of problems including a multitude of agreements for signage as well as lack of control over posting and review, and there are often lengthy approvals for posting signs.

Finally, gaining control over *change* is critical, but just as important is the need to control *content* and have a role in designing the narrative of pandemic management and leadership communication. As stated earlier, there is information on communication imbedded in a variety of other areas, and the success of communication is addressed in chapter 4.

## Small/Solo Librarian Environments

Smaller and solo library environments do not have the time to create extensive emergency-communication tools. Because of the size of the library, however, the number of employees with whom managers must communicate is less as well as the overall number of user groups and users. Smaller libraries typically also have fewer dollars available for significant signage as well as fewer stakeholders to assist in—for example—response teams, and managers have all of the leadership roles and responsibilities and—more than likely—few if any to whom they can delegate activities. Because of these issues, more importance must be placed on "if we had been ready," including that the prepared solo librarian has:

- chosen model signs that are required for emergency situations and created an initial set to post;
- identified a stakeholder who will assist in pandemic communication;
- completed basic emergency training and arranged for stakeholder training as well;
- identified likely partners to work with for shared roles and responsibilities during the pandemic emergency;
- identified a best-practices communication plan—with templates—and adopted it for the library; and
- prioritized those activities that are reasonable to achieve during the pandemic and designated a set of library activities to be suspended during the event.

# 7

# Management and Organizational Design

## *Unique Issues*

MANAGEMENT ISSUES, TECHNIQUES, and recommendations are found in many chapters in *The Post-Pandemic Library* and especially in any content related to human resources, communication, planning, and organization. In fact, for pandemic and post-pandemic libraries, the entire infrastructure for recommendations for dealing with management and organizational issues must be grounded in and begin with principles of management and organizational design. This chapter is designed to offer unique aspects for short-term, long-term, and possibly long-term management and organizational issues that surface and must be dealt with in these very difficult times.

Prior to addressing how management- and organizational-structure issues change, however, it is important to review the core or infrastructure or *primary* aspects. These include (with a nonpandemic focus): dealing with/ managing and coordinating change, operational planning, accountability and justification, management documents and documentation, and organizational design.

So, why a chapter *just* on these unique aspects and issues rather than just embedding issues into other chapters? The reality is that these issues vary dramatically in any emergency situation but especially during the extreme and unique pandemic and post-pandemic library environments, and almost more than any other area, the ongoing and possibly longer-term aspects may be "here to stay." In addition, due to the unique nature of emergency management (EM)—especially during pandemics—a number of management roles, reporting structures, and—basically— how work gets done and who does what are completely new. So managers should look for significant issues and thus changes that might be needed in:

- communication;
- human resources (HR);
- planning;

- partnerships;
- accountability and justification;
- continuing education/training (document infrastructure);
- management/organizational support systems; and
- documents and documentation.

Four critical processes that are not new in the organization but also vary, because of pandemic/emergency events, are:

1. group/team decision making (across and up and down the organization);
2. administrative decision making;
3. organizational design (temporary new structures with old structure suspended); and
4. budget (sources, record keeping, capital vs. operational spending).

So—given that most of the areas above are well known to managers of all sizes and types of libraries—it is concerning that anecdotal information, online forums, organizational webinars, and association programming have identified the fact that many if not most library managers today feel that they face more unknowns than knowns and they are at risk of failure for missteps while managing during emergencies. And—in addition to more commonly known management differences managers are dealing with—three things that are not *typically* present in the management of library organizations but happen in emergency situations, and especially more serious emergencies such as pandemics, are three of the most difficult things for managers to deal with: (1) uncertainty in primarily business-continuity decision making and operations; (2) *rampant* change; and (3) maintaining trust.

But why are so many struggling and appearing to be failing at managing during emergency situations?

The obvious answer is "management is hard," but, when the aspects of pandemic management are reviewed through the lens of typical management activities and aspects, one may find little that they specifically are at fault for and instead find that problems are everywhere and include: a lack of evidence, a lack of or too slow instruction from higher-up managers, poor communication, and an inability to deal with change and—especially—rampant change.

What should managers expect or look for, though? Management and organizational issues should be expected in the following areas:

*People come first.* Human resources—the most important area of any organization—must be immediately reviewed for relevant content for unique issues, the presence or absence of "what if" policies and procedures, already out-of-date HR content—or inaccurate policies, procedures, and practices. Much more attention is given to the most standard of HR materials in the more typical life of the organization, such as position descriptions, federal and state legal issues with articulated matches to organizational information, and—if lucky—performance-based evaluations and basic orientation or on-boarding information and continuing education for basic roles and responsibilities. If there is little or poorly maintained HR content, workers find it hard to make credible adjustments and changes with unclear outcomes.

*Change is typically chaotic.* Processes for change—in general—must be identified and followed because if the organization has been prepared for change at all, odds are, it hasn't been prepared for rampant change and certainly not issues as serious as long-term interruptions of services, greatly reduced engagement of workers and clients/patrons, the ceasing of many basic activities, and ongoing plans put in abeyance. Change is particularly difficult because during pandemics there are *many* more changes in long-standing policies and practices—many of which are health and safety related—and, whether it is easy to say or not, sometimes *not* changing means life or death.

*Communication is critical and must be altered and altered quickly.* Communication in most organizations is designed to be relatively standard; however, communications for emergency situations—especially pandemics—must be quickly and completely reviewed with goals for greater frequency, a balance of more directives and controls—possibly by external forces—and changes in not only how they receive information but also how they listen and act on information. And although communication content (those involved in design, content, and distribution) is more frequently vetted by more people than usual, communication must be faster, more frequent, and clearly designed for consistency and continuity. In addition, communications must now be distributed to more individuals and information builds.

*Other partners, neighbors, supporting entities, and so on, are involved and very likely affected by your issues.* There are many different types of partnerships in organizations, and when emergency situations arise, partnerships can be either central to an organization's service/resource delivery or of great importance/tangential to the operations. Whether they are a large or small focus, much more attention has to be given to partner pandemic behaviors and guidelines to ensure that no matter the value or parameters of the partner, they continue to fit into organizational life. In addition, partnerships—if tangential—should be part of the communication chain to be either involved, reassured, or put on hold, but must not be neglected and need to operate from an informed point of view.

*Good may come from bad.* Specific and well-designed opportunities for "growing managers" aren't found in great numbers, they vary dramatically in organizations, and—typically—managers must create programs to grow their own, given employment rules and regulations. During pandemics, however, a multitude of roles and responsibilities in management need to be filled—and immediately so—although many are temporary. And—if it is a smaller or solo organization—these opportunities can be a much-needed growth and nurturing process that can be used as infrastructure for guiding even one individual into the new and different work to assist a manager. If there is no infrastructure for either small or large organizations, benchmarked mentoring programs must be sought for a quick adaptation to the needs at hand.

*Accountability and justification practices may change but may not cease.* The majority of libraries gather data and use that data to make decisions. In fact, libraries maintain several and sometimes many levels of accountability and justification for their decision making in order to provide users and umbrella organizations rationale for actions and dollars sought, moved around, or just expended—not only for federal reporting but also regional, state, and local reporting, partnership dollars, and soft money, grants, and so on. During pandemics, however, not only must libraries continue with the required and desired assessment but they may also need to meet their new, different obligations as well as achieve outcomes. These processes add on pandemic and emergency-related forms, structures, formulas, and record-keeping practices and also reportage processes.

*Learning is always possible.* Continuing education, training, and professional development practices in libraries encompass orientation/first-day, first-week training, ongoing continuing education for infrastructure learning activities, and staff development for more in-depth, advanced, future, or specialized work and acculturation. There are a number of required EM content areas outlined in federal and state mandates, and workers have different levels of introductory or basic emergency training required to meet general needs. Although many organizations do have ongoing infrastructure training and development for EM beyond basics already, pandemics require significantly more training and continuing education for worker safety as well as care for resources, delivering services, and selecting, deploying, training, and using personal protective equipment (PPE) and other safety areas for worker interactions. Specific management training—in general—is often not part of required EM training, but continuing education and professional development content in best practices is available in communication, decision making, change, and organizational design. As standard and critical areas of management, these curricula can be pulled together to identify a full management training program needed.

*Management support systems are not plentiful in libraries.* Managers often "take care of themselves" last. That is, some libraries have a strong infrastructure of support with individuals in the organization identified as associate or assistant, middle managers who fill the role (recognized with titles, salary, and roles and responsibilities) of a support for the manager. Many libraries do not, for any number of reasons, including lack of training, funding levels, and scarcity of staff in general. This means that not only does the manager *not* have the support they need in more typical or normal times, but they also do not have the support during emergencies and—even more importantly—during an ongoing emergency situation such as a pandemic. If the manager has no one to whom they may turn to or delegate aspects of their work, it is likely that many aspects of business operations may not happen, or worse yet, emergency issues will not be dealt with. This is not a sustainable practice, as a support system is very critical for emergency situations; therefore, with no existing or temporary assistance roles being defined, managers must identity and communicate what isn't going to happen or what might be delayed and—if possible—provide timelines for how long—as they deal with the more important emergency situation. All of this being said, a structure of support outlined for difficult times allows for assistance for the manager, more consistent practices for business continuity, and opportunities to perform new or expanded practices for future positions or a return to possible expanded work. It should be repeated that it is not realistic, however, that new or expanded roles (especially those with unique training and responsibilities) be simply added on to positions, as the

profession—not known to pay adequately—needs to accept what is possible given time and talents.

Another primary aspect of assessment of the presence or absence of management support systems is the need for those in authority to not only assume responsibility for what they are doing but also, more importantly, identify who else (higher up, in temporary support roles, existing managers with expanded roles, etc.) is also responsible and what decisions they can make as well as those that are taken out of their hands.

*Successful managers articulate practices in writing, maintain integrity of content, and maintain alternative or multiple scenario documents ready for changes.* Documents and documentation are critical to every aspect of the organization, and the need to create temporary, update existing, adapt other, and then distribute content is extraordinarily great. Library managers need to remember they are running a business, and for all content such as human resources materials, communications, guidelines and standards, and budgeting, managers need to create the management infrastructure for all new, temporary, and permanent content. Also, document infrastructure for emergency situations is required and often involves moving away from narrative or descriptive content to embracing or at least incorporating technical writing, articulating targeted and measureable outcomes, and maintaining executive summaries as well as—if it isn't available already—categorizing content, maintaining glossaries and standardization of updating procedures with evidence-based content, credentialing of individuals involved, specific (often different) frequencies of distribution, and filing and archival systems. (See table 7.1.)

The other areas that are not new for managers but also vary, because of pandemic/emergency events, are as follows:

*Group/team decision making* is at the heart of the majority of library environments where—even if there are only a few or one in management—others (governing or advisory boards, stakeholders such as Friends, peers such as department heads or curriculum team leaders) are often consulted before major decisions are made. In pandemic group decision making as well as during practices of gathering content and opinions from others to make decisions, fewer or different people might be consulted or have roles delegated to them, typically processes for gathering or discussing might disappear due to accelerated timelines, and new or different training might be required or different expertise might be needed. These approaches and processes of assembling new, expanded, or reduced groups need to be communicated as much as the decisions and responsibilities need to be.

**TABLE 7.1**
**Managing Documents**

Publication Date: _____
Review Date/Revised Date: _____
Process Owner: _____

| Area | Done/ Will Be Done | In Progress/ Complete | Process Owner/Team Member |
|---|---|---|---|
| Is the institution responsible for creating pandemic documents? | Yes | Complete | Library administrator in partnership with the co-chairs of the pandemic team. |
| Comments: *Required at institution level and for the pandemic team and for the recovery period.* | | | |
| Are the pandemic and post-pandemic recovery documents needed? Completed? | Spring 20xx | Pandemic completed 5/1/20xx | Pandemic team co-chairs with library manager |
| | Summer 20xx | Post-pandemic to be completed on 8/1/20xx | (Additional may include any workers' union representatives, county pandemic team, state library—to qualify for relief funding, etc.) |
| Are the pandemic and post-pandemic recovery documents disseminated? | 4/15/20xx | Pandemic out on 4/15/20xx | Pandemic team co-chairs with library manager |
| | 7/15/20xx | Post-pandemic out on 7/15/20xx | (Additional may include workers' union representatives, county pandemic team, state library—to qualify for relief funding, etc.) |
| Are the pandemic and post-pandemic recovery documents periodically and systematically reviewed? | Monthly | Ongoing | Pandemic team co-chairs with library manager |
| | | | (Additional assessment and feedback will be welcomed from workers' union representatives, county pandemic team, state library—to maintain and accountability for relief funding, etc.) |
| Do insurance and risk documents need review? | Yes, 4/15/20xx  Review requested | Need reassessing on 7/1/20xx | Library manager, insurance representative, and Risk Office |
| Are new floor plans needed? Included in post-pandemic content? | Yes  Review requested | Due for completion 8/1/20xx | Library manager with area managers, risk officer, and pandemic team co-chairs |
| Are emergency responsibilities and expectations in job descriptions and performance plans required for HR? | No | Retain by worker, in department or area, and in library manager's office (by 7/1/20xx), updated every 6 months | Library manager, pandemic team HR subcommittee, co-chairs |
| Are budget categories identified for pandemic and post-pandemic needs? | Yes  Yes | Monthly review | Library manager, pandemic team co-chairs |
| Comments: *Ensure a clear account code division between consumable supplies for "the facility," "workers," and users.* | | | |

*Administrative decision making* is often reduced during pandemics and instead is comprised of a narrower process with highest-level managers using fewer teams, having teams but with fewer or different membership, and using fewer experts or consultative practices. This is typically a difficult process, as there is richness and depth in consulting a wide variety of people, but as evidenced by changed communication, changed team or group decision making, and reduced timelines, changes should be made carefully and should be clearly identified and justified in the process to retain trust of those in charge.

*The design of organizations*—or how people are organized to perform their work—varies. Common approaches in libraries—no matter the size—are seldom just one approach; that is, many libraries have some elements of their work divided by functions, some by size and subdivision into smaller areas or divisions, some combined for complex environments with a combined matrix approach of both functions and divisions with more than one manager of an area and cross-functional teams that work to integrate one concept across the construct, and some with a network with a group responsible for core services and products and then smaller expert groups handling unique aspects. All approaches—many of which are combined in libraries—vary based on expertise needed, size of the product or client base, or the diverse types of products.

Many of these designs are more bureaucratic than others even though most organizations strive for less bureaucracy to accelerate processes and ultimately decision making. It stands to reason then that during emergency times, the more complicated the structure and the more people involved in decision making, the harder it is to change quickly or implement emergency policies. Because of this, EM structures tend to—while in place—quickly either eliminate multiple levels or seek more representative approaches to workers participating in management. If organizational design needs to change for the short or longer term, the following steps should be part of the process:

- Standard protocols for making organizational changes—whether simple or complex, dramatic or devoid of drama—should be followed as much as possible to get systematic input and maintain trust.
- If speed is an issue, then a subgroup or representative membership for a decision-making pandemic group can be established for action (and even appointed by the typically larger group).
- If changes are wanted or needed, before being decided on, legitimate rationale should be established and discussed with all directly involved prior to decision making/major changes.
- Announcements for organizational changes (and their timelines and status) should be made by the team—with the rationale determined and clear changes identified with simple paradigm shifts, revised position descriptions, or timelines, and so on.
- Assessment for altered organizational approaches to services or processes should be incorporated into new temporary or long-term operations along with timelines for review.

Although it isn't required to make changes in an organizational structure for unique situations such as pandemics, managers must identify EM issues and needs to make sure all areas in the organization have specific

management oversight and—if not—have process owners identified. Organizations can also consider shifting roles and responsibilities within the existing structure as well as creating short-term, long-term, or permanent individuals, partnerships, workgroups, and so on. And, although existing departments, areas, or service- or workgroups should be able to address all issues for the well-organized environment, issues surrounding the most unique situations may necessitate unique training or roles and responsibilities for existing groups or revisiting goals and strategies for units or departments early in the pandemic timeline.

No matter what, however, changes being made should have support of the representative team and manager involved during and after the change is implemented, so not involving the team in the process initially can be disastrous. At the very least, an overview of the change should be articulated for those involved not only for the workplace but also for any communication and information needed for internal discussions (beyond departments) or customer service scripts. If changes made do not have the support of the organization in general, discussion and announcements should provide the rationale but also include qualifications others might have. And—because changes are subject to assessment anyway—if they are a pilot, state that, and if they have assessment built in, state that, making it clear who decided what and why. Ultimately, the more the organization is aware of what was done and why, the better. Common courtesy much less good business practice dictates that those for whom the organization is changing need to have an opportunity for input prior to larger announcements. Also, communication at the initial or lowest level needs to include substitute services or what they will do less of and how their position will change.

*Budget processes*—although many think this is an area that cannot change—have many changeable elements during emergency situations as serious as pandemics. These changes might include: changing or delaying outcomes, ergo changing budget support for processes or projects; money assessed for availability and flexibility; decisions on accountings and amounts for spending; shortcut practices for purchasing; and different recordkeeping for expenditures. Obviously, budget issues during pandemics are complicated and have "more" complexity such as a need to fund different or expanded services or formats and the amount of money spent on formats or services. Also it should go without saying that budget dollars are not plentiful in libraries in any categories of expenditures, and pandemics are not cheap. And, although libraries should have invested in EM "toolboxes" or kits prior to the event, most don't have all they need, and pandemic dollars are needed for safety for a multitude of reasons, including items needed based on the number of workers and (often) users, dollars needed for PPE and cleaning, furniture moving, and so on. Managers must pivot to requesting money from umbrella organizations, partners, and governing or advisory bodies as well as grants and external donor drives.

Finally, managers must pay special attention to deal with uncertainty, rampant change, and maintaining trust.

## Uncertainty

What role does uncertainty play in pandemic management?

Researchers focusing on the pandemic and the cause of this pandemic—COVID-19—struggle with a myriad of issues, including the nature of this specific virus, virus variants, the speed and method of transmission, the lifespan of the virus, treatment, and recovery as well as a myriad of other critical issues related to the virus and the economy, medical care, equity and the digital divide, and unemployment, to name just a few areas.

What all of these issues have in common, however, is uncertainty, and with uncertainty being a factor prevalent in nearly every issue, the workplace and workers are struggling trying to adjust, remain successful, and stay safe in a sea of uncertainty. It is natural for workers, therefore, to want certainty in some or any form or in any areas at work. Managers, however, are unable to easily provide *any* certainty.

### Why Is It So Important?

A natural amount of uncertainty exists in organizations for many of reasons; the least of which is the fact that workers can have different opinions and perceptions on the same topics or issues, even when these topics and issues have the same or similar evidence, the same goals, and the same design and delivery. In addition, workers have different expectations and needs as well as a need for different types of support for successful work performance.

It is unrealistic to expect managers to be able to clarify normal requests and to provide all workers with what they need individually or collectively. When the work situation is paralleled with the pandemic, it is impossible to find certainty in operations, recovery, worker roles and responsibilities, group and individual needs, and safety and security overall as well as deal with personal and professional fears of workers. And at the heart of general uncertainty is finding the answer to typically the most important questions: "When will this be over?" or—at the very least—"When will safety practices be refined to the level that people can easily resume at least some semblance of normalcy at work?"

When studying uncertainty, researchers identify complexity—and certainly the complexity of pandemic issues—as being a major factor due to the layers of the pandemic found in science, medicine, the economy, and society (local and global). In addition, most researchers guarantee that uncertainty will continue with many things never being resolved, and this must be faced by managers and—most importantly—workers. Managers, therefore, need to address it directly, providing a structure for determining issues surrounding control of not just day-to-day but also the future, techniques for grappling with uncertainty, and practices to assist workers—and even users to some extent—with what *is* possible to identify as "certain."

Managers can and should, however, make decisions with new approaches—clearly realizing and communicating that there is some risk involved—but should be careful to work with the data, facts, and evidence that are available to determine what is likely and probable to happen. Managers can and should move away from language and communication that either states or implies "certainty" and adopt practices for decision making that are thought out and logical—expecting to make mistakes and ongoing changes—while sharing concerns with workers honestly but exhibiting processes in place, timelines for communicating what is and isn't happening, and—overall—those things that are certain with an inclusion of what isn't, why, and how the organization and workforce continue to move forward.

To this end, uncertainty should be specifically addressed and managed as such:

- State the incomplete, sometimes mistaken, but certainly the limitations of data and research. Note what *is* changing with the latest information and why that might be and how it does and doesn't affect work.
- Explain that their specific organization—as one of thousands—can't be sure of a number of things and that certainty may never be possible. When needed, explain why decisions were made and why they weren't made in the face of uncertainty.
- Outline the complexity of the situation, admit what the organization's managers do and don't know, and address contradictions and inconsistencies.
- Acknowledge differing opinions in research, in the organization, and that their own managers have; then identify how those are addressed, how data is used as a basis for decision making, and how there are multiple possible solutions and aspects of each.
- Identify the breadth of data and evidence used and when, how, and why it is used. Prepare—as was done for the pandemic terminology glossary—the

list of opportunities and credentials of experts behind the data, evidence, and if used, those behind the best or effective practices chosen.

## Rampant Change

What role does change and especially rampant change play in pandemic management?

Obviously organizations change daily—although libraries have typically never been described as organizations with *rampant* change. Certainly most would agree that—using the old marketing tagline—"Libraries are not your father's (or mother's) libraries anymore." They do, however, change often, and it is a fairly common and not too unrealistic stereotype that typically those drawn to work in libraries—whether they have entered the profession or not—are *typically* not seeking rampant, unmitigated, or relentless change.

But many aspects of change indicate permanency, leaving things behind, or the classic "out with the old." Compiling definitions of *change* does not paint a starkly negative picture; however, to some or even most, many of these words are considered negative: "to make different in some way," "to make radically different," and "to undergo transformation, transition, or substitution."

That is due in part to the fact that most libraries may well have changes forced on them by umbrella institutions; by changing legislation; by new guidelines, standards, and directives; by users; by the market; by the economy; and—obviously—by emergency situations, to name just a few. And while in no way is all change bad, having change thrust on you can be a negative issue and one that typically implies that the organization has little control and almost certainly less control than it needs.

Managers must recognize that general resistance to change is more the norm in organizations, especially pandemic change that has been—more often than not—clearly thrust on the library, the results of which are *not* within the control of libraries. Reasons for disliking change, however, are broad, and managers need to consider and address the breadth of the negative reaction to the rampant change. Managers must—therefore—address the totality of the reasons why change is especially difficult during pandemics and a good start is to list those aspects of the change that might be present:

1. The goals or purpose of changes are not made clear—that is, beyond "you must do this because of the pandemic," discussing and presenting why changes have been made.

2. The changes are not accepted by the people who must function with the change or by those specifically responsible for making change happen.
3. If reasons are given, neither the reasons for change nor the benefits of the change are adequately or effectively communicated.
4. The timing of announcing the change was not explained or was wrong or perceived as wrong by those involved.
5. Reasons for change and substitute or new elements or activities are not fully explained to users, nor has the rationale been articulated in such a way that it can be communicated to users.
6. Appropriate "orientation" and training are not made available to those expected to enact the change.
7. No processes are put in place for evaluating either the process of instituting change or the success of the change.

They are, however, steps to take to make successful temporary or permanent change possible or highly probable, and depending on at what stage the organization is in regarding the pandemic, it is possible and recommended that these steps be considered for post-pandemic and reentry and the return to whatever "new normal" is next. (See table 7.2.)

Following these steps in the quick changes needed is important to illustrate to workers that managers can be trusted to handle the situation, that uncertainty has been reduced, and that changes are not painless but are greatly improved over thoughts and impressions of chaotic or rampant change.

## Trust

What are the most critical aspects about the role of trust in pandemic management?

You can't be a great manager or even a good manager without having the trust of the organization, but trust is often misunderstood and underestimated in importance. The manager, however, must have the *complete* trust of the organization during emergency situations, and especially in the most serious of emergencies—the pandemic.

Everyone in the organization must understand that longevity doesn't build trust in and of itself; titles don't translate to automatic trust; workers and users trust different people in different ways; building trust is deliberate; how to build trust can be researched, studied, and taught; and trust is a combination of character and

**TABLE 7.2**
**"Change" Steps/Techniques for Change**

Publication Date: _____
Review Date/Revised Date: _____
Process Owner: _____

| Steps for Pandemic Change Possibilities/ Probabilities | Involvement, Steps |
|---|---|
| Involve others in "changing," gathering data, and *analyzing* changes.<br><br>*Even though the pandemic afforded little to no time for planning, a critical step is immediate involvement of others.* | Who should be involved? Individuals? Departments? Function coordinators? Directors?<br>Managers should immediately identify—if not done already as part of the EM plan—the EM pandemic team to assist and/or drive operational planning for the library, worker and user content preparation, and changes coming.<br>Representation should represent every level of library employee and someone who manages as well as a member of the advisory or governing external group. The roster could include (keeping in mind there are large libraries with many departments and different levels and categories of workers, as well as many libraries very small to medium sized):<br>• At least two frontline workers and one from a single service if only that one service will be active during the pandemic<br>• One senior member as evidenced by experience in libraries<br>• One senior member as evidenced by longevity in the organization<br>• At least one entry-level worker<br>• At least two middle managers<br>• At least two users aware of services and resources representing target populations and special needs populations<br>• Community members with one from each partnership or the umbrella institution<br>• Pandemic team members from other teams in the environment including first-responder groups and institutional and local disaster-management teams<br><br>Teams should have:<br>• Job descriptions for each<br>• An outside facilitator<br>• A tight timeline for documents for gathering data, facts, and information to draft, seek approval, and distribute<br>• Limited numbers of meetings with longer product-oriented agendas and "homework"<br>• Glossary of terminology and templates for team-generated content<br>• Marketing and information packets for team members prior to meetings with goals, resources, service ideas, budget information, examples of previous events, and any of the library's risk-assessment reports<br>• A team web environment |
| Identify and inform (early) those who need to help *carry out* changes.<br><br>*Even though not all can serve on the team, those who are slated to be involved in various stages such as distribution, training, service delivery, etc., should be notified.* | All library workers should be invited to participate in document reviews for drafts, etc., as well as given access to the team's web environment. |
| Clearly define all roles in change discussion, the goals of possible changes, and their achievement indicators and measures for success. | Goals and processes should indicate that all workers have a role in pandemic planning, execution, and recovery with changes. Recommended steps can include:<br>1. decide on changes (multiple scenarios discussed);<br>2. draft chosen scenario, consequences, seek input;<br>3. implement changes; and<br>4. consider fiscal note/implications.<br><br>Achievement indicators/measures of success can include:<br>• timeline;<br>• reporting "out" strategy created/disseminated;<br>• goals met by all involved;<br>• outcomes proposed are reached; and,<br>• levels of satisfaction pre, post, and during (team, workers, users, etc.) |

| Steps for Pandemic Change Possibilities/ Probabilities | Involvement, Steps |
| --- | --- |
| Disseminate decision to change and the goals and outcomes for the change in writing. | Team designs dissemination including:<br>• process beginning/kickoff;<br>• team creates brand logo for quick identification and use during the process;<br>• web environment used to communicate and involve others in the process;<br>• public timeline "countdown" on web/in libraries; and<br>• executive summary of process with outcomes used for press kit. |
| Identify/assist others in identifying how the change will specifically affect them. | Individuals and teams, departments, and others need to know how *specific* things will change.<br>• Create paradigm shifts for service and resource changes related to individuals, teams, and departments for before and after change.<br>• Assess worker job descriptions for changes and create either new descriptions or paradigm shifts.<br>• Finalized changes (as much as possible) are reviewed with individuals and groups in meetings to answer questions, establish training dates, set timelines, etc. |
| Identify and address people's needs for dealing with change!<br><br>*If possible, disrupt only what must be changed to accomplish goals and/or outcomes for the change.* | What do individuals need for changes and/or changing?<br>• Conduct surveys to determine how workers deal with change in general.<br>• Identify ways to implement change given how workers self-identify their approach to change.<br>• Identify and clarify what does change and what doesn't change.<br>• Revisit vision, mission, and values to illustrate how changes dovetail with the organization's vision, mission, and values.<br>• Schedule follow-up assessment regularly to visit and revisit issues to provide opportunities for refinement and continued refinement. |
| Design flexibility into the change process, especially because the pandemic created the unreasonable "immediate" timeline and things will likely not be perfect throughout and will need to be revisited and changed. | Flexibility must be built into the statements of actions and the timeline, including:<br>• a careful look and expression to users regarding "immediacy" so users understand that all changes may *not* be made immediately;<br>• realistic timelines in place for the team to be able to honestly say that changes are in progress and *will* be forthcoming and when; and<br>• ongoing planned assessment so mistakes can be corrected, and multiple scenarios designed to afford choices. |
| Allow users some choices in time and effort to allow workers to take adequate time to assimilate new skills, procedures, support mechanisms, and the work behaviors needed to successfully institutionalize the change. | No matter how rapidly things have happened, the team needs to prepare for the changes after they have been decided. Actions to support this include:<br>• designing a timeline for "stopping" as well as "starting";<br>• identifying specific functions, areas that will cease (and likely when) as implementation plan moves along;<br>• allowing for a process for winding down to provide a chance to get used to *not* doing things;<br>• allowing for recognition for activities and functions to stop; and<br>• creating a checklist for archiving "old" such as data, forms, etc. |
| Identify good and bad aspects of change, address all sides, and whenever possible, focus on the data supporting, the need for, and the benefits of change. | Changes often drive opportunities as well as threats.<br>• Make sure—in advertising and marketing changes—that good and bad aspects, consequences, and benefits are honestly and openly articulated. Not all changes will be embraced, and that should be directly addressed.<br>• Standardize opportunities for input, actively seek input during changes, and make opportunities for feedback throughout the pandemic.<br>• Provide data and evidence used for decision making, and show how these were used (and by whom) to make decisions. |
| Establish timelines and parameters, and define the limits of the change.<br><br>*With recognition that most timelines are pure speculation, consider a staggered approach of identifying what will happen so that workers will know the direction but necessarily when it will happen such as within 90 days, by the end of the semester, by the end of the fall, by the beginning of the month, etc.* | The reality is we know a lot about what will happen, just not when. To capitalize on this, identify the timelines for your institution and any unique aspects for change timelines. Work with standards or guidelines and any other critical timelines, such as:<br>• worker timelines for events and adjustment periods;<br>• other institutional or community planning processes; and<br>• events to piggyback with for marketing and advertising. |

*(continued)*

**TABLE 7.2**    *(continued)*

| *Steps for Pandemic Change Possibilities/ Probabilities* | *Involvement, Steps* |
|---|---|
| Design adequate training for change activities and elements. | All orientation and training needed to get ready for the process needs to be identified. Specific training needed for the process includes: <br> • operational planning; <br> • change/the process of change; <br> • group work/working in teams; <br> • project management for implementing changes; and <br> • communications. <br> Although probably not all workers need to take the same training, all must be *aware* of all training and—given the pandemic—all *will* have to take basic training, and then some will train in additional areas. |
| Build in adjustment content and—if at all possible—timing for all workers involved. Pandemic training is critical, and ultimately workers will feel safe, but the discussions can be disturbing to those involved—especially as risks and vulnerabilities are identified. | Timelines needed for workers: <br> • Create timelines based on library worker expectations based on survey data and general feedback (verbal, complaint process, etc.). <br> • Build in flexibility—that is, managers should select timelines for change that *must* be followed and then build in choices for other staff so some of their changes might be flexible. |

competency, with ethics playing a prime role in illustrating trustworthiness. Not surprisingly, good work environments are places where workers trust not only the manager but also each other; and—typically—honesty is key to trust.

Those who study management, as well as those who study emergency management, consistently warn of the dangers of losing the trust of the organization, the users and partners, colleagues, and so on. To review this all, workers need to know what trust is, how critical trust is in the organization, what one does to gain trust, and what one does to lose trust. What few talk about is the most important thing after gaining trust: *regaining* trust when it has been lost. But when looking at regaining trust, it should first be noted that what one needs to do to gain trust back is *not*:

- repeating the same steps used when trust was established or gained;
- waiting until the current situation is over to attempt to regain trust;
- thinking that all that is needed is an apology that "it" (whatever "it" was) happened;
- waiting for (what probably is) the *negative* situation to go away; and
- waiting for *whomever* (the worker, the partner, who might be involved) to "go away."

### How Does a Manager Earn and Maintain Trust?

Those who research management have identified elements that must be present in the process of earning and maintaining trust.

- The definition of trust is clear.
- Trust is addressed in general as critical to the organization and is typically reaffirmed in a crisis—often redefining it in terms of the emergency environment.
- Expectations regarding trust are understood by all.
- Honest and plain language is used.
- Respect for those with whom you agree and those with whom you disagree is demonstrated.
- Transparent dealings and decisions (as appropriate and as much as possible) are expected and delivered in the organization always but especially in emergency and crisis situations.
- Mistakes or what is "incorrect" (if at all possible) should be—with a clear timetable—acknowledged, addressed, and corrected or—if it can't be corrected—explained, with an outline of how the organization will move on with or without the correction.
- Issues of control: things that can't be controlled and those that can be should be identified and verbalized—as much as possible—with consequences outlined (as needed) for both.
- The mission, vision, and values of the organization, during a pandemic, should be reiterated exhibiting the loyalty of the users and the workers to the organization. If temporary activities do not follow the organization's overall direction and commitment, managers should make it clear why not and when they will be reinstated and reaffirmed.
- Self-reflection should be practiced throughout the organization to assist administrators and managers in assessing the overall climate. During a pandemic, results of self-reflection (for all) guide the direction

of—in general—assisting workers, and specifically in designing and delivering training and continuing education as well as motivational techniques. Within this process, identified expectations and results as well as actions and accountability are an end result through practiced listening.

Losing trust is usually very specific to an incident or action taken; however, loss of trust is usually due to much more than "making a mistake" and can be due to:

- not identifying problems at all or in a timely manner;
- not taking actions needed at all or in a timely manner;
- demonstrated lack of competence (planning, communication, motivation, etc.);
- not admitting the manager roles as part of or the cause of the problem;
- a single act or an ongoing lack of honesty;
- no transparency in manager practices—and ignoring the lack of transparency affecting the organization when the lack of transparency comes from other internal, external, partner, or even user practices; and
- no accountability for actions of managers and the tolerance of no accountability from others in the organization—double standards.

## How Does a Manager Regain Lost Trust?

Managers should never wait to try to regain trust once it has been determined trust is in question, reduced, or worse: gone. And, contrary to many beliefs, specific steps can be taken to regain trust:

- Acknowledge trust is gone or in question.
- Identify the specific issue or problem causing or contributing to the situation (seeking clarification where needed).
- Admit the specific role the manager played in all or part of a problem or mistake.
- Be clear about what can and can't be fixed in the situation that contributed to or caused the lack of trust.
- Define a clear path for regaining trust and—if possible—correcting the mistake or situation that caused the issue.
- Create and discuss the timetable for "fixing" or "repairing."
- Focus on transparency for the reparation (with frequent mentions or announcements of where they are in the process and any other progress made).
- Identify behaviors that might or did cause the situation, and work with those who need to be aware

of and possibly receive training regarding these behaviors.
- If appropriate and possible, put processes in place so that the situation isn't duplicated.

When attempting to regain trust from their colleagues or workers, managers should remember to:

- use honest and plain language;
- demonstrate respect for those with whom they agree and for those with whom they disagree;
- identify and verbalize what—regarding the trust issue—can and can't be controlled, with consequences for each;
- practice listening and seek questions to clarify; and
- practice self-reflection in assessing actions and deeds.

## The Smaller or Solo Library and Management

In smaller libraries, the manager is also the leader and has—in fact—all of the other *primary* roles and responsibilities. It is, therefore, imperative that a manager's position description clearly list all of the librarian's primary roles and responsibilities in the smaller environment. It addition, the description should separate and more narrowly define those areas that may not typically be separated or defined—such as management roles separated from leadership roles or advocacy roles. And—all too often given the amount of work during normal times much less during emergency events—it is important that roles, responsibilities, and outcomes of actions, products, or activities be specifically listed throughout the description to recognize areas that can't be delegated at any time vs. areas that might be delegated during emergency events (for example). It is also important that content (for activities, products, etc.) that should be maintained be clearly identified—for example:

- Smaller and solo library environments should either benchmark, adopt, or identify and maintain a current list of EM materials and products (materials and companies or individuals as expert environments) to be able to source content quickly. (Examples of sources or products that must be pre-prepared and maintained might be EM practices identified, adapted, then adopted from state-agency-identified best practices, library cooperatives, Webjunction resources, and federal agencies.)
- Solo environments need to prioritize EM internal and external roles to determine if and when they need short-term and long-term assistance (from peers, stakeholders, vendors, volunteers, etc.).

- Smaller and solo library environment managers need to invest time in training identified external individuals or experts who can assist in business continuity and emergency communication, marketing, and public relations—critical areas that, given the workload, are likely to be reasonably delegated during emergency situations. This is especially important during long-term situations—like pandemics—where extended information must be distributed so that the library can manage and recover during the event but also so that the library's users can receive the assistance they need to recover.
- Managers need to identify areas, functions, and products of the library that can be accomplished with more of a project-management approach such as volunteer groups (scouts, Junior League, Red Cross groups) for (for example) specialized cleaning of print/paper and media materials, PPE integration into operations, and contact tracing.

### Finally—and, as Managers—if We Had Been Ready

- Managers of larger as well as solo librarian environments have current position descriptions with their primary and secondary management roles identified as well as specific distinctions between and among those job aspects that can be and should be quickly identified such as PR, marketing, communication, safety, and so on.
- Employees have activities identified and articulated in writing for (also) previously identified external experts in HVAC/ventilation, changing spaces to safely distanced spaces, and specifics as to their training needed.
- Support roles are clearly identified in larger organizations, and in smaller or solo environments, peers, stakeholders, and governing or advisory members are identified along with supporting roles and training needed to succeed.
- Managers are aware of their roles and have a strong awareness that they are middle-level managers in the larger organizational structure (the school, the college/university, or the city, county, or hospital/special library) and how they will work as middle managers—within the local and umbrella organizational structure of EM.
- All library workers—and any supporting workers during EM—are aware of and can identify their roles in management processes, including their roles in critical areas (coordinating volunteers, communicating with the delegated PR external stakeholder, etc.) throughout emergency events.

### Changing the Organization

Finally, changing the design of the organization is the lethal combination of change, uncertainty, trust issues, and shifts in decision making at the middle and highest levels. Given that it is very likely and necessary that managers, during shutdown or shutout (pandemic or otherwise) times, do make organizational changes—from the simplest of delegation of some roles and responsibilities to the creation of new structures within the organization and moving roles and responsibilities among the structures—managers need to focus on doing this the right way. Consideration, however, should be given to the level and type of changes as well as who gets what, what their titles are, what roles existing areas play in changes, and how long it will last.

Services given to "others" could be to managers or—if possible, given the overarching organizational structures and possibilities—to others temporarily identified such as a manager, assistant manager, coordinator, director, team leader, or process owner. And although typically organizations have guidelines for identifying either full- or part-time roles that are new or expanded, titles should include those that are not previously assigned or on a compensation or career track already in the organization. Hence the popularity of "team leader," or variations such as "chairs" or "process owners." Aspects of these organizational/structural changes in general must include written roles and responsibilities, a specific timeline or an identification of timing, and assessment processes. Specifically:

- These delegations or assignments based on different roles could be either temporary or permanent and be new or in place of or additions to ongoing, standard, or previously assigned roles:
  - temporary assignments;
  - process owners;
  - ad hoc chairs; or
  - co-leaders, co-chairs (shared roles).
- New management structures should be set in the context of the existing structure as to oversight, governance, etc.:
  - pilot status or first year or structured regarding pandemic timeline;
  - ad hoc department, ad hoc service;
  - matrix management (two managers have the roles of oversight from two existing activities—e.g., the circulation manager and the information literacy coordinator could be the matrix management for a pandemic pilot for circulating technology for use by patrons or students, etc.);

- altered decision making;
- a designated advisory group for the new service;
- an advisory group for all pandemic activities;
- expanded membership of the EM committee; or
- a new support team assigned to the EM team.
- The role is that of outreach such as:
  - A pandemic outreach coordinator—external to the library;
  - a library liaison to the umbrella institution's risk-management office;
  - a member of the county pandemic response team for the library; or
  - a library representative to the institutional technology department.

Even though the service might be temporary, additional aspects critical to the success of the project can include:

- branded initiative;
- unique/targeted marketing;
- different and more marketing techniques (e.g., piggybacked marketing);
- immediate, ongoing assessment; and
- roles of related and unrelated employees identified for clarity.

A common factor in organizations today is that the organization's management and leadership already suffer from the absence of a lack of structure; broad processes for designing services, resources, or products; or decision-making standards and protocols. If that is the case, pandemic or emergency situations rarely provide opportunities for dramatic improvement without guidance, education or training, or—at the very least—a knowledgeable mentor. If this is the situation in an organization, a number of things can occur:

- Management should—immediately before or during pandemic conditions or when shutout/shutdown decisions are reached—quickly design and distribute information on assessing services to determine successes, any fail points or weaknesses, and thus any changes needed.
- With hindsight, the organization's emergency plan should have identified issues that would be immediately considered when an emergency occurred through sanctioned group activities such as a SWOT or SOAR or focus groups using external facilitator, and so on.

With all of this in play, it is good practice to follow the change approach of establishing (such as the sanctioned group activities listed previously) the audit of the choice but articulated in a paradigm shift. This shift—at a glance—provides an overview; a before, during, and after; and terminology and establishes roles and responsibilities. (See table 7.3.)

Different organizations will have different categorizations and might include pre-, during-, and post-pandemic details for areas such as labeling, inventory, usage instructions, cleaning, supporting users, staff training, identifying complaint processes, defining conflict-management processes, assessments, and more specific timelines.

**TABLE 7.3**
**Managing Organizational Change**

Publication Date: _____
Review Date/Revised Date: _____
Process Owner: _____

| Service<br>Laptop Checkout | Pre-Event<br>Laptop Checkout | During Event<br>Tech Checkout and Support | Post-<br>Event |
|---|---|---|---|
| Service keywords | Technology circulation, internal | Tech checkout, support, external | TBD |
| Department | Library services | Partnership—library services; institutional technology | TBD |
| Process owner | Library services | Co-ownership | TBD |
| Service design | Internal, two weeks | External for thirty days, four months at a time | TBD |
| Service information/web content | Library services | IT | TBD |
| Record-keeping/forms | Circulation desk forms, circ module | Pandemic student-use forms (co-designed) | TBD |
| Goals/outcomes | Supplement user needs | Provide tech device and wireless for user needs; for business, school, study, pandemic relief, employment, etc. | TBD |
| Reportage | Library services—monthly, annual | Co-reportage (content used in grant reportage, community updates, marketing) | TBD |
| Assessment | Monthly, annual | Weekly thru pandemic | TBD |

*(continued)*

**TABLE 7.3** *(continued)*

| Service<br>Laptop Checkout | Pre-Event<br>Laptop Checkout | During Event<br>Tech Checkout and Support | Post-<br>Event |
|---|---|---|---|
| Marketing | Branded with library; piggyback on marketing plan events/activities | Branded with pandemic relief logo, piggyback on "community" marketing and PR | TBD |
| Length of service | Fifteen-year service +/ongoing | Pandemic relief program | TBD |
| Support team | Library services with IT | LS and IT jointly | TBD |
| Budget—current issues | Existing units with peripherals | Existing and new units; peripherals | TBD |
| Policies | Library services | Library services, IT, pandemic relief grant funding guidelines | TBD |
| Procedures | Library services | Library services with IT | TBD |
| Service Change-1 | Internal only | Internal and external | TBD |
| Service Change-2 | Checkout timing | Expanded checkout timing | TBD |
| Service Change-3 | Funding | Shared funding | TBD |
| Service Change-4 | Fines and fees assessed | None | TBD |
| Asset documentation | Library services; continued asset reporting for existing tech | Co-asset tracking; counting for pandemic relief tracking for new tech | TBD |
| Funding/grant design | Library services, grants office | Grants office, pandemic response team, library services, IT | TBD |
| Maintenance repair | Library services | IT | TBD |
| Replacement | Library services | IT | TBD |
| Training, workers | Library services | IT | TBD |
| Training, users | Library services | IT | TBD |
| Student learning outcomes | Library services | Library services will track for their service aspect; IT? | TBD |
| Evaluation of organizational structure | N/A | Library services, IT | TBD |

# 8

# Leadership during Extreme Emergencies

## *The Pandemic*

LEADERS INSPIRE and exhibit loyalty to the profession, the organization, and its vision and values and to the library's services and track record of commitment to their constituents. Although in most professions, it is important to distinguish between management and leadership roles and responsibilities, it is especially important during emergency events that these roles are identified, assigned (if they aren't already assigned in the organization), and carried out for the length of and after emergency events including business continuity and recovery. In fact, one can point to any one of a dozen aspects of pandemics that make them unique in the realm of management and leadership, but two of the primary differences include (1) the need for in-depth, extensive leadership to be present and continuous and (2) the need for leaders to have knowledge about the cause of the event itself and—in a more serious case such as COVID-19—know what the pandemic virus is, what it "does," how it progresses, and—most importantly and as much as possible—about how the pandemic virus is and will be affecting workers and users.

So how is leadership in a pandemic defined, and why do pandemics call for more in-depth and unique attention from effective leaders and leadership activities?

The best leadership definition is one that combines a number of critical elements in one statement with elements focusing on meaningful *influence* and *motivation* at the highest levels. Specifically, *leadership is a dynamic relationship based on mutual influence and common purpose between leaders and collaborators in which both are moved to higher levels of motivation and development as they affect real, intended change.*

And why do we need the strongest level of effective leadership with influential and motivating leaders during pandemics? If the library is flooded, or if the library is damaged by fire and/or smoke or is displaced by pestilence, or earthquake—to name more common types of

emergencies—these situations *may* well last a long time and *can* cause the library to shift into a new normal, but seldom do those responsible for leadership have to have in-depth knowledge about water, flooding, seismic activities, fire, or smoke. Nor do leaders have to—for long periods of time, typically—deal with *ongoing* life and death precautions nor with the mental health issues (caused or affected by the event) of workers no matter where they are working during the event.

In pandemics, however, morale issues can be multilayered and very difficult to address. Positive leadership content and advice must come from informed and often in-depth statements. It is critical, therefore, that those in leadership roles learn as much as possible and as quickly as possible about the underlying causes of primary and secondary issues—for example—about the behaviors of what caused the pandemic such as the new disease or virus, virus variants and *their* behaviors, transmission and preventive behaviors for workers and users in public and private workspaces in organizations, effects of viruses on materials found in spaces, effects of viruses on workers and users, requirements for maintaining viral-free facilities, and the choices and consequences of the variety of treatments—to name just a few areas. Part of the problem, however, beyond the breadth and depth of content is the diversity of content (the truth, rapidly changing facts, rumors, and falsehoods), the distribution of information and research (including channels and timing), identifying the credentialed voices to listen to and seek leadership from, organizing the content critical to success, and—even more unusual—the political issues related to the virus and the cause and treatment of the virus. And although all have a strong relationship to leadership content, one of the most difficult areas for this pandemic are those political issues rampant in the news and entertainment media.

So although this pandemic is not the first where library leaders must deal with political issues, COVID-19 presents a long list of issues including blaming one group of people and the related dangerous consequences, musings on and recommendations for different treatments and who should take them, and data conflicts throughout continuity and recovery. So although workplaces are typically not where politics should be or are addressed, this pandemic requires that leaders engage in leadership actions in a careful but honest way while choosing the right language to address topics without having to defend or take a political side.

To specifically identify other and all leadership issues during emergencies, one needs to look at emergencies themselves, and because there are more than thirty different types of emergencies, leadership approaches must tailor themselves to certain aspects as needed. What does this mean?

Because pandemics are so different, there are very few if any training materials on leadership during pandemics, and what is there (crisis management, extreme management) is applicable but in a smaller sense. Examples include the following:

- Location: Weather events or weather-related events in or near the library or umbrella institution or in a part of the environment or surrounding area seldom affect all of the library's users (excluding massive events due to major weather events or infrastructure failing such as Hurricane Katrina), but pandemics affect every location, which—obviously—poses extreme and unusual burdens on workers and users as well as their family members, friends, and relatives and the income of most people.
- Population: Emergencies tend to affect the population in only a few areas (although the definition of a pandemic includes its reach beyond its birth area) or the population served by the areas affected—homes and families, schools and children, businesses and homes during floods, and so on—but pandemics affect every cultural and ethnic group and all economic levels and all ages, typically at different times during the pandemic, and always at almost every age. Library populations or those for whom the library is "responsible" are well known to library administrators and planners based on the library's use of scans to create user profiles in the service areas of the umbrella institution or the business or the community—to determine needs. Pandemics then affect—literally—all of the users and nonusers and, because the breadth and depth of service areas and users is great—all need leadership related to library services and resources.

- Single and/or ongoing event: The effect of emergencies on people or property and timing can be more easily predicted with research and study after the initial onset of the emergency. But even though flooding might later cause mudslides and fires might cause not only smoke but also water damage (for example), typical emergencies do not come in many waves over an extended period of time. In addition, pandemics and their stages have unpredictable timing so the effects of these stages or waves on victims is unclear, so rather than figuring in just one event, a pandemic can be multiple events with very diverse problems associated with each; in essence, pandemics affect everything, everywhere, and everyone at any time and thus include travel between and among locations, so transportation processes, homes, workplaces, and primary and secondary sustenance and support environments. Leading people during these times is complex at best, and the amount of work illustrates the need for leadership activities to be carefully identified and possibly delegated out to several in the organization.

So leadership must be knowledgeable and constant as well as systematic, and it must continuously morph for new stages of the same virus or different stages for variants infecting populations or people, different ages, locations, and timing. And, pandemic leadership must also be more directive (and typically management is more directive as well), as leadership messaging has to—as much as management—not only lead but also motivate people to take the correct 24/7 steps to a safe outcome.

### Must Managers Also Be the Ones to Lead?

No—managers do not have to be the only ones who lead, especially during emergency situations, and especially during an all-consuming pandemic emergency situation. It may not even be possible for the one in charge to be both the primary manager *and* leader. But whether or not they are both, the top manager leading or the top manager partnering with someone else (second in charge, stakeholder of governing environment, health official, frontline representative, etc.) to lead together—their specific actions, their communication, or their role modeling—some say that organizations cannot successfully survive an emergency event without a specific plan to both manage *and* lead. As in management, however, it is not uncommon to need to identify leadership opportunities for workers and delegate to have others assist in leading at different levels. The level of detail needed to identify what needs to be done and how it might be delegated *and* who has both the time and the expertise is best accomplished by the identification of all of the different aspects of management and leadership, including attributes, the debate over what it is and isn't, and the identification of roles, responsibilities, and behaviors as well as matching these with the possibilities.

## Attributes

Management attributes as well as leadership attributes can be identified separately from each other—for the most part—and most leadership attributes for study and learning are embedded in other higher-level training. Typically, and often inappropriately, however, *management* and *leadership* are used synonymously, so it is probable that those needing to identify leadership areas for advanced knowledge or mastery would need to cross to management curriculum to find all areas of competencies and attributes desired. Typical leadership attributes that overlap with management are communication and change, but those especially critical in emergency situations include flexibility, inspiration, innovation, courage, and initiation of change.

## The Debate: What It Is and Isn't

Management and leadership issues also include several debate questions:

- Do the differences cause conflicts between the two primary roles?
- Can someone be taught how to manage?
- Can someone be taught how to lead?
- Can someone be good at management but not leadership and vice versa?
- Can these critical areas be delegated to others? Can they be taught together? and
- Should these important elements—for example, in communiques—be separated out (with a management distribution and a leadership distribution), or must they be integrated into one message? Are both needed during all communication timelines?

Once these and other debate questions have been addressed, then three primary issues of pandemic leadership must be reviewed to see how and what roles managers and leaders play and what actions play the larger roles for handling chaos, dealing with rampant change, and addressing illness and death.

## Handling Chaos

Although no organization wants to admit to being in a chaotic state, the first few weeks or months of a pandemic or public-health emergency guarantee chaos. During this time, while those in charge are trying to learn as much as they can about the disease or virus itself, very little can be decided and very little business-continuity planning can be done.

Those in charge—in the earliest stages—first use their management and communication skills to outline what they need to find out and communicate scenarios for going forward, as it is critical that workers find it easy to see that definitive decisions can be made and that managers are taking steps to organize what the organization needs to do for business continuity. Almost immediately, however, leadership language must begin to assure workers that they can still trust those in charge and that those in charge have their best interests at heart.

## Dealing with Rampant Change

While one would hope that decisions can be made relatively quickly, and while it is possible to "fill in the blanks" for scenarios, managers (using their leadership skillset) quickly find out (and communicate to workers) that rampant change will be the norm and then identify a series of tools and tasks for workers to use, including the formation of an internal response team focusing on the leadership of the library and appropriate leadership language to use and avoid. Managers then employ tools that assist them, such as determining what workers say they need and identifying organizational cultural elements to work on. Motivating—a primary leadership activity—must then be the primary focus to influence workers to use tools to deal with change and provide guidance on how the work will progress to operate based on its values.

## Addressing Well-being, Illness, Death, and Positive Mental Health

Unfortunately, pandemics cause those in charge to be put into the incredibly difficult positions of dealing with both worker and user well-being, illness, death, and existing and future mental health issues brought on or exacerbated by the pandemic. The fact that workplace rules and regulations (HIPAA) make it very difficult to communicate information and concerns surrounding these situations and issues, leadership activities must—working with privacy guidelines—focus on grief, appropriate benefits, and equitable treatment as well as individual and team recovery.

## Overall Leadership Roles, Responsibilities, and Behaviors

While it sounds difficult for one person to act in two capacities, it is necessary in the majority of library organizations that lack middle management or even assistant or associate status positions. With this being said, many of the highest-level administrators focus on leadership while designees focus on management. Those highest-level leadership roles during pandemics specifically include the following:

- integrate, articulate, and motivate those in the organization based on vision, mission, values, strategies, goals, and outcomes;
- influence direction and commitment of workers based on the organizational vision, strategies, and so on;
- influence and motivate external relationships such as governing boards, advisory boards, partners, and stakeholders;
- motivate users, constituents, and—as possible—nonusers;
- embody and exemplify organizational values;
- begin and lead discussions on organizational values, direction, and mission;
- facilitate accomplishments (motivate, support, etc.);
- influence others (marketing, public relations, leading discussions, etc.) regarding the overall vision and directions and the organizational plans; and
- exhibit "personal power" (the specific personality or style that others follow because they trust them and share their organizational and professional values).

A final concern for defining and identifying aspects of management and leadership is the need for leaders to grapple with expanded (and improved) leadership areas such as global societal competencies. These areas, added to leadership attribute lists, include changes in expectations for behavior and performance and—consequently—drive required for continuing education and training at the very least and also drive to review the organization's vision, mission, and values and the breadth and scope of leadership motivation and influence. Those seeking these new aspects for leadership lists will find a variety of categories that are more narrowly derivative of equity, diversity, and inclusion.

### What Styles of Leadership Work in Both Larger and Smaller Organizations?

Given that there are many leadership attributes and that lists of leadership behaviors and roles and responsibilities are so long and getting longer, and that leadership is critical in pandemics, *and* that leadership is constantly changing, one needs to figure out—for leadership education and training—if there is one particular type or style of leadership one should strive toward—and most importantly, a style that would work in all types of organizations as well as all sizes of organizations.

The simple answer is *yes*—and rather than one specific style of leadership such as a collegial style—leaders must learn about four basic styles or approaches to leading and then—given the situation—apply the characteristics of the appropriate style to the organization. In fact, one of the easiest examples comes from an emergency event story; that is—if a leader identifies themselves as a democratic or collegial style of leader, their approach would be to:

- bring their existing advisory team together—possibly adding or subtracting members given the nature of the situation, the expertise needed, any confidential issues, and so on;
- assign attendees pre-meeting activities such as pre-learning about the situation (the cause, the mandates, required timelines, etc.);
- identify (often using a discussion or problem-solving technique or process) parameters, what actions are needed short term, immediate issues, health issues, and so on;
- lead (or having another facilitate) the group brainstorming issues, ideas, research, and so on;
- gather all opinions of what is possible/what should or might happen and prioritize possibilities (again, using a specific technique or process);
- vet prioritized ideas through others; and then
- choose an approach.

This would certainly work in a variety of situations but definitely for leading a building initiative or capital campaign, handling the implementation of plans for dealing with large budget problems, or almost any other major project whether it involves good news or bad news or major changes, but during emergency situations—especially those with large numbers of unknown factors, as in the first days or even months of a pandemic—this is *not* the most effective way of putting a plan in place or even parts of a plan. Instead, the one primarily in charge should:

- choose a team to discuss the situation—not necessarily all managers—possibly adding or subtracting members given the nature of the situation, the expertise needed, any confidential issues, and so on;
- assign attendees pre-meeting activities such as pre-learning about the situation (the cause, the mandates, required timelines, etc.);

- identify (often using a discussion or problem-solving technique or process) parameters, what actions are need short term, immediate issues, health issues, and outcomes needed, as well as how this is *not* managing the situation but rather leading people as it begins, through it as necessary, and so on;
- lead the group in presenting facts, research, what we can and can't do;
- identify opinions on what we can, can't, and should do; and
- prioritize a list of possible directions.

A leader, then, choosing an approach alone or with a small group of advisors or a trusted associate, identifies the issues and chooses the best approach to putting things in place. Typically, this involves choosing to use characteristics of the four basic styles of leadership not only in the beginning but also through the event. Leaders benefit from—especially with a new team or in a new environment—mapping out how these elements will be used based on what characteristic is used.

Those in charge who practice situational leadership exhibit different elements of the four basic leadership styles at different times and in different situations. Typically, only *one* of the styles is defined for an overall leadership style, but given whatever situation is at hand, bringing as many strong and positive characteristics and elements from each of the styles when leading others is how this approach is successful, as all of the four styles—some more than others—have good and bad elements. (See table 8.1.)

### TABLE 8.1
### A Recommended Approach to Leadership (for Any Size or Type of Organization)

| Elements/Activities Illustrating Styles and Techniques | Context/Examples of What Works during Pandemics |
|---|---|
| **Dictatorial/Autocratic/Authoritarian/Tell** | **Dictatorial/Autocratic/Authoritarian/Tell** |
| • There is a strong ongoing focus on task accomplishment and those in charge are demanding of workers and worker products.<br>• Directions and communication focus on individuals and not teams.<br>• Those in charge—rather than persuading or motivating—distribute directives that require specific worker compliance and behaviors.<br>• If mistakes are made and products are late or incomplete—for example—identifying what is wrong includes those in charge identifying who is at fault, placing blame with more directives for behavior changes.<br>• Feedback is not sought nor desired and sometimes not allowed to be shared throughout the organization.<br>• Workers aren't "developed" when found making mistakes and corrected. | • During pandemics, leaders need to be firm in confirming the values of the organization in order to place task accomplishment in context.<br>• Leaders need to clarify that although team structures are important, there is more individualization during risky times so teams are critical but individual roles and responsibilities will be clarified.<br>• While management language outlines directives that require compliance, leadership language places compliance in perspective based on values, mission, etc. All mandates can benefit from including this leadership language.<br>• In addition to leadership language illustrating perspective and context, language should assist in illustrating which values are driving some decisions (the mandate approach) out of the organization's control that negates feedback at implementation and how new tasks and changing practices—when incorrect—will be immediately corrected, for ensuring workers and users are safe during business continuity and then recovery. In fact, leaders often find it difficult to couch "zero-tolerance policies" with their less dictatorial traits.<br>• While effective leaders are seldom also seen as autocratic (much less referred to as dictatorial), this is due to pandemics having far more mandates, rules, and regulations governing services, delivery, and access. Leaders must encourage and motivate with careful language—as always—but within the parameters of the situation. |
| **Team/Democratic/Collegial/Sell** | **Team/Democratic/Collegial/Sell** |
| • This type of leader leads by positive example.<br>• The leader fosters a team environment where all workers are developed as well as encouraged and given opportunities to reach their highest potential, both as individuals and team members.<br>• Individuals and/or teams are encouraged to reach goals as effectively as possible.<br>• Leaders motivate groups and individuals and strive to strengthen team members and individuals. | • Leaders, during emergency events, especially during public health issues, are often seemingly absent so it is significantly harder to "lead by positive example." Leaders can overcome this by using more examples of others and narrative in general leadership content. In addition, leaders typically telling people what they *are* doing is helpful to provide different layers of context.<br>• While teams are the focus of this style and teams are harder to work with when risk is associated, leaders can emphasize the overall team, identify specific parts of the whole by verbalizing what individuals are doing, and also consider relaxing and identifying a hiatus on goals and timelines so that people feel understood and that they are pulling together although it isn't a visual in reality. |

*(continued)*

**TABLE 8.1    (continued)**

| Elements/Activities Illustrating Styles and Techniques | Context/Examples of What Works during Pandemics |
|---|---|
| **Country Club/Consult** | **Country Club/Consult** |
| • Leaders will work with groups to discuss products needed, then delegate and leave groups to accomplish tasks and complete products. <br> • Leaders encourage the team to accomplish its goals. <br> • It may be difficult to determine who—if anyone—is in charge or will be held accountable. <br> • Individuals and teams do not typically observe leaders weighing in to identify and correct mistakes, and if mistakes surface, the leader does not exhibit many if any punitive powers. <br> • Leaders decline to be punitive for fear of jeopardizing relationships with individuals and team members. | • Leaders work with individuals and groups to identify products needed with far more "you must" and little discussion. Although groups do not then create their own goals, it increases success if leaders identify the areas where workers *do* have choices and flexibility as well as any relaxing of organizational guidelines that can make it easier on workers (e.g., reportage, dress codes, identification of who is in charge, breaks, and schedule length). <br> • One area that many leaders and workers like about libraries is the perception of a more easygoing and nonpunitive environment. While Country Club leadership supports this, during emergency events, leaders need to be clear on where this is and isn't in play during the event. This should typically be outlined in writing, along with "can't control" issues relating to identifying mistakes and punitive measures not for making a mistake but for not following directions, choosing not to do something, etc. |
| **Laissez-Faire/Join In** | **Laissez-Faire/Join In** |
| • Leaders do not work with groups but "delegate and disappear." <br> • Work is accomplished however an individual or group sees fit. <br> • Devoid of typical team processes or work guidelines, leaders detach themselves from individuals and teams. <br> • Unable to determine who might be in charge of products, teams, etc., teams may waste time as they suffer through power struggles. | • An organization that provides services cannot be sustained in the long run—and often not for the length of the event—if there is little organization or leadership or just those in charge who join in, delegate, and then disappear. In fact, the lack of choices for what and how work is done in emergency events is difficult for both leaders and workers, and leaders must strive to keep themselves and their workers engaged. <br> • Leaning in to leadership is often the most difficult role for Laisse-Faire/Join In or "laid-back" leadership, as it is time-consuming if leaders do things the "right way" and actually lead. The most difficult aspects of this leadership come when organizations have a hierarchy of workers, as—during riskier times, for example—frontline staff (both classified and professional) are treated differently and must pivot to controlled work. Leaders should take care in not only implementing required changes but also identifying for workers who is doing what. Most difficult for leaders who have prided themselves on no hierarchy, practices that lack equity are hard to upend when organizations attempt to recover. |

Taking specific characteristics or elements from different approaches to craft successful leadership approaches is identified as situational leadership. This approach is especially helpful during times of chaos and emergency situations; however, the success of this often depends on what leaders have already done to gain the trust of library workers. In fact, the more successful the leader is, the more trust they have already built in their organization. That is, workers are less likely to be shocked that the leader is firm and moves ahead without consulting them if the leader has explained to workers in the past that this may have to be an approach when time is of the essence or the seriousness of the situation is paramount.

Choosing the right leadership style for pandemic emergency situations includes being familiar with the four classic styles, assessing situations as they come up, and then choosing specific elements of one or more of the classic styles for leading to use as a guide for moving forward. Expert leaders listen and observe the situation and weave those elements into their handling:

• The seriousness and restrictions of the situation may drive them to be firmer and definitive in their approach. "Remember our values? This is how we will proceed based on our mission and commitment to our community."

• The organization's low morale may cause a leader to release control and let the workers create a path. "Times are hard, and all of you have worked tirelessly to deliver the tech support our users need to be successful during the pandemic! Your next project is up to you! Pick something important to you, and work together to make it better for either your co-workers or your users."

So, if trust is at the heart of successful leadership, when does instilling trust occur, and how does that happen for leaders?

While the discussion of successful *management* also includes the importance of trust and the role it plays, it's important to be specific about how leaders lay a solid foundation of trust. Overview issues to revisit about trust include the realities that titles and longevity don't translate to automatic trust and that building trust takes time, is deliberate, and must be focused across the organization for individuals and workers in teams.

People "trust" others and situations in different ways; that is, if each worker is asked to finish the sentence "I trust my leadership because ... " many different and conflicting answers would be given. So although managers have specific lists for keeping the trust of their workers, what do *leaders* do specifically to build trust?

Trust is said to be present in organizations when leaders speak plainly and honestly about the workplace, the work product, general activities, and specifically about issues as they arise. Honesty—a foundation of trust—begins with honesty about the situation at hand but even before that with honesty about themselves and their actions. Specifically in emergency events, leaders are honest when:

- they admit the situation at hand is a serious one;
- they are clear about how they would like to handle it, but may not be able to, given the facts of the situation;
- they say they do not know something;
- they admit they made a mistake or misstep and then identify steps to correcting things; and especially
- they admit they cannot lead or communicate as they usually do, but instead, they must lead differently, and here is what workers must expect.

This is especially important in pandemics, when there is much—at the beginning and throughout—that is not and may not be known. Other trust activities designed to build trust include:

- asking for feedback in general or even more than usual as well as allowing disagreement and negative feedback (during emergency events, the most successful feedback is systematic and targeted feedback);
- admitting mistakes and identifying when correcting mistakes is possible, as well as the timeline and activities for correcting; and
- supporting assessment and self-reflection in general but especially during unusual and difficult times.

And although leaders have to be careful in making promises, they can say, "While I can't promise you that this will be over in a certain amount of time, I can assure you we are in this together for the long haul, and no matter how long it takes to emerge, we will be proud of how we maintained those critical services we provide." Leaders should also:

- recognize success of work products and—within that work—of both individuals and teams; and
- assess for failures and—when found—recognize a failure for which they are responsible.

If leaders feel that any recognition of their own failure may *not* work out for the best for them, they can easily identify areas—for example—where they feel like they should have done things differently. This goes a long way to instilling trust and stating that it's okay to fail in all or part of a situation.

It should not go unnoticed by many that the practices outlined are predicated on the leaders being a "known" quantity by either experience or reputation, which appears to negate a new permanent or even temporary leader being successful at any time, much less during emergency events. This is not true, and there are a number of ways—even in the most serious of situations—that leaders (new leaders or those known for something other than leadership) can succeed. These ways include a review of the three most important elements of leadership: communication, assessment (if they are new or the event is completely new), and timing.

## Communication

Communication (a necessary competency to master)—in knowledge, skills/abilities, and attitudes—is at the heart of good leadership. This is especially important in emergency events, as workers and the wide variety of other people such as users, partners, stakeholders, and vendors—to name just a few—are in disparate locations. And this is a welcome relief for leaders or those who aspire to be leaders, even though they may dread or simply not be skilled at in-person interactions that more than likely include presentations, speeches, and so on. Contemporary elements of effective leadership with communication include these ten elements that can be in place for leaders new to the organization, new to leadership within the organization, or new to the field:

1. Remote communication leadership techniques
2. Honesty (know/don't know, can/can't, control/no control)
3. Audience identification (internal, external [primary], etc.)
4. Timing and terminology for direct distribution of leadership content

5. Terminology for interpreting information from others such as umbrella organizations
6. Marketing/public relations/branding or the "communication" of the organization
7. Technical writing/instructional design of communication
8. Information/data visuals (paradigm shifts, infographics)
9. Specificity of audience information for processes and products
10. Specific terminology to convey context with scripts

### Assessment

Although many in the profession today are not familiar with events even remotely similar to the pandemic, leaders must work with managers to establish the variety of types of assessment critical to the leadership of the initiative. Because assessment is often closely entwined with management and they (obviously) are "performed" by the same person or people, the list below offers management and leadership elements as well as just leadership elements.

### Management and Leadership

- remote assessment—techniques, modes, methods
- creating bridges for information for comparing or contrasting ("apples to oranges")
- matching data to audience—processes, products
- redefining existing and defining new measures of user success and your role in that success
- visual representations of data

### Leadership

- choosing focus (pick one or more) from benefit, value, worth, impact (address "intangible" and people/expertise first)
- terminology for data interpretation
- marketing/public relations/branding (new or the "moment")

### Time

Many leaders do not take "time" or timing into account as much as they should. And the reality is that a leader can have the perfect presentation with perfect terminology, but if their delivery is too late or too early, it doesn't hit the necessary mark and could skew or even negate the message. This is an especially difficult mastery during an emergency event, where timing issues are fast moving and correct timing can be the avenue to success. And timing isn't just providing the right information at the right time but can be part of research, participating in the larger umbrella organization or community process, as well as identifying and consistently using the right visuals, language, and process for identifying issues, showing progress (or not), and striving to weigh in regularly even though there is little or any progress or if there is only difficult or bad news. Leadership timing issues include primarily leadership, but also, as with communication, leadership and management actions, activities, and characteristics can go hand-in-hand:

### Leadership

- even with no dates, creating big "picture" to guide
- immediacy/being ahead of the game
- honesty and timing (know/don't know and when)
- standardized content (terminology, definitions, subject headings, forms, documentation)
- frequency (systematic with good and bad news, closure/no closure, etc.)

### Management and Leadership

- consistency (selected terminology used throughout)
- expectations—workers' and products' outcomes identified
- expectations—users identified (primary, secondary, etc.)
- clarity (terminology, rationale, etc.)
- access (tracking, grouping/categorization, etc.)

### If We Had Been Ready

Even if organizations had new leadership or reassigned others in the organization to be leaders, a number of factors should be in place at any given time regarding leadership success:

- Leadership roles and responsibilities are clearly defined in general and are defined for ad hoc or temporary opportunities within emergency and disaster plans to assist in—for example—general motivation of internal workers, general motivation of identified external groups (peers, users, Friends, volunteers, stack maintenance workers, etc.), and assessing more unusual but also needed areas such as tracking organizational culture during emergency events.
- Ad hoc/temporary leadership roles and opportunities are identified and matched to professional-development content and program goals (e.g.,

"Upon completion of the one-day seminar, attendees successfully completing the day-long content and the post-activity work will have the skills necessary to lead the communication effort for the volunteer team during emergency events").

- Emergency orientation and training identify processes required to take advantage of leadership roles as well as providing guidelines to accept leadership roles. Pathways—in general and during emergency times—are clearly defined and articulated for workers to gain leadership competencies and take opportunities for leadership experiences.
- Measures of performance success for short-term and long-term leadership are defined for emergency situations, including timelines and methods of evaluation.
- The organization's mentor program includes emergency-management mentors equipped with the attributes and skillset necessary to prepare employees for ad hoc leadership activities and support.
- Smaller libraries also have opportunities for leadership assistance by identifying individuals in the organization (peer workers, stakeholders, advisory and governing board members, etc.) to partner to lead or co-lead specific elements of emergency activities. And, although this takes time to create beforehand, it is time well spent to match and train previously identified individuals to step in on temporary or ad hoc bases.
- Plans are in place for leaders and leader activities for limited areas such as project-oriented work with volunteers, designated groups of stakeholders, and fund- and Friend-raising for pandemic expenditures not specifically related to recovery but to morale, culture, team building (Friends, foundation members, ongoing projects such as annual inventory, new student orientations, recreational activities to reward volunteers during emergency events, and ongoing book sales).
- Ad hoc or temporary leaders or co-leaders lead groups such as advisory (but not governing) board meetings, attend press conferences, are members of emergency-management county/area workgroups, and liaison with external vendors and commercial workers.

### And in Smaller and Solo Library Environments

Leadership in smaller environments is identified as one of the primary roles and responsibilities of the person identified as the manager. Due to the expertise needed by the leader during an emergency such as a pandemic, position descriptions for leadership roles must be specifically identified and include areas such as but not limited to the morale, motivation, and retention of a positive organizational culture for workers—regular staff (no matter how few); temporary, volunteer, and project-management workers; boards (advisory and governing); stakeholders such as foundation or Friends; partners; vendors; community contacts; decision makers; and media/press contacts.

In addition, communication areas (overlapping with management) are critical for any size of environment but also critical in smaller and solo environments and especially important during emergencies such as public-health crises especially due to the (more than likely) smaller physical environment. And, although appropriate communication critical to effective, successful leadership is time-consuming, best practices offer many templates and examples of content and documents that should be part of emergency preassembled practices.

This content should take the form—as much as possible—of Swiss cheese documents with the skeleton of content created and easy integration of fill-in-the-blank current and frequently changing information. These templates include both management and leadership information, but—given limited time available to, for example, solo librarians—they are outwardly focused with an emphasis on leadership content. This uniquely curated information (much of it online) can take the form of products in a variety of formats designed and maintained to be completed and used throughout the event. They also combine management content, but during pandemics, small/solo environments divide up management as keeping services going, planned hours of services available, and so on, while leadership becomes external communication for both user outreach and stakeholder and governing and umbrella organization accountability. Within leadership content, there are significant areas and avenues where the smallest organization—if structured and prepared in advance—has effective leadership when delivered through and often enhanced by:

- blog content (more personalized information);
- media content for streams and channels (allows for emotion to be part of the discussion and can use packaged content to piggyback on media);
- postings for social media accounts (library avenues, often delegated but particularly effective in reaching all ages and types of users);
- information in the form of humor, self-help, and do-it-yourself (for workers, volunteers, users);
- dashboards with data (general and library specific);
- infographics (visual representations of services, materials, facilities, and projects and can be general or library specific);

- YouTube media (allows for emotion to be part of the discussion, can be personalized, can be prepackaged or piggyback on others);
- interviews (delivered through a variety of media) with workers, users, management, identified spokespeople as stakeholders (services, materials, facilities, projects, allows for personalization to be part of the discussion);
- signage—for individuals, groups, activities (generic, Swiss-cheese, targeted); and
- PowerPoint presentations, programs (prepackaged, able to be personalized for targeted groups such as umbrella decision makers, stakeholder groups, Kiwanis, Rotarians, etc.).

As much as possible, solo libraries or libraries in smaller communities, smaller institutions, or smaller service areas embedded in larger environments can succeed by taking time before emergencies to explore, identify, and personalize best practices, form relationships, establish partnerships, review documents for content, and even participate in or lead "drills" with other emergency response areas. Proactive behaviors not only add to the expertise, attributes, and competencies but also contribute to workers being viewed as professionals operating in well-managed environments who are prepared not only for their everyday best but also for the worst. In addition, the more prepared managers and leaders are, the greater the opportunity for the library to have more autonomy in choosing how to move forward.

# 9

# Pitfalls, Problems, Mistakes, and Failures

ORGANIZATIONS, whether they are partially or completely open (given whatever *open* might mean), must deal with pitfalls, problems, mistakes, and failures—even though there may be no "recovery" moment for the smallest to the biggest issues. To be specific, managers and leaders cannot wait for emergency issues (especially during pandemic events) to be "over" before issues are dealt with—in any area. At the very least, issues need to be recognized and initially addressed, and at the most, they need to be solved and, if possible, corrected.

Obviously, the overall addressing of issues is an important part of the management process at all times, but given the uniqueness of pandemic and post-pandemic situations, fail points, weaknesses, and gaps need to be immediately addressed or—for more important or serious cases—*spotlighted*. This initial response must be taken because organizations need to immediately assess and—if appropriate—alter or revise policies, practices, and procedures as well as the behaviors of workers and possibly users as well. And—besides "solving" the situation itself—all managers and leaders recognize that trust in the organization, its managers, and its leaders must be preserved in pandemic or very serious situations, and one very real aspect of trust is admitting and then addressing issues to maintain trust. No matter the size of the issue, even the smallest one can erode what is critical to recovery: trust in management and leadership.

To recognize pitfalls, handle problems, correct mistakes, and deal with failures, what must the focus be, and what steps must be taken?

- *Speed of recognition*: In identifying specific and related underlying aspects of situations in an attempt to make sure—if possible—things are addressed *during* pandemics and given that weekly reviews may not be enough, the key is a quick recognition

that the situation has been pointed out and that the issue then moves to the next step in the process. Whether it is clear whose fault it is, speed in addressing "other people's" situations is critical as well, because it is likely that the issue may end up including the organization because they did not recognize and start the process. Managers want to try to make sure the issue does not prove to be detrimental to all those aware of the situation.

- *The process of investigation and assessment*: It is not unusual—during more unique and serious times—that simple or lower-level problems build in intensity and—if not addressed with a thorough assessment—foster more serious negative situations than usual.

- *Responsibility*: Roles and responsibilities for the situation or elements surrounding an issue are important to identify, as it is not uncommon for problems, mistakes, and failures of *other* people (departments, institutions, partners, users, etc.) to quickly surface and be exacerbated by the situation at hand. Identifying who has primary responsibility regarding the issue—even if it is not clear yet what level of impact there may be—is critical to avoid negative impact on the library and workers as well as library users.

So how *are* these—sometimes sticky—situations handled? Organizations should decide if the standard problem-solving processes are in place during an emergency situation. Having this initial discussion will provide workers with a reminder of how problems are handled or issues are addressed typically and point out the unique aspects that may dictate an altered approach. Given the other factors in play, if organizations aren't fast enough, thorough enough, or investigative—or if the organization isn't *typically* self-aware and few (if any) people take responsibility for decisions made or steps taken—then the approach must change. Instead, making it through emergency situations quickly requires the following:

- Fast, systematic, and consistent management of the issues must take place (e.g., communication should be distributed as quickly as possible, a process owner should be identified, and a quick overview of the process should be shared—again—if the process has not been discussed frequently or recently or not at all).
- Initially without laying blame, those affected should be informed the organization is aware and working on the issues, and so on (e.g., an initial announcement should address the situation and invite those knowledgeable to assist as needed, and the timeline for completing the process and—if possible—reaching closure should be communicated).
- Evidence should be gathered across the spectrum of the issue (e.g., individuals are interviewed across the process or areas related to the process, those typically for as well as against issues should be involved, and anonymous involvement should be made available).
- Care and concern for those affected (more than usual) should be taken to keep them informed of process steps (e.g., a manager's approach should be to address the topic in frequent communications, provide notification of process progress, and offer a variety of discussion and feedback options with those involved in the situation).

Keeping in mind that managers and leaders have to accept the fact that problems may exist and—even more difficult—that they may exist due to weaknesses or issues existent prior to the pandemic, overarching managers and leaders should be involved from the beginning or from the initial level of awareness. If some or many within the organization recognize their higher-level management or leadership may have problems accepting these types of situations—or if others recognize that less-than-desirous decisions had been made in the past—then the organization should take great care to identify the process owner, even considering someone outside the standard chain of command or the department. Therefore, the process owner and others should consider the following:

- Trust—in and of itself—should be addressed, and the organization's managers and leaders should have direct conversations with workers about trust and the need to trust the process being used. These discussions can often imply—rather than specifically stating—that although there may already be trust factors or there may be organizational issues that stand in the way of some or any success, work-

ers need to become aware of the process so that trust can be instilled in the process. Consider appointing a team (two coleaders) in areas where problems have been identified to provide an initial system of checks and balances.
- Provide a documentation process for areas that are unique to the emergency situation with the thought being that beyond the pandemic, the problems must be addressed.
- During emergency events or pandemics, consider having an ad hoc single process owner for all problems brought forward as a signal to staff that there *is* an approach. This process owner—chosen with broad input and, if possible, unique training—should be seen as being more in line with solving conflicts for the duration of the unique situation. Also, the organization must identify what this single process owner can and can't do and what their advisory or governing limits are.

It is important not only to determine specific problems as well as how to solve them or recover from them, but also to determine—first—why problems might happen and what categories of problems there are. This is especially important when it is determined that one (and often more than one) problem is repeatedly occurring. Clearly, if there *is* a pattern, the organization is likely to see more of the same or escalated problems. Determining these patterns is the step to not only handling one situation but also stopping or reducing other or future problems. Patterns to look for include the following. (*Note:* For purposes of this discussion, all issues, problems, mistakes, and so on, are being identified as problems even though something might not technically be problematic for the organization.)

### Plans (Absence of Plans, Older/Old Plans, a Mix of Plans, No Emergency Planning)

Organizations quickly find—going into an emergency situation as serious as a pandemic—that the absence of an operations, short-term, long-term, or disaster plan—or any other type of plan or guide—immediately and constantly brings problems to light. And while "in the beginning or even the middle of a pandemic" is not the time to begin to craft a plan, nor is it really the time to update old plans or coordinate existing plans. In fact, in the absence of current plans, it is better *not* to update existing plans or continue putting an older plan together; rather, team or individual process owners and/or managers and leaders should identify the things that need to get done or areas that must be addressed and also identify what will stop during this time. Using that approach in different areas, functions, departments, and so on, ensures that everyone is automatically talking about the same thing, and with a project-management approach—with one leader or a team of leaders of the process, the organization can more easily coordinate what will and should happen both from a management/leadership point of view.

For organizations having no plans, having no up-to-date plans, or being in the middle of planning, other recommendations have included picking a benchmark plan from someone else and personalizing or adapting that plan to keep the organization going forward while dealing with problems. Using that approach, however, is typically not successful, as plans may be similar but not similar enough and certainly *not* exact to what an organization needs or can work with. The reality is that not just any plan will do.

The only benchmark or best-practice plans that would work "automatically" or quickly are general emergency plans (examples are available from the profession, the association, or from local, state, or federal agencies, such as FEMA). These expert plans are designed for flexibility and scaling to size and for providing the context and framework so that the organization can follow the process and fill in their path.

In addition, during and after COVID-19, there are and will continue to be extensive documents, examples, and so on; therefore, managers should look to national associations and state agencies for content. Using these two areas—along with their own community's content (local FEMA from county government, city public health, higher education statewide governing and advisory boards, and K–12 state agency initiatives)—organizations will find a good foundation for framing questions, providing guidance, and documenting their own decisions for the future.

## Knowledge/Training (Lack of Knowledge and Training, the Wrong Knowledge and Training)

Although it is fair to say that the majority of library professionals do *not* learn how to handle an emergency or even the basics of emergency management (EM)—through either formal management programs or continuing education—the reality is that most current or new professionals have no knowledge either. With that in mind—in the short term—the organization should identify specific individuals and have them trained together to be the process owners. They can also seek a mentor organization among similar environments, and they should request a "seat" on the local EM council or board (typically FEMA, county, city, and K–12 and higher education representatives) and use content recommended for that local group—again—for the best context and consistency.

In the long term, managers should invest in training for one or two/team staff members (not the top-level administrator or manager) to take the reins. This person—identified as soon as possible—should assist in assessing the most recent examples of where this training and their service can assist the team.

*Example:* Actions taken during the pandemic—no matter the stage—should be identified and vetted to see how additional leadership training (for those not in leadership positions) might have assisted in decision making, transitions, and recovery. In addition, the person identified to become the organizational expert can assist with identifying, creating, and delivering training to workers.

## Management or Leadership Void

Not having someone who excels at or is even comfortable with leadership in general or in pandemic times can almost be identified as one of the more serious—if not the most serious—pandemic "situations." Not only will there be new problems, but there will also be reoccurring problems caused by the pandemic and problems stemming from pre-pandemic issues. If a lack of competent leadership exists, or if a leader fails to recognize and deal with incompetence around them, then those in charge of functional areas or more "middle" management or "leadership" should choose scenarios for what is acceptable to them for leadership in general but, more specifically, decision making regarding problems and then provide those to top-level management to give them choices.

This menu-driven-scenario approach is typically welcomed but must be consistent and clearly communicated. This also means that middle-level managers must work quickly to see what *is* possible and communicate that "out" and up. If this ends up the primary way the organization handles these situations, middle-level managers and those in leadership roles must document directions and scenarios, and they must be prepared to lead and communicate clearly what the appropriate choices are with additional pros and cons as needed.

## HR Content (Absence of HR Content, Older/Old HR Information/Content, No Emergency Content, HR Content Not a Match)

One of the weakest areas in emergency situations is human resources (HR). Many organizations must use the umbrella organization's content even though it may not address most of those unique needs. Because of the great diversity in laws, legislation, and guidelines, as well as the shortcomings of both state and federal content (too general and broad), no one source can offer it all. Following that initial realization, state agencies and public health departments will try to meet needs and update and distribute HR information needed, but obviously many libraries are within umbrella-management situations, and—of course—these umbrella structures fail to provide what the library specifically needs.

### How *Will* the Organization Solve Problems and Address Issues and Mistakes?

There are many problem-solving models that offer a series of steps. Obviously, in EM situations, the timelines are not easily adhered to—given the nature of emergencies and also given a number of other inescapable issues (e.g., gathering facts, forming consequences, etc.). It is important, therefore, to look at every step to see what might *not* happen as well as what might happen.

### Identify and Define the Problem (Who, What, When, Where, Why)

In a more serious and complicated EM situation, and especially when so few librarians or other workers are experienced or knowledgeable and (for example) don't know the terminology, there are typically fewer opportunities to clearly identify and define the problem. Knowing the right questions as well as the approach to finding good answers is the beginning of the process, and forms or templates should be used to provide guidance and consistency.

### Gather and Assess Information and Data (Facts, Rumors, Events, Actions)

The uncertainty of pandemics and the lack of information on recovery for post-pandemic decision making make it hard for managers to sort out all of the information and data and to settle on facts and dispel rumors. As for other areas where these detailed steps are an anathema, forms and templates should serve to provide consistency. In addition, the more the organization is in need of new information, the more important it is to have a process owner (or a team of process owners) to manage these processes.

### Develop a Profile of Those Involved (Primarily Involved, Secondarily Involved)

It is typical, possible, and understandable that more than one person might be involved in making mistakes and causing or being involved in problems during the serious emergency situations—for example, the pandemic and post-pandemic. The process of gathering data, information, and facts includes identifying not only all involved

but also their level of involvement and whether or not they were involved in a primary or secondary way and in what stage of the event. (Profile information should include discussing all aspects of the events with those profiled in a documented informational discussion rather than an accusatory discussion.) Conducting the best interviews in this step of the process might better include individuals trained to conduct discussions and—if possible—those not involved in or familiar with the individuals or issues.

### Create a Set of "Can" and "Can't" Statements (Do and Don't, Is and Isn't)

Although identifying what people can't do (when identifying what they can do) is typically optional for decision-making steps, it is necessary during serious emergency situations. Problem-solving processes during extreme times should be rapid and include the broadest possible identification and discussion of possibilities to determine the consequences of choices, and because emergency situations are often controlled by legal, legislated, and—in general—more controls for safety, and so on, this is now a critical step in the decision-making process.

### Establish Consequences for Possible Solutions (Solutions, Recommendations, Strategies, Directions to Take)

Establishing consequences for each possible choice includes not only vetting these choices at the beginning of the process and identifying can and can't choices but also outlining consequences of both. This broad look takes time, but it avoids unnecessary delays and increases the likelihood that the correct or the most correct decision is made early in the process.

### Choose and Implement One Direction (Choice, Solution, Approach)

After the direction or correction is chosen as the solution, the designated process owners/decision makers map out the approach, typically working through the data gathered to decide if any individual already involved needs more focus as well as how specifically they might rectify the facts, rumors, and—most certainly—the outcome.

### Evaluate Actions (One-Month Return, Six-Month Return, Continued Failure throughout the Process, Timeline Dictated by the Emergency Situation Itself)

Although the problem being managed may well appear to be solved and does not reoccur, no matter the timing, the path and choice(s) need to be evaluated to assist in the determination of patterns of similar or related problems, those involved, and the likelihood of consequences originally identified as well as—post-situation—increased training needed. This evaluation should be integrated into the beginning of the process with one step being the early definition of expected outcomes and what success "looks like."

## How Does the Organization Manage Problems and Situations and Track for Patterns?

There are many ways to track problems and mistakes, and it is especially important to record the problems, issues, and mistakes to provide documentation for the organization's decisions as well as decisions made by others that affect the organization. EM documentation, however, has somewhat different (in-depth or substantive) issues than documenting problems or mistakes during nonemergency times. These differences are critical to the EM process and include:

- tracking timelines chosen, adhered to or not;
- referencing new forms or forms used back to previously used or new HR content;
- creating glossaries of terms unique to EM to provide context;
- choosing terms from the organization's glossaries for each path and discussion taken;
- using standardized forms throughout the process;
- following the process for those mistakes identified for all involved (i.e., for all levels and types of problems and by all involved in the process);
- studying patterns to determine baseline data; and
- matching patterns to training to identify training successes, failures, and future requirements.

Tables 9.1 and 9.2 contain examples of completed problem-/issue-documentation forms.

Obviously, to reduce problems throughout the process, a checklist for preventive measures should be established to provide consistent attention to what is critical. Although most emergencies have the same or similar checklists, the pandemic generates unusual situations and—therefore—a different, unique checklist.

The prevention checklist is designed to identify those things that reduce or eliminate problems to attempt to bypass them, reduce them, and keep them from causing additional problems moving to and during post-pandemic return to services.

The categories in the chart are common causes of problems during and after pandemics, but it is not an exhaustive list. For example, additional categories could be localized and include:

- unique physical facility issue;
- unique staffing issue (number of workers, availability, access, etc.);
- lack of/reduced resources (less space available, fewer computers available, length of use of space less than desired by users, suspension of certain services, times of user research assistance, etc.);
- management choices such as hours open and so on;
- critical community needs identified;
- local institutional or governmental accountability;
- service agreements; and
- funding levels.

Table 9.3 contains an additional completed problem-/issue-prevention checklist/form.

Problems that occur repeatedly often need to be documented for workers in a quick overview. A paradigm shift from "it was" to "it is now" provides workers with a quick reference and status of corrections/changes.

It is especially important to quickly and carefully document and distribute management processes related to trust in workers through all stages of the pandemic. In addition, this content offers a snapshot of a future or post-pandemic reality, reduces uncertainty and fear, and reduces repetitive questions on length of time for changes for both worker and user questions.

Table 9.4 depicts a paradigm shift for pandemic and post-pandemic problems/issues and changes.

### Smaller Solo Environments

Making mistakes—no matter how big or how small the organization—calls for fast action, care, and concern for all involved and documentation to ensure the resolution is tracked and the mistake isn't repeated. With that in mind, however, solo or small environments call for a variety of issues to be determined. These issues include the following:

- How does the manager determine the root cause and fix something that needs to be fixed without endangering relationships of users, other temporary employees, or workers, board members, or peers who may be assisting during a pandemic or a more serious situation?
- Once sources are determined, how is a solution communicated or put into effect without offending or causing concerns of other possible workers or users?

**TABLE 9.1**
**Pandemic—Those Affected: Issues/Problems/Mistakes/Complaints (In-Person, Hybrid, or Remote Work)**

Date: _11/26_
Review Date/Revised Date: _11/30–12/5_
Process Owner: _JBT_

**How affected:** *Worker technology (identified as needed for the worker or user technology paradigm) was not being upgraded in a timely fashion or at all. Remote connections were consistently failing and workers had to bring equipment in for assessment. While scheduling these sessions, the administration distributed information prohibiting return to campus until xx/xx/xxxx.*

**Affected\*** Circle all relevant:   User   Workers   Volunteers   Subcontractors/Vendors
Stakeholders   Other

*\* Completing this form will provide a process for investigators and decision makers to take the widest possible look at those affected by the problem and thus identify in-depth information about the issue as well as distribution lists for communiques for announcing/communicating decisions.*

| Date Occurred; Reported | Issues/Problems/Mistakes/Complaints | Process Owner/ Contact |
|---|---|---|
| 11/25–11/26<br><br>**Done/**<br>**Initials**<br>*JBT; 12/1* | *Issues/Problems*<br>• Maintaining worker technology is of critical importance throughout the pandemic and into the post-pandemic.<br>• Problems must be reported and rapidly solved to remove all impediments to workers in any work and especially those supporting remote services.<br>• The process of technology upgrades is outsourced and typically well organized.<br>• Worker complaints total—25 percent to 40 percent of the workers.<br>• Four people (typically) are process owners of technology upgrades and worker use of technology: [name 1], [name 2], [name 3], and [name 4].<br>• Vendor maintenance processes include outsourced representatives providing monthly (or more often) in-library upgrades and providing—on demand and by appointment (as needed)—individual worker support.<br><br>*Investigation (interviewed selected workers, three process owners, and the vendor client representative)*<br>• [Name 1] and [name 2] did not inform vendors of remote workforce relocations and closure.<br>• *Vendors went to the facility and were denied access; reports were filed.*<br>• *Vendor client services did not review the problem reports for the company.*<br>• *There is no written process/procedure for tech upgrades with vendor.*<br><br>*Choices included:*<br>• [Name] from IT will serve as the process owner for assisting workers in using the institution's technology for business continuity.<br>• Vendors schedule visits with managers, and workers make appointments for drop-offs, fixes, and pickups.<br>• Vendors schedule distanced on-site work (seeking special permission from Risk Management on xx/xx/xxxx).<br>• Worker template for email apologies, links to appointment scheduler and safety info.<br>• Evaluation includes worker satisfaction survey in thirty days, then sixty days and meeting with vendor client representative to review any ongoing reports. | *Director of technology manager, user services; remote service coordinator* |

**TABLE 9.2**
**Problem to Post-Problem and Recovery**

| | |
|---|---|
| Date: | _11/26_ |
| Review Date/Revised Date: | _11/30–12/5_ |
| Process Owner: | _JBT_ |

**Issue:** *Library opened up too many services and too much space in first pandemic stage. Worker and user complaints communicated to managers and board. Contact-tracing data yielded three possible infections.*

**Affected**: *Frontline workers, maintenance/cleaning service, and users observed in use of services to date (attendance at [program 1] and at [program 2], and delivery of senior van from assisted living on xx/xx/xxxx with twelve people for one hour of browsing).*

| Issue, Problem, Mistake, Failure | Elements | Choices/ Changes/Recovery |
|---|---|---|
| Library foyer<br>• is opened temporarily with a small bank of computers and tables in the foyer set aside for materials' pickup<br>• contact tracing at the door for users and for workers together<br>• limited access<br>• limited number of users allowed in at one time | • Usage low in a.m.<br>• Higher with senior visit in p.m. (one hour).<br>• Community cases high.<br>• Workers concerned, complaints voiced (significant #).<br>• Testimonials sought. | • Pandemic team leaders gathered data.<br>• Workers surveyed.<br>• [Name] consulted health department.<br>• Pandemic team leaders designed Plan B.<br>• Monthly team/board meeting held one week early.<br>• Testimonials delivered to board, managers. |

**Solution:**
• Beginning xx/xx/xxxx, hours open reduced to three days in afternoon M, T, W, with four days closed.
• Workers moved to intermittent work schedules with volunteer shifts.
• Cleaning increased during and after.
• Services reduced to computers, and computers moved to foyer; materials picked up outside only. No study tables used inside.
• Library sought/received donations of outdoor furniture for patio distancing for seating.
• Wireless left on full signal 24/7.
• Parking-lot/stay-in-cars use advertised.
• No group visits.
• No programs.
• Increased PPE for workers.
• PPE offered to those using the services available.

**Follow-up Steps:**
1. Marketing is expanded to push online, announce move from Plan A to Plan B for safety concerns.
2. Data gathering increased.
3. Team meeting held more often (every two weeks).
4. Team meeting with board held more often (every three weeks).
5. After first two weeks, workers resurveyed.
6. Decision to be vetted given data on xx/xx/xxxx.

**TABLE 9.3**
**Prevention—Problem Prevention and Status**

Date: _11/26_
Review Date/Revised Date: _11/30–12/5_
Process Owner: _JBT_

**Issue:** *What are we doing for prevention? Media request, governing board Q&A on xx/xx/xxxx.*

**Affected:** *All shifts of workers; users coming to the library; governing board members answering questions/visiting; media audience (@15,000k readership as of xx/xx/xxxx); support crews for cleaning, delivery.*

| Area, Process, Action | Where, What | What, By and With Whom? | Status/Date |
|---|---|---|---|
| Clear, current, consistent signage throughout | Signage at front door, circ desk, ref desk is typically clear and consistent and up to date. Signs should be vetted every two weeks for consistency, terminology, placement, etc. | • Circulation staff<br>• Reference staff<br>• Meetings with workers scheduled to work in public service areas<br>• Assistant manager assesses all stat sheet comments | X<br><br>xx/xx/xxxx |
| Instructions for patrons | Desktop computers, entrance sign-in station, study tables, point-of-use at checkout | Check weekly with:<br>• Head of reference<br>• Manager, volunteers (front door)<br>• Circ desk manager | X<br><br>xx/xx/xxxx |
| Worker environments | Circ common space and meeting rooms are risk assessed for distancing; shared spaces are assigned; cleaning protocols used | Check weekly with workers in spaces | X<br><br>xx/xx/xxxx |
| Pandemic and post-pandemic user service scripts for assistance and complaints | Public service desks, phones, phone messages, email responses, chat content, text exchanges, etc. | • Observation within practice<br>• Monitor complaints<br>• Monitor comments in recordkeeping<br>• Discussion in staff meetings<br>• Random survey of users | X<br><br>xx/xx/xxxx |
| Templates, forms for exchanges | Pandemic and post-pandemic forms and templates | Review forms and templates by pandemic steering group/team for "independent" assessment | X<br><br>xx/xx/xxxx |
| Pandemic and post-pandemic conflict-management process | Users and workers; among workers; managers and workers; managers and users; managers and upper-level or umbrella-level administrators or managers; managers, partners, etc. | • Review through observation<br>• Review complaints filed<br>• Topic during staff meetings | X<br><br>xx/xx/xxxx |
| Organizational climate survey | Workers; managers | • Minutes of regular staff meeting discussions<br>• Climate survey of workers<br>• Worker focus group | X<br><br>xx/xx/xxxx |

• How is trust maintained in small situations where calling attention to negative issues will—more than likely—identify individuals more quickly or even unnecessarily or illegally?
• How does a manager get help in handling problems during emergency situations?

So many libraries are small or solo environments, and larger libraries are divided into branches, departments, or functional areas, so the likelihood is good that many problems or mistakes can be traced back quickly to one or two people. In addition, no matter the size or type of the library, geographic area, or service and resource area, it is possible that users can be easily identified for their role in mistakes and problems. Therefore, when confidentiality can easily be compromised unintentionally,

larger or more umbrella processes should take over to create a reasonable environment for an organization to not only run smoothly but also solve problems and issues that might arise in serious, emergency times. To make it possible to solve problems and current mistakes, managers can do the following:

Create reporting mechanisms such as emails, suggestion boxes, and feedback forms that allow for anonymity. This creates an environment of confidence since forms and instructions can explain how situations are handled.

Aggregate opportunities such as "flipchart evaluations" in public areas of the library can be used to gather information on the fly; the chart advertises the opportunity but can also steer people to feedback forms to provide avenues for reporting both small and large problems.

**TABLE 9.4**
**Problem to Post-Problem/Recovery**

Date: *11/26*
Review Date/Revised Date: *11/30–12/5*
Process Owner: *JBT*

| Problem, Mistake, Failure (What Happened?) | Recovery (How Will Things Be Now? Handling, Solutions, etc.) | Comments | Dates, Length of Time of Changes/Actions |
|---|---|---|---|
| 1. Starting Plan Library began pandemic by providing too many hours of service, too much space, and no choices for worker schedules, locations. | Changed Plan Library lessened hours, reduced circulation and one-on-one research assistance, and ceased programs for youth and school visits. | First worker survey very negative; Second worker survey data showed comfort level rating of "5" (out of 7) restored. | During and post-pandemic until Health Department lifts hours curfew and social distancing is reduced (was 6'). |
| 2. Starting Plan Need to reduce negative worker feedback for initial response. | Changed Plan Need to reduce negative worker feedback for secondary response. | More training is needed for workers to have remote success. Panel with representatives on worker safety. | By xx/xx/20xx, there will be a return to full hours of service and fully scheduled workday for workers. |
| 3. Starting Plan The library's teacher pack service for home schoolers, partner schools, charter schools, public K–12, and public and private higher ed was reduced in number and delivery given CDC guidelines and need to quarantine. Area teachers from 37 percent of the schools complained about content that was now unavailable for classroom use. | Changed Plan Pandemic team scheduled to: • gather ideas from other libraries on how they are delivering course packs/teacher support materials; • create a workgroup—including frontline workers and teachers—to discuss how the service might resume; and • meeting scheduled with teachers and library staff from representative area schools. | Decision on whether and what to pilot (as it means cleaning and quarantining materials) to be made by [name 1] and [name 2] by xx/xx/20xx. | Pandemic and possibly post-pandemic for sixty to ninety days until quarantine data is reduced for # of days required. Full service back in place by xx/xx/20xx. |

Communicate what happened, once it is reported, and that can be sent to everyone assisting in the work in the library (e.g., temporary workers, Friends members, board or council people helping out, volunteers, etc.). This more blanket correction can be third party, such as "It has come to our attention . . ." and "The library has been told that . . . so here is simple way to address *x* if *y* happens again."

In any pandemic or emergency discussion meetings of those assisting at the library, include a standing agenda where people attending can bring up things they have seen or that have been reported to them for discussion and solution rather than identification of who did something.

Identify when you—as the manager—have done something wrong, and work with others (workers, volunteers, etc.) to identify what it was and how it might be fixed or handled differently.

And finally, identify with those "present" the levels and types of mistakes that are common, are expected, and must be reported quickly with no issues associated with making these mistakes. This gives those in the library the terminology they need to discuss problems and rank or sort them and put them into context and perspective.

**Is It Brain Surgery?**

Popular phrases when someone makes a mistake are "Well, it's not brain surgery" and "Everyone makes mistakes." And—although these statements are absolutely correct for what we do—the reality is when there *are* a number of health and well-being issues, those that typically *do* come with pandemics as well as public health issues in workplaces today (and we've been told many more to come), managers must find ways to identify and solve them. They must walk the fine line of attempting to ensure the health of workers while striving to provide acceptable spaces for the public.

Managers must also find ways to ensure that the organization and its services and resources can withstand the test of mistakes and problems in general and especially in public health crises. The library needs to be a place where people want to work and feel it is a good place to work, since they aren't there for the money, and that is a process that takes time and great care and attention.

# 10

# Service Access and Delivery

ALL TYPES AND SIZES of libraries offer core or foundational services and these services are often the hardest to maintain during emergency events because—given our strengths—they include access to spaces for browsing, research, instruction for individuals, small groups or large groups; studying; in-person programming; technology usage (in-library and loaning); and expert assistance with research, information, and technology. These one-to-one activities or group activities coupled with the access needed to spaces, technology, and so on, are often the first services to disappear or be delayed in difficult times.

And—although making these services available during emergency events such as pandemics—is not always within the library's decision-making purview—libraries must approach their situation by first identifying their core or primary services, identifying their secondary services and the individual aspects of both the core and secondary services, matching what they offer to what their constituents need in general and especially what they need during the emergency event, and then identifying what is and isn't within their control for moving forward.

Once these service aspects are identified and it is clear what libraries can provide, they want to use the gathered information to inform constituents, administrators, workers, users, nonusers, stakeholders, partners, their "community"-at-large, vendors, subcontractors, and the media. In addition, this information also supports the detailed information needed to show safety compliance for the library to plan for their services, workers, and users but also for reportage for emergency response teams. These steps also support documentation needed for internal transfer of funds, institutional and umbrella organization budget requests, and soft or grant money applications as well as for deploying gift and donation money and for soliciting new dollars from community or institutional—primarily external—funders.

Finally, the information from this data provides the content and justification needed for any specific language that can be used with governing or advisory boards, the umbrella institution, and the media, and if the library chooses to do so, they can use it for the creation of a marketing "campaign" to more easily communicate the direction the library has been given or has chosen for this unique time.

Once the core and secondary services for business continuity are decided on, the various activities within the services provide a structure for (1) how operational plans have to change, (2) planning timelines, and (3) continuing work on goals, strategies, and outcomes and what needs to change to continue gathering data for core service evaluation. The identification of what can and can't happen also provides aspects of alternative or parallel services that must be enabled within existing worker schedules and abilities or new or different schedules or abilities.

Before core/primary and secondary services can be finalized and aspects of these services can be completed, however, there are helpful processes to assist in the review of services. The SWOT approach tasks individuals or groups with looking at "something," meaning a facility, a collection, an ad campaign, or—in this case—a service to identify strengths, weaknesses, opportunities, and threats. Following the discussion and completion of the template, a team—which can vary based on what one is "exploring" or assessing—reviews the four elements or areas outlined, then weighs the importance, impact, data presented, and so on, to see how they might proceed. While one might not understand how a service can be weighed or its importance assessed or its aspects reviewed, template areas *can* be weighted for importance, cost, data, popularity, a match to available staff, and so on, and then a decision-making team can decide—for example:

- whether or not the strengths outweigh the weaknesses;
- whether the entire service should be stopped temporarily and the factors that need to be in place before it is brought back;
- whether not the busiest or "most used" part of the service can be sustained but in a different format; and
- whether or not an aspect is *relatively* busy but will be sustained because its users are the most critical/most in need.

SWOTs are older processes and ask participants in discussions to narrow down their feedback and be specific about visualizing all sides (negative and positive). SWOTs typically do not ask specific questions or trigger questions, but in the case of an emergency event, questions are added in this process to expedite the discussion and to guide it throughout the discussion to assist the library in deciding about this service during this event—and in this case, business continuity.

**TABLE 10.1**
**SWOT**

Are the delivery and support services currently available for technology checkout adequate during an emergency? Are they appropriate?

Publication Date: _____
Review Date/Revised Date: _____
Process Owner: _____

**STRENGTHS**
*Trigger Questions*

**Administrator Feedback**
1. What services that the library currently offers are already designed to respond to expanded user needs during a pandemic?
   a. Technology circulation?
   b. Online live assistance for tech support for library technology circulating?
   c. After-hours assistance?
2. Are the current policies and procedures flexible enough to accommodate an expanded service?
3. Are funds available to expand service should the need arise? ROI issues?
4. Which users take advantage of the current service?
5. Which users are currently identified as needing the service?
6. What is the wireless access/connectivity across the community?

**Worker Feedback**
1. Are workers comfortable with their abilities for:
   a. Technology circulation processes?
   b. Online live assistance for tech support for library technology circulating?
2. Are expanded hours of assistance needed (e.g., phone messages requesting assistance, complaints on securing successful service at home)?
3. Which users do frontline workers see taking advantage of the current service? (e.g., Are there repeat users? What are the ranges of users taking advantage of the service?)
4. Do users seek wireless access information? The access itself?

**WEAKNESSES**
*Trigger Questions*

**Administrator Feedback**
1. Have any complaints reached the administration regarding this service?
2. Is the service cost effective as it is currently designed (e.g., loss rates, replacements, use vs. investment)?
3. How was this service ranked in past user surveys? High? Low?
4. What is the longevity and currency of the service?

**Worker Feedback**
1. What are the repeat complaints workers encounter at the circulating desk? Equipment aging? Hardware not robust? Wireless issues?
2. How many losses do workers experience in any given month? Is the equipment gone? Peripherals?
3. Are there deficits in numbers available? When do these typically occur?
4. What recommendations would you give your administrators for changing or shrinking or expanding the service?

**OPPORTUNITIES**
*Trigger Questions*

**Administrator Feedback**
1. Is soft money available for expanding a tech circulating service?
2. Is a partnership with [company name] possible to introduce wireless hotspot expansion?
3. Are there unrealized experts among workers who might lead a training initiative?

**THREATS**
*Trigger Questions*

**Administrator Feedback**
1. Could or should another department take the service over in a pandemic situation? If yes, then please provide two reasons why.
2. Is it possible that the library cannot support expanded growth? Provide two reasons why.
3. What have been the challenges faced in providing the library's services?

| **OPPORTUNITIES** *Trigger Questions* | **THREATS** *Trigger Questions* |
|---|---|
| **Worker Feedback** 1. Does the library need to introduce wireless hotspot expansion? 2. Are you or anyone you are aware of expert in a tech or tech-support area? 3. What could existing workers and/or you bring to a training initiative for workers? 4. What training should workers have immediately if provided the opportunity? Funding? | **Worker Feedback** 1. Do you think—with your experience at the front line for this service—that another department should take over the service in a pandemic situation? If yes, then please provide two reasons why. 2. Who might provide the service better in emergency times? 3. What do frontline workers need to better provide this service? Training? Experience? 4. As a frontline worker, what challenges have you faced in providing this service for the library? |

Typically considered more of a top-down process, the SWOT chart in table 10.1 pushes the organization to expand the top-down process by deliberately identifying administrator as well as worker feedback questions. SWOTs offer a wealth of information, including:

- the different and similar views of each of the two groups;
- how they compare and contrast with each other;
- how the service(s) might "look" within the continuity and post or recovery stages;
- what data come into play;
- what anecdotal information is available; and
- opportunities for self-reflection by each group and group member given their view of the organization, service, expertise, and possible training.

Another approach—"SOAR"—tasks individuals or groups with looking at a topic to identify strengths, opportunities, aspirations, and results. With a SOAR, a team can not only assess how the service or aspects of the service are doing but also review how all or part of the service can be altered or projected to do more, or succeed using another approach. The SOAR can also be helpful in taking a group along a path whose results can include:

- aspects of the service that can be kept; and
- suggested measures for aspects of the service that might continue and how to evaluate them.

Additional strengths of using these approaches is in evidence when the specific questions asked for each category are tailored to meet the specific needs of the situation. This is especially important when more restrictive times are at hand and the questions can act as initial delimiters to narrow down responses. In addition, if the processes are used by small groups or individuals who wish to compare information to find common denomi-

nators, trigger questions added for each section for both groups offer a structure that allows for feedback that can be more specifically compared and contrasted.

SOARs—a newer process (see table 10.2)—allow a group to plan strategically with a positive focus that focuses on the current strengths of the organization with a foundational discussion of visions for the future. For use in a pandemic, this approach is primarily a planning tool, not for overall but rather for the length of the pandemic, including post-pandemic services and services during and after recovery. SOARs are considered more of a top-down approach to collaboration and offer a wealth of information, including:

- the foundation or strengths of services;
- strengths and expertise of those who offer services;
- how research and data illustrate service impacts;
- opportunities for self-reflection by each group member given their view of the organization, service, and expertise; and
- service futures during, post, and in recovery.

### Pandemic Services: Closed, Revised, Continued

An unexpected—but, in many libraries, welcome—consequence of the pandemic was that many services were studied, found to be core, and continued with or without changes. Other services were also studied and put on hiatus, reduced, or revised, and then, as business-continuity practices were determined to be just as—if not more—satisfactory, those services were reduced or ceased. And while the altered services may get new life down the road, significant review and justification attempts have been excellent exercises for libraries as they assess use, impact, success (based on original goals and ongoing outcomes), cost-effectiveness, and—in as many situations as possible—whether or not the target audiences are having their needs met. So—although

**TABLE 10.2**
**SOAR**

Are our services able to respond to/in a pandemic?
What do we want to see in our emergency service delivery?

Publication Date: _____
Review Date/Revised Date: _____
Process Owner: _____

| Strategic Intent | STRENGTHS | OPPORTUNITIES |
|---|---|---|
| Group, Collaborative Discussion Based on Impact and Outcomes | What are our greatest assets going into this situation that will enable us to handle a serious threat (that could include a shutdown/shutout)?<br>1. Identify three assets or strengths of the library that will specifically provide support needed during the pandemic.<br>2. Provide two examples of strengths exhibited by the library's successful response in the past few years.<br>3. In thinking about your role as an employee, identify two things that you bring to this difficult situation that could benefit others or improve or benefit services. | Are there any opportunities for success in our emergency-management response structure? What opportunities do people want?<br>1. What one "big success" could the library realize or "big goal" could they achieve during the pandemic?<br>2. If you could pick one thing to change moving forward that would work within the pandemic, and possibly beyond, what would it be?<br>3. During this time, and now that you might *have* the time, what would you like to improve on in your role in the library? Any training identified to help? |
| Appreciative Inquiry | ASPIRATIONS | RESULTS |
| | What do we think should happen in our safest environments during a pandemic/shutdown/shutout?<br><br>1. In a safe and virus-free setting, what three things do you think will contribute to that safety?<br>2. What will *you* do to assist the library in creating a safe environment? Before you come to work? While you are at work? | What are the measurable results we want to have happen in a pandemic/shutdown/shutout? How do we know when we have success?<br>1. Name two aspects of safety that you think you would be able to measure when we reopen our spaces.<br>2. What three things do we need for users to do to assist in creating a safer environment for both users and staff? |

assessment of services is not thinking outside the box and libraries have done this for many years—what librarians tend *not* to do is to cease a service completely, and in doing so, inevitably a constituent goes without all or parts of a service.

The future, however, will find many different approaches to offering some services—many of which are scaled down—and a bigger and broader focus on empowering people to use services available and possibly much better for them. The process of making these difficult and possibly ongoing decisions, however, has included a wide variety of discussions and could include the SWOT and the SOAR as well as an audit or inventory of each service—some of which are driven by physical areas, some by furniture, and so on.

A full audit of spaces is needed for—at the very least—the first two stages of the pandemic identified as to availability and required actions by users and workers. The completed example chart in table 10.3 presents each area and all spaces that drive services with the initial plans for lack of, revised, or new service delivery. Timelines are left off but would be added as the "community" changes. No designations are made by type or size of library deliberately, as this is designed to be a master list. Obviously the smallest library of any type or kind has represented

areas in table 10.3, as does the largest public or academic library.

## Pandemic Services: Created

Pandemics are admittedly untenable public-health crises that take—literally—tens of thousands of lives for years on end. This unprecedented situation became—for many nonprofit and commercial entities—the mother of invention, as individuals and groups struggled to maintain their businesses while others changed their mission and direction; for example, nonprofit services and resources designed for recreation and entertainment transitioned to organizations now focusing on sustenance, health, and wellness, and in many cases (and certainly in the case of libraries), organizations expanded their services to support those in need for their livelihood, health and welfare, medical pandemic-issue assistance, and also one-on-one assistance for those needing general information, resources, library services, and opportunities for research.

All types and sizes of libraries—at the start of the pandemic and throughout—have experimented with the widest variety of services—resurrecting some older services and activities as well as instituting safe ways to deliver cur-

**TABLE 10.3**
**Service Accessibility—Temporary, Permanent**

Publication Date: _____
Review Date/Revised Date: _____
Process Owner: _____

| Department/Area/Function | As Is | Pandemic Changes/Temporary: all PPE required no matter what the government spaces dictate; contact tracing required at the door | Pandemic Changes/Post-Pandemic: all PPE encouraged no matter what the government guidelines dictate; contact tracing required at the door as long as possible; staff can still wear PPE and socially distance |
|---|---|---|---|
| **Collections** | | | |
| Browsing shelving; disinfecting project continues | | No browsing by users | Possible browsing designed row-by-row with one-way aisles; usage/capacity designated by government or less |
| Resources/Materials—Print/Paper: disinfecting project continues | | Inaccessible | Accessible intermittently with quarantines on handling/use (see chapter 2) |
| Resources/Materials—Media: disinfecting project continues | X | Inaccessible to in-person; requests taken by e-processes; materials pulled and circulated by outside lockers | Accessible intermittently with quarantines (twenty-four to forty-eight hours longer than for print/paper) |
| Realia: disinfecting project continues, but not all can be cleaned—items that can't be cleaned are not accessible | | Inaccessible; disinfecting project begins | Inaccessible until a significant amount of time with herd immunity (three to four months); disinfecting project continues; realia that can't be cleaned moved to storage |
| Other—Archival, Genealogy, Rare Materials, Manuscripts, Maps, Sheet Music, etc. | | | Reduced access to items (Paper? Historic? Special PPE needed? Unique training for users needed? Mediated digital or in-person use can be requested? Possible—as can't be cleaned or wiped?) or access denied until herd immunity (three to four months) is in play and collections reopen. |
| **Furniture** | | | |
| Public Seating—Inside: disinfecting project continues | | Inaccessible | Reduced numbers of tables and chairs; limit per hour and # using |
| Public Seating—Outside/Patio: disinfecting project continues | X | Socially distanced; registration at capacity designated by government | Socially distanced; registration at capacity designated by government |
| Workspace/Library Worker Office/Staff Bathrooms/Seating: disinfecting project continues | | Accessible intermittently; hot desks ceased; disinfecting project continues | Accessible intermittently with rotating use of limited timelines; hot desks ceased; disinfecting project continues |
| Others Areas—Play Areas, Leisure Seating, Outside Recreational Items, Outdoor Seating (Flexible Use) | | Inaccessible | Play areas closed; leisure seating permanently socially distanced; outside recreation and leisure socially distanced |
| **Spaces** | | | |
| Open Seating/Study: disinfecting project continues | | Closed; inaccessible | Reduced numbers of tables and chairs; limit per hour and registration at capacity designated by government |
| Small-Group Rooms: disinfecting project continues | | Closed; inaccessible | Inaccessible until a significant amount of time with herd immunity; space used to accommodate library workers |
| Individual Spaces (tablet chairs, study carrels): disinfecting project continues | | Closed; inaccessible | Reduced numbers of tables and chairs; limit per hour and # using; when herd immunity is growing, these numbers of chairs will be introduced back in systematically; registration at capacity designated by government or less |

(continued)

TABLE 10.3 *(continued)*

| Department/Area/ Function | As Is | Pandemic Changes/Temporary: all PPE required no matter what the government spaces dictate; contact tracing required at the door | Pandemic Changes/Post-Pandemic: all PPE encouraged no matter what the government guidelines dictate; contact tracing required at the door as long as possible; staff can still wear PPE and socially distance |
|---|---|---|---|
| Other—Museum Areas, Display/ Exhibit Spaces, Meeting Rooms, Public Gardens, User Storage/Lockers, Library Storage, Water Fountains, Small Construction (little libraries), WeWork Spaces, Balconies, Porches, etc. | | If the library is open, spaces smaller than [designated size] within the library are closed; anything open is socially distanced | Follow government guidelines per size of space/ capacity, meeting rooms closed for meetings but open for testing or study or teaching sessions, library storage (limited to one per space/# of square feet), public lockers are closed |
| Public Bathrooms | | Closed | Closed |
| **Public Service Delivery/Workstations** | | | |
| Circulation Desk | X | Queue established with social distancing, PPE installed | Queue established with social distancing, PPE installed |
| Reference "Desks" | | Closed in-person; appointments only for virtual assistance; email; chat reference still available during library hours of service and until midnight at announced times; drop-in live assistance available during library hours of service | Social distancing; PPE installed; appointments only |
| Tech Assistance | | Closed in-person; appointments only/ virtual live assistance only; available during library hours of service | Social distancing; PPE installed; appointments only/virtual and in-person |
| Other—Small Business Research Assistance, etc. | | Closed | "Partner" workers staffing conform to the library's governmental guidelines |
| **Student Technology/Public Workstations** | | | |
| Desktop PCs | | Closed in-person; inaccessible | Integrated back into user access through first thirty days post-pandemic or [designated stage] and government guidelines; by sixty days tech checked out using locker pickup, no inside use |
| Laptops | | Inaccessible | Integrated back into user access through first thirty days post-pandemic; by sixty days tech checked out, no internal use, as cleaning protocols are not as successful on charging devices |
| Personal Devices | X | Wireless on; outside use in PPE; socially distanced patio areas | Integrated back into user access through first thirty days post-pandemic; by sixty days tech checked out, no internal use |
| Power/Charging | X | Wireless on; outside use in PPE; socially distanced patio areas; hot plugs unlocked/available for personal devices | Integrated back into user access to circulating units through first thirty days post-pandemic; by sixty days tech checked out, no inside use, as cleaning protocols will not be successful on charging devices |
| Other—Simulation Training, etc. | | Closed | Simulation training—using hardware and public workstations—follows the desktop computer guidelines for individuals |
| **Teaching/Presentation Spaces** | | | |
| Computer Lab; Computer Classrooms | | Inaccessible to the users; if approved, librarians will teach remotely through the lab | Integrated back into user access through first thirty days post-pandemic; registration at capacity designated by government |
| General Classrooms; Information Literacy Teaching Spaces | | Inaccessible to the users; if approved, librarians will teach remotely through the lab | Integrated back into user access through first thirty days post-pandemic; by sixty days tech checked out, no internal use but some appointments taken |

| Department/Area/ Function | As Is | Pandemic Changes/Temporary: all PPE required no matter what the government spaces dictate; contact tracing required at the door | Pandemic Changes/Post-Pandemic: all PPE encouraged no matter what the government guidelines dictate; contact tracing required at the door as long as possible; staff can still wear PPE and socially distance |
|---|---|---|---|
| Age-Level Activities | | Inaccessible to the users; if approved, librarians will teach remotely through the lab | Integrated back into user access through first thirty days post-pandemic; by sixty days tech checked out, no internal use but some appointments taken |
| Other—Recording Studios, Film Studios, etc. | | Closed due to size, user proximity | Follows the government guidelines |
| **Innovation Spaces (Discovery Activities, One-Button Studios, Maker Spaces)** | | | |
| Maker Room | | Inaccessible; not offered in-person; virtual presentations only and broadcast from spaces | Inaccessible; not offered; postponed |
| One-Button Studio | | Inaccessible; not offered in-person; virtual presentations only and broadcast from spaces | Inaccessible; not offered; postponed |
| Discovery Center | | Inaccessible; not offered; postponed | Inaccessible; not offered; postponed |
| Other Entrepreneurial Spaces for Small Businesses (App Design, Etsy Owners) | | Closed | Open to individuals scheduling space; quarantined between uses for four hours |
| **Partners (Tutoring, Supplemental Instruction, etc.)** | | | |
| Workshops, Small-Group and One-on-One Tutoring | | Not offered; postponed; inaccessible; virtual use with registrations only | Slowly integrated back into socially distanced, public meeting room use |
| Other—Clubs, Special Collections, Government Groups Offering Services (IRS, Job Fairs), Nonprofit Assistance (Food Stamps, Job-Seeking Skills), etc. | | Closed | Open as soon as allowed given user needs:<br>• Job fairs<br>• Job-seeking skills<br>• Social services<br>• Vax support |

rent services and use resources such as print/paper materials and electronic devices. At the heart of any service review, however, should be the library striving to keep the expertise of library professionals front and center to make sure that decision makers, communities, and users as well as nonusers are aware that—without library professionals—the majority of services cannot happen.

Revised and new services include a wide variety of ideas from all types and sizes of library settings. Although it may be years before changed or new services are completely vetted for success with decisions to cease or retain, the list is *impressive* and includes the following.

## External Delivery/Remote Delivery

Initial goals of most libraries included keeping the flow of print/paper materials and other resources going. When pandemic data on transmission began to include the "shelf life" and type and rate of transmission of the virus on print/paper, cloth, plastic, and other—primarily porous—surfaces, libraries began to sanitize in earnest as well as quarantine materials from forty-eight hours to—at one time—two weeks (if surfaces were not cleaned).

While this led to assessments of cleaning products and processes—as it should have—the immediate problem became the reality of transmission from person to person while they were providing the resources. This was dealt with by requiring appropriate PPE for workers and users as well as external lockers where materials were stored for pickup and drive-up/appointments for curbside pickups of bags and packages (including resources and instructions for cleaning and return). Additional approaches including using car/taxi delivery services; the library bookmobiles or entertainment or information mobile resources for expanded services or for existing services to expanded areas; piggybacking on existing delivery services (nonprofits, commercial drop-offs/lockers, and the postal services through the general mail or using postal locations). Other settings for drop-offs included popular hangouts in communities (much like curbside pickup of food) and religious settings and general, larger places such as community halls, movie theaters, and local schools/after-school services settings. Materials transmitted this way included specific requests as well as packages bundled based on—for example—genres, bestsellers, nonfiction, subject areas such as cookbooks, and crafts/

DIY. They had longer checkout periods with suspensions of checkout caps and any fines and fees. Returns could be to any one of a number of places identified on master lists where libraries and partners arranged for drop-off/pickup locations.

## Internal Delivery

Libraries in special, school, and academic settings took requests and bundled specific titles as well as general-assignment materials—such as science experiments, geography, and computer coding—and delivered these to classrooms, offices, labs, after-school programs, home schoolers, faculty rooms, study spaces, hospital rooms/patient centers, doctor offices, and play areas. These packages—checked out *en masse*—were sanitized, and not only instructions but also cleaning packets were often included since these settings were typically not home environments. They had longer checkout periods with suspensions of caps of books out with no fines and fees. Returns could be made to many places identified on master lists where libraries and partners arranged for drop-off/pickup locations.

## Pared-Down Use of Facilities/Spaces in Facilities Reengineered

The diverse issues of library facilities are legendary and include:

- many libraries have no spaces large enough to socially distance;
- many libraries' entire facility is too small to meet the guidelines for the required number of feet for social distancing;
- it is often not possible to move furniture in some spaces;
- libraries with hardwired technology cannot easily—or at all—move the technology to provide the required social distancing;
- many libraries have no open spaces such as meeting rooms or outdoor spaces/patios with or without the needed furniture;
- weather is obviously an issue for many unplanned outdoor spaces that have no overhangs, roofs, or heating/cooling mechanisms;
- some libraries do not have the amount of technology needed to provide even reduced services; and
- some libraries do not have wireless inside or possibly inside but not outside.

With these issues in mind, those that *do* have all or part of these opportunities used their spaces for patios with wireless to be socially distanced and opened up for reservations for limited hours of use/services; meeting rooms had minimal, socially distanced furniture set up to accommodate reservations for limited hours of use/services; in some locations, shaded or covered parking lots—used with or without people in cars—and external wireless were opened for users to drive up and use their own devices; gardens, play areas, and contiguous park or museum settings with outdoor venues partnered with libraries to provide reserved/limited-use spaces; and libraries set up kiosks and temporary outlets in larger, socially distanced spaces with wireless routers that could be used for library users (mall areas, city hall spaces, county facilities, hospital waiting areas, fairgrounds, and some outdoor food venues that felt that partnering with the library could sustain their business through the pandemic).

## Asynchronous Services

Many libraries already offer asynchronous reference, tutoring, and so on; expanded hours; or expanded types of services with their existing messages or use of free online messaging and chat; email (return with guaranteed times); posting to bulletin boards with return information in a more confidential venue; Facebook messaging; other social media platforms; and fax machines.

## Synchronous Services

Libraries use teleconferencing; FaceTime; telephone and radio broadcasting; free and fee online video spaces and products; the telephone; and live chat and messaging.

## Self-Directed Services/Guided Services

Self-directed services can either stand alone or enhance other services with pathways and/or online guides designed to lead users through processes to assist them in getting the resources or information they need; media streams or podcasts as popups for online or web-based delivery with choices for users; recorded FaceTime or smartphone content; apps; or QR codes directing users through spaces to get the resources or information they need.

Specific events include webinar software for story times, youth or teen discussion forums, lap-sit times for parents or caregivers; consulting for dissertations; information-literacy tutorials or live workshops; IRS assistance through live broadcasts; hangout spaces (FaceTime, Zoom, or Google) for telemedicine for those users without telemedicine access or delivery mechanisms elsewhere; maker meetups (FaceTime, Zoom, or Google) with users getting kits through curbside pickup *or* designing maker events with materials used from home; and author interviews streamed to book clubs—to name just a few events!

So—although some of these services are not new in some or all content or delivery—the goals have always been to continue to provide services that speak to the value of what libraries *do* provide—and to strive to meet the needs of constituents of any and all ages, in all income levels, at all learning levels—meeting them at their point of need.

If we had been ready—where these services are needed by constituents—they are available:

- Infrastructure wireless is in place throughout libraries, outdoor spaces, and adjacent areas.
- Partnerships with area supporters are in place to offer backup programming.
- Libraries offer a wide variety of pickup after-hours services to meet needs of constituents.
- Recreational and cultural programs in the library are streamed simultaneously for remote users.
- Live media venues are used by the library to provide reference and research support during the hours the library is open—and beyond.

- Instruction and teaching on how to use the library and its resources are available remotely on demand or by appointment.
- Asynchronous and synchronous reference and research are available, and assistance in finding and using resources is available beyond the library's service hours.
- Connectivity is available as a device for access outside the library sphere.
- A variety of equipment/hardware and technology resources circulates outside the library to meet constituents' needs.
- Libraries—as educational institutions—support the broadest curriculum with pathways provided in a variety of formats (K–12, lifelong learning, public, academic, home schooling).
- Pathways and online guides exist for users not on-site (home schoolers, homebound, classrooms in schools without libraries).
- Remote-user mobile environments exist (like bookmobiles) to support services and resource delivery.

# 11

# Public Relations, Marketing, and Branding

THE ROLE AND IMPORTANCE of library messaging or library communication—public relations (PR) and marketing and, if possible, branding—during difficult times such as emergency events and most recently pandemic times cannot be minimized. And while creating awareness, capturing and engaging constituents, and advertising resources and services are always important, the focus during these particularly difficult times should include but not be limited to:

- expanding messages about the institution's services in general;
- focusing on critical services and resources;
- increasing awareness of unique features of services (contactless services);
- introducing or educating constituents of access (service areas or area changes such as altered hours, new "open" hours, hybrid hours);
- expanded or new digital environments; and
- focusing on the unique expertise and commitment that workers in libraries bring to their constituents.

Also, in any communication or messaging during difficult times—and especially public health emergencies—all content must be carefully crafted and continuously assessed.

And, while any new images, any focus, or any new or altered messages chosen do not supplant the institution's central or core vision, mission, roles, or values, it is important in the earliest stages of pandemics that the institution reviews the current message and, if it doesn't meet pandemic-level needs, then they need to find—at the very least—temporary messages that provide recognition of the situation and characterize how some classic roles may (for example):

- still be available, with small changes or business as usual;
- temporarily be on hold;
- identify what must change (and possibly why) but how it is available in alternative or hybrid approaches; or
- announce what is new and how it will meet needs.

### Defining Library Messaging—Pre-Pandemic

Libraries—based on the type and size of library—have dramatically different messages with great variance in modes and methods and differing degrees of success. Today's libraries typically, however, employ public relations (PR) and marketing using many techniques with many expanding messages from branding resources and services overall, creating awareness of their physical facility, emphasizing their web environment, and with a special focus on a unique or special service or their library overall. It is especially important to note that within a pandemic environment where institutions often partner to manage the situation, libraries may not have complete control over the critical communication they use as they have to mirror others, creating their messages as part of the community and partnerships in which they exist as well as in tune with the emergency event information.

In discussing these important activities, the following issues should be considered:

- The professional literature of library and information science identifies *marketing* as an umbrella term over *PR* and *advertising*, *branding*, and so on, and while marketing is typically seen as an activity supporting buying and selling, libraries employ the same techniques, such as market research, to create awareness, indicate value or usefulness of their "product" to the "market" or the constituents, and encourage use of resources and services to meet needs. Although many in the profession do not support commercial marketing or branding for libraries, most libraries realize that they have "competitors" for their services and certainly competitors for their funding. So, while many librarians do want to brand, they are on board with more contemporary techniques such as relationship marketing (targeting how services meet specific user needs) and telling stories highlighting value, benefit, worth, and impact. In addition, libraries take great care to market the roles they play in supporting their primary constituents and especially during unique events such as:

- illustrating how academic libraries support student success and required student learning outcomes for remote learning during emergency events;
- providing evidence of how school libraries assist their students in successful scoring on standardized tests and in meeting learning outcomes—delivered remotely through the district's learning-management system and using the library's online e-resources;
- showing how public libraries contribute to a tax base of a community or provide critical support services such as job seeking, worker training, or technology to constituents identified by socioeconomic status during events that include a strong recovery or have a severe economic downturn or in their support of social service agencies now having to provide services in centralized one-stop settings; and
- serving as a special library with specific support content for health professionals and their patients needing unique public-health information or as a cost center for businesses providing activities that can be categorized as billable hours.

- Typically, the term *advertising* is not used in libraries; rather, it is used synonymously with broader definitions of *marketing* in for-profit environments. Librarians say they "market" the library; however, typically, they don't say that they "advertise" the library, services, or programs. In reality advertising *is* one part of the overall marketing initiative, and messages (communiques to target groups) the library distributes do "advertise" services in general as well as specific programs and services. Library "advertising" or messaging is especially important for constituents at risk in public-health crises who

need—but don't have access to or are not aware of—certain services libraries *do* provide, such as robust web access, office productivity resources and services, extensive cultural, entertainment, leisure-time support, and cutting-edge technology with technology devices and (often) connectivity to use at home.

- During emergency events, libraries need to be aggressive in having their communications manager (as part of the emergency response team's communications effort) be able to not only design messages but also interpret content for library workers and constituents. In addition, communications or PR workers in libraries need to be part of any group assembled to discuss and decide on leadership, management, and general constituent information at all levels including the coordination of visuals, terminology, timing, and consistency.

- Only recently have libraries been interested in specifically branding the library, although they have long included—for example—logos and taglines for the library in the process of designing and deploying a marketing initiative (e.g., "Your library: the information place"). Branding during public health crises is important, as this approach is a single focus on a product or services and communicated by taglines or logos. The brand—designed to distinguish the product or service from others—might be used to distinguish the emergency-event service or product as different from typical library PR, marketing, or even the library's usual focus or brand. This focus makes it easy to communicate unique needs to constituents as well as determine effectiveness and create an easier path to assessment.

Marketing—often the umbrella word for all marketing activities including public relations, messaging or advertising, and branding—provides the structure for what we offer and how we offer it based on market research. During the pandemic, library marketing includes the entire marketing process of identifying constituents or target populations, determining need, and matching what the library has for those targeted individuals or groups, but then it veers from standard practices to narrowing the messaging down to what the library offers during the pandemic.

Messaging or advertising—as one aspect of marketing—includes determining content or "copy," images, and context for users, nonusers, and—for example—decision makers, to highlight unique aspects of the library that are available for constituents. During the pandemic—advertising might focus on expertise available to users—for example—to create awareness of how the library specifically supports constituents during emergency-event conditions. Marketing content should also include templates the organization uses to provide guidance for acceptable content—keeping in mind that often the library's pandemic or public-health content may need to coordinate with an emergency response team internal to the organization or external and comprised of many types of institutions.

Public relations—an integral part of the marketing process—maintains the library's vision, mission, and overall reputation but within the context of the emergency situation. Odds are the library will not change its vision or mission but may instead choose to focus on the reputation of the library and how it is available to assist people during the crisis. PR—beside focusing on the library's overall role in the environment or community—for example—may also focus on a *new* way to look at the library as valued or valuable or a benefit or critical pandemic support for information for treatment, staying successful in school, circulating technology, or connectivity. Also, and even more importantly, during difficult times such as a public-health crisis, library PR might choose to build on the vision and perception of the institution as a trusted and valuable institution, while using that image to capitalize—with specific rhetoric—on the critical and possibly unexpected roles the library can play in the pandemic: first responder, primary educational support for remote learners, or a one-stop location for small business support.

Branding—one part of marketing an institution—can be used to "sum up" who the library is and what it does, and a pandemic brand might sum up who you are at the time of need. With general examples such as "See the world from home" or "Don't forget to read," the library can communicate what it can do for specific constituents such as "Information you can trust" or "Emergency information you can trust 24/7" or "Need pandemic information at 2:00? Call the library." The brand can also distinguish the institution from other "competitors" in the environment in the most general terms such as the place to temporarily access connectivity or enhance tech use. Rather than a completely new pandemic brand for the library, a brand could piggyback on existing branding information with an expanded tagline or an image with a twist.

Decisions on marketing changes need to take into account an estimated length of the time of the event or effects of the event, or specific business continuity based on the seriousness of the event. Short-term events would not warrant a complete change or new content and might not need a rebrand given the shorter length of time and (hopefully) the temporary nature of the event or impact of the event. Examples include:

- a weather or a nature event where the library becomes a shelter-in-place or point of departure or—coupled with other services—a temporary location for care or social service; and
- a longer-term but well-defined event such as a fire in the facility that has a specific beginning and end and the library has clearer parameters for time, continuity, repair, and reopening.

Pandemics or other health crises, however—given the uncertainty, the seriousness of the situation, the need for the library to make changes (many dramatic) to remain in service, the impact on the library's business continuity, and the length of time—present a good time to review the brand to see if the library within the pandemic should be branded or rebranded. If the library has no brand and if it is possible to move quickly, establishing the "pandemic" brand is very helpful in changing perceptions of the spaces and services, raising awareness, and showcasing expertise.

So how else do PR, marketing, and branding differ in difficult or pandemic times?

- Altered or new messages or images do not have to be and shouldn't be chosen with permanency in mind. This varies from nonpandemic or emergency decision-making—that is, creating a marketing presence is not something the library takes lightly or does quickly; therefore, in more normal times, content and focus need to take into consideration longer-term use.
- While the marketing process for the library involves a significant number of people (with smaller environments bringing in external stakeholders, constituents, and peers), fewer people in a shorter length of time will have to choose the pandemic approach. This shorter and smaller approach should still be carried out according to standard marketing processes, and especially—given the uniqueness of the situation—with a recognition of the overall perception of what the library is now and the perception you want others to have of the library at the end of the health crises.
- The "new" approach process should pay great attention to peer and area marketing and brand choices so the library can benefit from related messages. In fact, the recent pandemic approach was modeled after the terrorist language of situation status, escalation, and so on, with ranges of color indicating when the more serious problems or situations might be happening or could happen. These images were successful for terrorism alerts, and the approach had automatic interest, was easier to update, and

had easy-to-understand graphics and a universal terminology. It made sense that a recent successful approach might be a good visual to build on (safety in public spaces was the initial message).

- A "new" pandemic message may be derived from the current message; however, many libraries greatly deviated from standard services to provide pandemic support. With the newer approach to using the facility, it also made sense for a completely new approach that allowed marketing content to build on the fact that the library, a community, an institutional presence, or constituent mainstay was still there and even more a part of possible recovery and, in this case, pandemic recovery.

- Any new marketing, advertising, PR, or branding approaches must be able to be deployed immediately in existing and emergency platforms. To achieve this, universally understood images, uncomplicated language, and being easy to replicate and distribute are critical to the pandemic approach and success. In addition, any messaging during pandemics and other related emergency situations needs the more directive approach that lacks subtlety for a quick adoption and—hopefully—fast recognition.

- Typically, marketing doesn't come with qualifying information, but pandemic messaging for public institutions such as libraries can include a different tone or tenor—such as an expressed regret or apology for the inability to be open or allow user access or provide full services—to minimize conflict or concern over lack of access and gain acceptance not only for the message but also for the level of services temporarily unavailable.

- Obviously—post-pandemic—organizations can return to previous approaches, so closure for existing PR or images or personalities or a "goodbye" or archiving, retiring, or transition as the library moves to a different, newer pandemic approach is *not* needed. Rather, existing information can be suppressed with new links and new pages providing the current and possibly temporary content and approach.

- Public health messages are accompanied—in some areas—with references to local, state, or federal rules and regulations. Libraries, therefore, should cite or "credential" messages; for example, new messaging should reference any overarching institutional, local/community, state, or federal requirements, statements, laws, guidelines, or directives. In addition, and also unique to the situation, messaging might need to have dates included on the copy so that workers will be able to add or replace content and constituents will be able to determine if they have the latest information.

Those seeking to review and revise the library's marketing—for the pandemic as well as (more than likely) post-pandemic—should prepare a snapshot of what the marketing status is within the organization now (including before and during the pandemic). A particularly valuable discussion is one where administrators, middle managers, and representative library workers take a close look at what is happening now/pre-pandemic, but independent of each other, and then individual comments are aggregated and groups or representatives of groups come together to assess what was effective before, evidence or data indicating successes, any changes that were made that were particularly successful, and the post-pandemic marketing future.

Although it is hard to maintain an updated, completely accurate marketing plan, the organization should strive to keep the infrastructure of marketing information current. A particularly important piece of marketing plans is the ongoing list of opportunities for marketing distribution. The audit of the infrastructure provides a quick approach to choosing what will work for the pandemic (see table 11.1).

In trying to determine post-pandemic directions to create new or return to previous marketing information, assessment activities need to occur to determine effectiveness *during* the pandemic. And, obviously, "pre-pandemic" marketing effectiveness is different from "during-pandemic" marketing effectiveness. While pre-COVID-19 levels of marketing and PR effectiveness are determined by literally dozens of different ways of gathering information, several common ones are meeting goals and outcomes, attendance (in-person, first-time, and return users), new users/signups, online user data, observation, reviewing data-gathering sheets (resources used, programs attended), general customer feedback, target population feedback, overall satisfaction levels, and so on. During COVID-19, questions to answer—put simply—are: Did you keep or increase users? Were your new or expanded resources used? Did you meet "typical" needs? Did you meet pandemic needs? If you did, why? If you didn't, why not?

Measurements for successes during a pandemic should focus on:

- approaches to maximizing awareness of pandemic general resources and services (direct advertising to target users and those requiring uses such as home schoolers, K–12 administrators, team leaders and teachers, small businesses through associations, social services' clients through agencies);
- success of matching available services and resources to need (pre, during, and post usage numbers, surveys, testimonials, comparing old and new data);

**TABLE 11.1**
**Marketing Infrastructure—Pandemic**

Publication Date: _____
Review Date/Revised Date: _____
Process Owner: _____

*Note: By no means is any list below a complete list. Each section could have an "etc.," and no commercial or purchase or subscription space is included in the chart deliberately such as buying ad space (online, print media, etc.), and while this approach can be taken, it would be listed on a separate chart or in a separate section of a marketing plan.*

| Infrastructure | Examples—What is and could be used, noting that these are ideas for large and small as well as all types of libraries |
|---|---|
| Unique Marketing—Special Events Emergency Events Public Health Crises Pandemic | Unique Issues and Locations: Critical aspects of emergency event marketing content—Official levels of emergency event; seriousness of emergency event; stages of emergency event through the emergency response team; speed/time needed for creating awareness; chosen governmental agencies (CDC, FEMA, OSHA); ongoing data/dashboard; speed/time needed for informing; speed/time needed for changing behaviors (required PPE and behaviors); institutional changes based on event; avenues of communication available given network of EM managers—see emergency response team, type of information (instructions, levels of awareness of business continuity, alternate use); target populations, needs met/messaging to meet needs |
| Universe of Marketing Possibilities | Communiques including scholarly communications blogs, OER newsletter, parents weekly updates, childcare providers e-lists, links from other websites, newspaper columns (weekly features/monthly features), discipline-specific departmental e-lists, homepage, podcasts, media streams, special services pages, pop-up announcements on resources pages, intros to interactive service sites, student newspapers, faculty group newsletters, CMS institutional page, CMS dashboards, pre-event announcement copy, community group announcements, mailouts through other entities (billing, advertising, etc.), Libguides banner, marquee website announcements, church newsletters/bulletins, educational channels, blogs, online catalog user communiques, notifications on print/paper mailouts, internal signage, external signage/nonprofit, external signage/for-profit, partner signage, partner email lists, phone messages, individual faculty/teacher emails, social media, foundation newsletter, alumni news. |
| General Marketing—Typical Events | Homepage, pop-up announcements on resources pages, pre-event announcement copy, "community" group announcements, mailouts through other entities, banners, marquee website announcements, TV/cable/institutional channels, blogs, online catalogue user communiques, notifications on print/paper mailouts, internal signage, external signage/nonprofit, external signage/for-profit, partner signage, partner email lists, phone messages, social media. |
| Terminology Range | • Online communications—permanent (homepage, etc.)<br>• Online communications—intermittent<br>• Print/paper—signage, posters, snail mail letterhead, flyers, handouts, bookmarks<br>• Social media—the institutions<br>• Social media—general postings, partners<br>• Social media—general postings<br>• Presentations—virtual, in-person<br>• Presentation (handouts)—virtual, in-person<br>• Media/platforms—TV, live web streams, recorded spots |
| Timing | Publication date(s), submission date, editing date, frequency, systematic/consistent distribution, variables in distribution, approval process—internal, external. |
| Use of | Large single announcement/link, full text of message/link for more info, banner, popup, informing temporary change, informing long-term change, access information, general marketing information. |
| Submission Parameters | Length, format, mode of submission (online, file, copies), goals, requests for using, deadline for submission, template/forms to complete. |
| Contact Names, Addresses, etc. | Publisher, reporter, editor, manager, administrative assistant, director, coordinator, addresses for mailing, email address, name of affiliate entity, fax numbers, phone numbers (landline, cell, FB/Twitter). |
| Audience/Profile of Recipient or Reader | Locations, geographic designations, zip codes, ages, income, life status, work environment, work experience, reason for reading (information, entertainment, etc.), language spoken, reading level, tech expertise. |
| Readership | Institution, partners, .com, .edu; all employees, institution partners, .com, .edu; all constituents; target populations; residents; parents of constituents; caregivers of constituents. |

*(continued)*

**TABLE 11.1   *(continued)***

| Infrastructure | Examples—What is and could be used, noting that these are ideas for large and small as well as all types of libraries |
|---|---|
| Viewership Data | Locations, geographic designations, zip codes, ages, income, life status, work environment, work experience, reason for reading (information, entertainment, etc.), language spoken, reading level. |
| Ranking/Likelihood of Success in Reaching Audiences | Have not assessed, some numbers of respondents indicate they have been referred, extensive interest was generated by use of the mode and method, % of users indicating the source they used, # of users indicating the source they used, attendance at the event that was the subject of the message, use of the resource or service that was the subject of the message, testimonials, opinion, cost, match of timing, match of user needing to reach. |

- minimizing user complaints (capturing user/constituent commentary, interview schedules at random, focus groups with random users); and
- typical data gathering delivered in new venues (outdoor program attendance, use of drive-up/pick-up services and resources, constituents using virtual environments).

Not typically a cornerstone of library marketing, more *previews* of services and resources should be part of pandemic marketing in order to respond to needs and move more quickly, to identify what recent or altered subscriptions or access are coming, to quickly and consistently invite and gather feedback and ongoing perceptions of specific needs, to minimize conflict for what isn't able to be used as well as assist in the identification of what may yet be missing from services and how to provide alternative services. This increase in types and styles of PR and advertising include:

- posted notifications of what is coming—typically—weekly;
- projections of times for services;
- descriptions of processes for bringing in new or altered services; and
- identification and focused marketing of tools for helping people during and for the return and post-pandemic including:
  ○ paradigm shifts identifying typical processes and substitute processes;
  ○ paradigm shifts identifying typical resources and substitute resources;
  ○ old floorplans to new floorplans;
  ○ areas outfitted with PPE to match ever-changing governmental guidelines;
  ○ projected return of hours available for what and when;
  ○ suggestions for substitute assistance (alternative places and processes for story times, homework help, use of meeting rooms); and
  ○ tips on best times for using resources, visiting spaces.

### Careful Messaging during Emergency Events

Libraries strive to provide as much as they can for their constituents and in the best way possible. They want to be the first and the best and offer the assistance students, parents, families, professionals, children, graduates, seniors, and so on, need to be supported in their goals and pursuits. It is tempting, therefore, that after libraries carefully make all necessary legal changes and comply with all mandates, they build terms into marketing that constituents want to hear such as "safe spaces" or "virus-free areas" or "sanitized libraries" or "risk-free services." The reality is that no such assurances are possible, nor should they be made in any library messaging. In addition, as regulations relax, workers do *not* want to be put in the position of having to police their areas, keeping restrictions in place that are no longer required in public spaces, or dealing with the conflict around restrictions no matter how necessary or minimal. We simply can't guarantee, promise, or allude to "safe," "risk-free," or "virus-free" zones for ourselves or others.

We can and should say what we *are* doing in language that indicates maximum adherence to rules and regulations, such as:

Library constituents are asked to maintain social distancing required by community standards. To assist in this process, signage, floor markings, and sign-up processes are used to queue up, stagger, and offer multiple opportunities to users to get the help they need, in recommended methods.

Use of meeting rooms now and through [*date*] is still restricted to meetings *but* is available to the alternative services including monitored study and tech/web usage on a first-come, first-served basis for no more than [*number of hours*] at a time. Desktop tech "rests" for [*number of minutes*] after each use, and users are given wipes to use before and after their visit to assist in keeping library spaces clean.

Help us help you by signing up to use the job-placement area to meet your needs and write that perfect résumé to find your perfect job. Presentations by service experts are made on the hour from 1:00 p.m. to 4:00 p.m. every Tuesday, Wednesday, and Thursday to small groups of no more than eight participants in the Phillips meeting room. Participants may bring their own device (with a keyboard) or are able to check out laptops to assist them in the program and in designing a résumé immediately following. Attendees should move to the room fifteen minutes before the event and sit in marked seats. Masks are welcomed, and if you would like to wear one but don't have one with you, please take a complimentary mask from us!

Also, successful public-health marketing can strengthen a library's reputation, increase a library's base of support, expand the number and types of positive perceptions, and bring in new groups of users as well as stakeholders. If new messaging is not possible, however, at the very least libraries should pull or qualify existing messages to minimize disappointment and conflict when regular resources aren't available. If this is the case, libraries should substitute signage, messaging, and postings or provide redirects to simple choices and instructions. Simple changes could include:

We're closed for your safety. Visit our online resources at _____.

We're working remotely to help you. Get the help you need at _____.

Closed now, but opening again on [*date*]. Until then visit us at _____.

No fines, no fees, and 24/7 online assistance at _____.

Because of the chaos and uncertainty that has come with this pandemic, institutions should:

- consider using "what we have and what we don't have" for post-pandemic messaging (first three to six months) (note: this more negative PR messaging is typically *not* recommended for any/all messaging, signage, etc.);
- *not* estimate timelines for returning specifics (such as opening small-group rooms) but instead—in all types of libraries—use "temporary" or "TBA" (to be announced) for returning information;
- for those services that are now "gone" or "off limits," include what the alternate use is, such as quarantining items, safety, and so on;
- call attention to what is new—both positive and negative—to reduce conflict from surprises, and so on (e.g., drive-up services, fabric chairs removed, queues for checkout, appointments and scheduling for using research workstations); and
- consider—in a few targeted messages, in announcements, and on signage—apologies for changing, removing, and so on, in addition to referenced rules, guidelines, and mandates as well as dates for posting.

Additional examples of what works best or a snapshot of the very least of what pandemic marketing should include can be identified after the organization addresses the issues in table 11.2.

Finally, carefully constructed marketing strategies from the pandemic planning group (representative members of advisory groups, the decision-making team, and stakeholders and constituents, etc.) provide managers with pathways to preserving the library's reputation, ensuring strong levels of awareness, familiarity, and knowledge of pandemic business continuity. Effective communication of the role of library and staff expertise during this pandemic makes constituents, workers, administrators, and other internal and external groups fully aware of library roles and responsibilities in both using and working in the library environment.

**TABLE 11.2**
**Pandemic Marketing "Snapshot"**

Publication Date: _____
Review Date/Revised Date: _____
Process Owner: _____

| Area/ Function | Marketing Pre-Pandemic | Marketing during Pandemic | Marketing Post-Pandemic (first three to six months) |
|---|---|---|---|
| Library/ Overall with Hours of Service | Web (each page), doors, local newspapers, book drops, bookmarks in books out, phone message, email signatures | Web/COVID-19 page, doors blocked out, book drops, local newspapers, phone message (all other phone messages off), email signatures, community TV/COVID-19 message emailed to groups ID'd as biggest users | Fewer hours so *big* marketing push to reeducating with community TV, posters, school flyers (return to drop-off), web (all pages), all phone messages, safety featured for post-opening in mailouts, advertising, and on doors |
| Services— General | Web page for services, local newspaper features monthly, flyers to send out when needed, unique flyers to target groups such as assisted living, some social media postings and outreach | Web/COVID-19 page, local newspaper feature, community TV/COVID-19 spot, messages and print/paper posters mailed and emailed to groups identified as biggest users such as elder care/ assisted living, private schools, all social media postings and outreach | Focus on top three: local newspaper features, community talk shows, email and snail mailout to targeted pops of three services being emphasized; safety featured for post-opening in mailouts, advertising, and on doors; increase social media postings and outreach; post-pandemic recovery web content; video stream tour of facilities, services |
| Services— General Reference | Web page for services, local newspaper features, school flyers | Web/COVID-19 page push virtual/ live, community TV/COVID-19 spot, messaging (email) for home schools, more social media postings and outreach | Focus on one of top three: emails to some users (teachers, private schools—safety featured for post-opening or video stream); post-pandemic recovery web content |
| Services— Research Appoint-ments | Web page for services, newspaper features, school flyers, home schools, targeted educational-level emails (all doctoral students, etc.), faculty PR to put on syllabus, student orientations, seasonal signage, CMS posting | Web page for services/virtual/live assistance, targeted educational-level emails (all doctoral students, etc.), faculty PR to put on syllabus, notification on CMS, student life or PPT or video stream, IL web content, faculty e-list | Hours offered shifted to include more live, synchronous, web page sign-up, texting appt. times, permanent CMS posting/tab, presentation in faculty meetings/depts., live offered to home schools, IL web content, faculty e-list |
| Services— Age Level, Children | Web page for services, school newspaper features, school flyers, home school, targeted educational level emails to parents, teachers, caregivers, linking from mirror sites in schools, after-school programs, seasonal signage | Web content linked from COVID-19 page, school website links requested, home school e-list, targeted educational level emails to parents, teachers, caregivers, linking from mirror sites in schools, other child-related such as after-school programs, seasonal web info | Web content linked from post-COVID-19 "return" page, school website link announcement, home school e-list message, targeted educational level emails to parents, teachers, caregivers, linking from mirror sites in schools, other child-related such as after-school programs, seasonal web info |
| Services—Age Level, Youth | Web page for services, school newspaper features, school flyers, home school, targeted educational level emails to parents, teachers, caregivers, linking from mirror sites in schools, after-school programs, seasonal signage, messaging on homework help/live 24/7, social media | Web page for services, school newspaper online features, community clubs for youth, youth church groups newsletter posts, emails with live engagement with youth library advisory group, home school, targeted educational level emails to parents, teachers, linking from mirror sites in schools, event signage (movie releases, marketing youth resources—graphics, games), messaging on homework help/live 24/7, social media | Web page for services, school online newspaper features, emails to community clubs for youth, youth church groups newsletter posts, emails with live engagement with youth library advisory group, home school, targeted educational level emails to parents, teachers, linking from mirror sites in schools, event signage (movie releases, marketing youth resources—graphics, games), messaging on homework help/ live 24/7, social media, socially distanced return of youth advisory group to plan return to youth events |

| Area/<br>Function | Marketing Pre-Pandemic | Marketing during<br>Pandemic | Marketing Post-Pandemic<br>(first three to six months) |
|---|---|---|---|
| Services—<br>Special<br>Pops | Web page for services, newspaper features, school flyers for any unique educational environs, seasonal signage, associations, entities for special pops support | Other languages needed? Web page for services, community groups newspaper online features, church groups newsletter posts, event signage (movie releases), social media, messaging for short-term pandemic support in other languages | Other languages still needed, requested, or used during the pandemic? Web page for services, community groups newspaper online features, church group newsletter posts, social media, messaging for short-term pandemic support in other languages, or video stream in other languages |
| Services—<br>Instruction/<br>IL | Web page for services, newspaper features, school flyers, home school, targeted educational-level emails (all doctoral students, etc.), faculty PR to put on syllabus, student orientations, seasonal signage, CMS posting | Web page for services/virtual/live assistance, targeted educational-level emails (all levels of students, etc.), faculty PR to put on syllabus/on CMS, general notification on CMS, student life or PPT or video stream, IL web content, faculty e-list, video streams | Web page for services/virtual/live assistance, targeted educational level or discipline-specific emails (all levels of students, etc.), faculty PR to put on syllabus, general notification on CMS, student life or PPT or video stream, IL web content, faculty e-list |
| Services—<br>Facility,<br>Small<br>Rooms | School newsletter, library web page, signage in library, signage in related departments, student testimonials used in print and video streams, CMS announcement, student life/partnership announcements, popups on reference web page | Announcement of closure and alternative use (quarantine materials, furniture repositioned for social distancing, staff single offices, etc.); messaging of closure and apology in school newsletter, on library web page, and on COVID-19 page signage in library; signage in related departments; student testimonials used in print and video streams; CMS announcement; student life/partnership announcements; popups on reference web page | Announcement of *continued* closure including why, apology, and alternative use (quarantine materials, furniture repositioned for social distancing, staff single offices, etc.); messaging of closure and apology in school newsletter, on library web page, and on COVID-19 page; signage in library, signage in related institutional departments; signage on doors; student testimonials used in print and video streams; CMS announcement; student life/partnership announcements; popups on reference web page |
| Services—<br>Facility,<br>Meeting<br>Room | Library web page, meeting room brochure, correspondence with community groups, CMS announcement, student life/partnership announcements, partner agreements, partner correspondence, social media, faculty and staff mailout | Announcement of closure and alternative use (quarantine materials, furniture repositioned for social distancing, staff office space, etc.); messaging of closure; status of business continuity; apology on web page and on COVID-19 page; CMS announcement; partnership messaging; social media and faculty and staff mailout | Announcement of *continued* closure including why, apology, and alternative use (quarantine materials, furniture repositioned for social distancing, staff office spaces, etc.); messaging of closure and apology with status of business continuity on library web page and on COVID-19 page, signage in library, and signage on doors; CMS announcement; partnership messaging; social media; faculty and staff mailout |
| Services—<br>Programs | Web page for services, newspaper features, school flyers, home school, targeted educational-level emails (all doctoral students, etc.), faculty PR to put on syllabus, student orientations, seasonal signage, CMS posting | Web page for services/virtual/live assistance, targeted educational-level emails (all levels of students, etc.), faculty PR to put on syllabus/on CMS, general notification on CMS, student life or PPT or video stream, IL web content, faculty e-list, video streams | Web page for services/virtual/live assistance, targeted educational-level or discipline-specific emails (all levels of students, etc.), faculty PR to put on syllabus, general notification on CMS, student life or PPT or video stream, IL web content, faculty e-list |

*(continued)*

**TABLE 11.2** *(continued)*

| Area/ Function | Marketing Pre-Pandemic | Marketing during Pandemic | Marketing Post-Pandemic (first three to six months) |
|---|---|---|---|
| Services— Facilities, Discovery/ Innovation | Library web page, youth program web page, discovery and innovation program and circulation brochure, correspondence with maker clubs/previous attendees, CMS announcement, school messaging, home messaging, social media, student group mailout | Announcement of closure and alternative use of discovery space (quarantine materials, making PPE, furniture repositioned for social distancing, staff office space, etc.); youth program web page; messaging of closure and status of business continuity re: maker programming hiatus; kit checkout; apology on youth page, web page, and on COVID-19 page; CMS announcement on general programming; school messaging; social media; teacher and faculty mailout | Announcement of *continued* closure including why, apology, and alternative use of discovery space (quarantine materials, making PPE, furniture repositioned for social distancing, staff office spaces, etc.); youth program web page; messaging of hiatus and apology; status of business continuity and maker programming hiatus on library web page and on COVID-19 page; social media and web content on general programming; school messaging; teacher and faculty mailout |
| Services— Outreach | Library web page, links to COVID-19; outreach web page; correspondence with leaders of groups the library typically visits to provide outreach; CMS announcement; school messaging; home messaging; social media; student group mailout; internal groups such as departments, partners, and users of outreach services; handouts and brochures for all community visits and programming | Library web page, links to COVID-19; outreach web page; correspondence with leaders of groups the library typically visits to provide outreach; CMS announcement; school messaging; home messaging; social media; student group mailout; internal groups such as departments, partners, and users of outreach services | Library web page, links to COVID-19; outreach web page; correspondence with leaders of groups the library typically visits to provide outreach; CMS announcement; school messaging; home messaging; social media; student group mailout; internal groups such as departments, partners, and users of outreach services; handouts and brochures for all community visits and programming |
| Resources— Print/Paper | Library web page, links to COVID-19; web content links to resources with page and popup notifications, advertising or instructions, CMS announcement, school messaging, social media, targeted, discipline-specific emails to individual and departmental faculty, genre web pathfinders, curriculum support web content/Libguides, specialized messages ("if you like this," bestsellers, homework help, study guides, etc.) | Library web page, links to COVID-19; web content links to resources with page and popup notifications with closure notifications, advertising or instructions, CMS announcement, school messaging, social media, targeted, discipline-specific emails to individual and departmental faculty, genre web pathfinders, curriculum support web content/Libguides, specialized messages ("if you like this," bestsellers, homework help, study guides, "recovery" guides, OER, etc.) | Library web page, links to COVID-19; web content links to resources with page and popup notifications with continued closure notifications, apology and possible return, advertising or instructions, CMS announcement, school messaging, social media, targeted, discipline-specific emails to individual and departmental faculty, genre web pathfinders, curriculum support web content/Libguides, specialized messages ("if you like this," bestsellers, homework help, study guides, "recovery" guides, OER, etc.), media equivalents to print |
| Resources— Digital | Library web page, access instructions, links to COVID-19, web content links to resources with page and popup notifications, advertising or instructions, CMS announcement, faculty professional development, school messaging, social media, targeted, discipline-specific emails to individual and departmental faculty, genre web pathfinders, curriculum support web content/Libguides, specialized messages ("if you like this," bestsellers, homework help, study guides, etc.) | Library web page, access instructions, links to COVID-19, web content links to resources with page and popup notifications, advertising or instructions, CMS announcement, faculty professional development, school messaging, social media, targeted, discipline-specific emails to individual and departmental faculty, genre web pathfinders, curriculum support web content/Libguides, specialized messages ("if you like this," bestsellers, homework help, study guides, "recovery" guides, OER, etc.) | Library web page, access instructions, links to COVID-19, web content links to resources with page and popup notifications, advertising or instructions, CMS announcement, faculty professional development, school messaging, social media, targeted, discipline-specific emails to individual and departmental faculty, genre web pathfinders, curriculum support web content/Libguides, specialized messages ("if you like this," bestsellers, homework help, study guides, "recovery" guides, OER, etc.), media equivalents to print |

| Area/ Function | Marketing Pre-Pandemic | Marketing during Pandemic | Marketing Post-Pandemic (first three to six months) |
|---|---|---|---|
| Resources— Technology, Internal | Library web page, access instructions, web content links to resources with page and popup notifications, advertising or instructions, CMS announcement, faculty professional development, school messaging, social media, targeted, discipline-specific emails to individual and departmental faculty, genre web pathfinders, curriculum support web content/Libguides, specialized messages ("if you like this," bestsellers, homework help, study guides, etc.) | Library web page, access instructions, web content links to resources with page and popup notifications, advertising or instructions, CMS announcement, faculty professional development, school messaging, social media, targeted, discipline-specific emails to individual and departmental faculty, genre web pathfinders, curriculum support web content/ Libguides, specialized messages ("if you like this," bestsellers, homework help, study guides, "recovery" guides, OER, etc.) | Library web page, access instructions, web content links to resources with page and popup notifications, advertising or instructions, CMS announcement, faculty professional development, school messaging, social media, targeted, discipline-specific emails to individual and departmental faculty, genre web pathfinders, curriculum support web content/Libguides, specialized messages ("if you like this," bestsellers, homework help, study guides, "recovery" guides, OER, etc.), media equivalents to print |
| Resources— Technology, External | Library web page, access instructions, CMS announcement, school messaging, social media, curriculum support software, usage Libguides, student and faculty workshops | Library web page, links to COVID-19 page, reduced access/instructions, apology and alternative use (if any), CMS announcement, school messaging, social media, usage Libguides | Library web page, links to COVID-19 page, stages in returning access/ instructions, continued apology, CMS announcement, school messaging, social media, usage Libguides |
| Resources— Realia | Web page for services; home school e-list; targeted educational level emails to parents, teachers, caregivers; linking from mirror sites in community; after-school programs; seasonal signage | Web content linked from COVID-19 page; closure with apology, etc., to home school e-list; targeted educational-level emails to parents, teachers, caregivers; linking from mirror sites in community | Web content linked from post-COVID-19 "return" page; impact of post-pandemic stages with info on realia care and cleaning; reduced access info to school website link announcement; home school e-list message; targeted educational-level emails to parents, teachers, caregivers; linking from mirror sites in schools; other child-related such as after-school programs (broad messaging if library chooses to— for example—check out realia to childcare, parents, after-school, etc.) |

# 12

# Returning to Begin Again

I N ATTEMPTING TO SUM up a list of recommendations in "Returning to Begin Again," a review of content led me to update many comments and add as well as subtract ideas, and—I might add—it had only been two weeks since I'd written the original final chapter. As I read, I was quickly reminded of one of my managers wistfully saying in a May meeting many years ago, "I can't wait for the fall when we won't have anything going on." I quickly asked her to *not* say that out loud again, as—so far—I had never seen a completely peaceful or even low-key fall, and I don't think the profession has had a "slow year" in the last two decades.

What that memory did afford me, however, was a look back at not just the basic structures we have dealt with, but also those things that comprised updates, changes, revisions, measures, and beginnings and endings throughout the years—and there were many. These elements or happenings or activities we have experienced and tried to manage have come from everywhere—aging buildings, new buildings, bad administrative decisions, new administrators, new positions, new staff, staff leaving, changing politics, successful projects, failed projects, the ever-changing marketplace, and innovations, new ideas, and risk taking.

In fact, this sometimes-circus-of-a-profession led me to choosing "change" as the primary area to teach, learn about, and not just deal with but also attempt to master. And many years ago, I began to focus on change—in and of itself—with my goal to attempt to control as much as possible about rampant change at work and, when that wasn't possible, try to organize it with charts, graphs, visuals, identifying value, accountability, data, more data, and dealing with, learning about, structuring, finding comfort in, and seeking change, as well as ultimately looking ahead instead of looking back and focusing on what you can and can't do, and then

finally, opportunities for renewal. So—yes our few weeks out turned into months and then over a year—unbelievably—but organizations moved ahead light years—or at the very least recognized and addressed many difficult issues along the way in accelerated periods of time.

I realized many years ago that I don't want a new normal, but—now—I do want a classic case of reinvention and beginning again with a long, hard look at policies and practices and what's left and what to save from the old *and* the new. So avoiding the word *normal*, we face a new beginning with many opportunities in how business can be done, what we feel comfortable with, and what we have now found out we are capable of. Reading widely and especially outside the profession, we are being told the good news and the bad news (science, nature, public health, and travel and tourism, to name just a few areas), including the following bad news:

- We are entering into a period in history when there will be even more strains of viruses and influenzas—new and transforming—many of which are spillover—that is, transmitted from animals to humans. *Our fall flu season, where we wash our hands a little more often, should be treated much more seriously, and even though we can't control people's sanitary habits individually or at home, we can and must control the care for our work environments.*
- This virus, its variants, and other new viruses will continue to be "long-haul" viruses where not only do they last a longer time but also those infected may recover but continue to have lasting and very serious effects. *This means our workplaces, socially distanced in 2020 and 2021, should remain as such and not return to cramming our users and workers into small spaces.*

- There will be a growth in "super" viral strains where previous vaccines and more typical "flu shots" won't be effective—hence, continuous research for vaccines is here to stay. *Libraries and information centers need to commit to ongoing systematic education, even if it is only maintaining public-health content sites in general or for local spaces—to contribute to creating and sharing accurate representations of what is happening and our role in the changes.*

- Growth in travel continues—logically—to result in rapid spread of existing and new viruses—even with all of the newly instituted safety practices in the travel industry. *A carefully monitored education program for users and workers needs to take place during high travel times for the foreseeable future, and within the guidelines of governmental regulations, managers need to generally remind workers of return-to-workplace behaviors after travel season. Workplaces and managers should examine their own approach to "sick time" to ensure the benefit is seen as one, and that taking or using this benefit is not cause for punitive behavior toward them by managers or team members. In addition, choices of diverse schedules for work locations needs to continue to provide workers with alternatives to coming in to workspaces the 40+ hours a week most work.*

- Geographical areas will move back and forth from open to closed during recovery as moderate gains continue to be misinterpreted and areas relax safe practices too soon or not enough and negate gains. *Travel and tourism industries should be first to commit to and continue new health and safety practices so that peaks and valleys of infections will lessen. Integrating small, consistent steps for public health is often more successful in stopping the spread of disease instead of full starts and full stops of safe practices.*

- Herd immunity is not on the near horizon and may not happen the way it typically does, due to not only medical but also societal issues including the lack of vaccinated people; premature returns to "completely open"; relaxed behaviors; politicization of individual viral and vaccination response; the virus itself mutating and making it difficult for natural immunity to take over; unknown issues for residual health effects and treatment; and different locations (commercial and nonprofit businesses, cities, counties, states, regions, and countries) handling things dramatically differently. *Legislative practices and rules, regulations, and guidelines need to be examined to find the balance of personal liberties at all costs vs. free speech being interpreted as the right to yell "fire" in a crowded theater.*

Scientists—while optimistic about the near future—are honest in saying that COVID is here to stay, and as variants come into being, different ways to manage them will be needed. Projections include that there is likely to be, at the very least, annual surges through 2025, which more typically will track along seasons with summer reductions in infections and cold weather increases.

The good news includes the following:

- Rituals such as handwashing, social distancing, and wearing masks are significantly more common and practiced more "comfortably" and naturally.

- Even though early numbers of 70–80 percent of people saying they now want to work remotely has dropped and will continue to drop to around 30 percent, it is still a significant number, which assists in reduced transmission and management challenges but renewed and better-used workspaces.

- Data show that many people in infected areas are now more careful in public settings, thus contributing to lower transmission rates (if practices continue).

- Continued contact tracing—even at reduced and less invasive levels—is projected to be significant help in identifying transmission possibilities quickly, reducing more serious cases, and identifying those who need treatment earlier.

- Organizations are building more protocols into daily work and life, and umbrella organizations need to build in standards and rewards for adhering to positive protocols moving forward.

- Public health officials are continuing to learn about the virus, virus variants, evolving and more successful treatments, and creation and use of vaccines through ongoing, focused research.

### Returning to Begin Again

Entering a workspace—whether it is a new space, a renovated space, or one that has been vacated for some time—requires a few steps be taken to assess whether or not areas have what they were supposed to have or what workers and users need to be successful. This space assessment should be done, however, by those typically scheduled to work in the space as well as some who have never worked and are likely *not* to work in the space. In addition, following the completion of a "work walkthrough" checklist, there should be role playing with some acting the part of users who—upon entering the space—need to use the library for a number of activities, but typically and most importantly, assistance from public-service areas. These spaces begin inside the buildings but typically outside a primary entry door to ensure that *all* signage is correct.

Missing or incorrect signage or labeling, placement or distancing, or any other issues or questions that might come up are noted on the checklist, and then rather than being corrected then and there, identified questions or possible problems are grouped together to be addressed all at once. Additional areas for discussion include num-

bers of people staffing areas at one time, moving constituents between desks or among spaces, points of contact, and any additional typical constituent services. While often the most critical way to proceed, teams of people from other libraries or other departments can play the roles for simulation of services to increase the likelihood of catching every nuance.

**TABLE 12.1**
**Returning to Begin Again—Work Walkthrough**

Publication Date: _____
Review Date/Revised Date: _____
Process Owner: _____

**Public Services/Circulation Desk**—This set of questions can also be used for information-only desks or for concierge assistance locations either in the library or immediately outside the library.

| Work Walkthrough Questions | Question Specifics | Answers or Questions to Lead to Answers |
|---|---|---|
| 1. In the previous library circulation space, how many people were assigned to the circulation desk on any one shift?<br>2. Why were those numbers of workers scheduled?<br>3. Is any unique expertise needed to work shifts? Maker kit information? Tech support? Language skills? | What—in general—did the worker(s) handle?<br>• The phone?<br>• People in line to check out?<br>• Reserve collections?<br>• Any security gate infractions?<br>• Directional questions?<br>• Referring users to reference?<br>• Taking fines and fees?<br>• User sign-in for shared-space users?<br>• Circulating all items including technology?<br>• Any basic tech instruction?<br>• Checking in technology that has to be assessed?<br>• Help with other area tech (printers, scanners, "I'm lost" questions, ID questions)?<br>• Data/recordkeeping other than tech-driven data? | With new spacing is there the necessary line-of-sight needed or do worker-to-user instructions have to change? |
| 4. How far away are circulation employee and worker cubicle/office space from the circulation desk? | • Will it be easy for people working in cubicles to be a backup for busy times? Nearby? Easy to signal? Will they be able to hear the security gate signal?<br>• Is distance easy to keep?<br>• Do masks prevent understanding?<br>• Does PPE provide protection but not enough contact with users to understand needs?<br>• Is there space for PPE for handing out to be stored at the desk? | The greater the spaces, the more signage and the clearer the instructions must be.<br>What must new customer services scripts cover? |
| 5. What items are needed at circulation for the new desk? | Workers should have a floor plan to either hand out or quickly be able to mark with the intent of easily moving constituents from one location to another. On the back of the map, staff should have a comparison of areas for users so they can have context such as:<br><br>Previous library      New Library<br># of study rooms      # of study rooms<br>Children's library      Children's library<br>Stairwells—two-way      South entry stairwells—up only<br><br>Service points should be numbered or lettered from the map to the list. This is especially critical because the user surveys want specific things from the previous library to be available in the new. This side-by-side is proof of continued services and resources.<br>Library should also create a new hours and services brochure(s) to provide the hours—if they are a return to the same or are varied.<br>There should be PPE for workers and access to PPE for users should they need any.<br>Desks should have queues with "in" and "out" for getting help and choices for getting cleaned materials. | How will circulation desks change?<br>• Categorize directional information/handout<br>• Maps as handouts<br>• PPE and public health safety information |

*(continued)*

**TABLE 12.1** *(continued)*

| Work Walkthrough Questions | Question Specifics | Answers or Questions to Lead to Answers |
|---|---|---|
| 6. Communication between public service desks needs to be specifically identified. How did staff communicate before?<br><br>7. Customer service from the circulation desk? | If it is too hard now to get people's attention, etc., managers should decide on a buzzer/bell that "dings" or a phone call between desks that will work to get attention and impart information from desk to desk. A bell or buzzer is recommended for getting people's attention quickly when circulation staff need quick backup for security gate infractions, etc.<br><br>Create a "we're back" FAQ for constituents. Such as:<br>• Who can help me with computers?<br>• Where can I get a reserve item?<br>• Where can I drink my coffee?<br>• How/where do I book a study room?<br>• How long can I use a computer?<br>• Where are the printers?<br><br>A preliminary FAQ should be done prior to opening; then circulation and reference staff should note use of the FAQ and additional questions needed. It is not unreasonable for the FAQ to change after the first few days of service as you identify what constituents want that you didn't think of before.<br><br>Consider—for the first two weeks after the opening—having a greeter who assists constituents as they come in the door. Libraries often have these greeters after a new opening with significant changes—especially when the area has grown—and they often provide greeters during the first weeks of the first two semesters that the new library is open. | • Design customer scripts for handoff protocols<br>• Categorize "counting" handoffs to capture staffing levels and expertise needed<br>• FAQ web presence<br>• FAQ handout<br>• Training packages—self-directed for staff to experience throughout the year |

**Reference Desk**

| Work Walkthrough Questions | Consultant Comments | Librarian Answers |
|---|---|---|
| 1. In the pre-COVID library space, did only one reference librarian staff the reference desk at any given time? Was there a double staffing or a designated back-up librarian at any specific times?<br><br>2. How far away are librarians' offices from the reference desk? Manager offices? | What—in general—do people who staff the reference desk do?<br>• Provide phone reference?<br>• Assist people at PC workstations?<br>• Support circulation staff when security gate infractions occur?<br>• Scheduling in use of spaces such as quiet study rooms?<br>• Assisting users with technology? Laptops? Other?<br>• Zoom reference or research questions from users?<br><br>How will all of these functions take place in the new space?<br>How will librarians not on reference provide backup for reference? Does the manager need to assist at reference? | • FAQ web presence<br>• FAQ handout<br>• Training packages—self-directed for staff to experience throughout a year<br>• Brief history of staffing, media newsletters<br><br>What is changing should be noted. For example, when the reference desk person calls for the manager to handle a question or deal with a situation, the manager will come to the location to assist, and users are not to be sent to anyone's office or told to wait outside someone's office. |

| Work Walkthrough Questions | Consultant Comments | Librarian Answers |
|---|---|---|
| 3. What items are needed at the reference desk? | Staff should have a floor plan (such as the one for circulation) to either hand out or quickly be able to mark with the intent of easily moving constituents from one location to another or among several locations. On the back of the map, staff should have a comparison of areas for users so they can have context, such as:<br><br>Previous library      New Library<br># of study rooms      # of study rooms<br>Children's library      Children's library<br>Stairwells—two-way      South entry stairwells—up only<br><br>The map should have a service point (numbered or lettered) from the map to the list. This is especially critical because the user surveys want specific things from the previous library to be available in the new. This side-by-side is proof of continued services and resources.<br><br>Library should also create a new hours and services brochure, even though the hours will be the same or if they are a return to the same or are varied. You will have new users, and it's been a while since the old library was open. | Items audit list/buying list embedded in risk spread sheet<br><br>Products:<br>• Customer service scripts<br>• Self-directed training<br>• Information brochures for services<br>• Documentation/ guidelines<br>• Tech list needed to have success downloading, using, and measuring content and meeting services |
| 4. Communication between public service desks needs to be specifically identified. How did staff communicate before? | The new library space is too large to easily get people's attention, etc. Staff should decide on a buzzer/bell that "dings" or a phone call between desks that will work to get attention and impart information from desk to desk. A bell or buzzer is recommended for getting people's attention quickly when reference staff need backup. | • Handouts articulated<br>• Simple instructions for identifying spaces and who uses the what/where of reference. |
| 5. Customer service from the reference desk? | Use the FAQ at circulation for the reference desk as well. Such as:<br>• Who can help me with computers?<br>• Where can I get a reserve item?<br>• Where can I drink my coffee?<br>• How/where do I book a study room?<br><br>A preliminary FAQ should be done prior to opening; then circulation and reference staff should note use of the FAQ and additional questions needed. It is not unreasonable for the FAQ to change after the first few days of service as you identify what constituents want that you didn't think of before.<br><br>Consider—for the first two weeks after the opening—having a greeter who assists constituents as they come in the door. Libraries often have these greeters after a new opening with significant changes—especially when the area has grown—and they often provide greeters during the first weeks of the first two semesters that the new library is open. | • FAQ<br>• Information brochure<br>• Customer services scripts |

**Public Services—Library Desktop Workstations**

| Work Walkthrough Questions | Question Specifics | Answers |
|---|---|---|
| 1. Beginning in [month], there will be fifty seats in the main part of the library with desktop workstations and one to a table. They have PPE on them, cleaning packets, and signage on how to clean. | • Is it clear to users where to sit?<br>• Is it clear to users where they can't sit?<br>• Does desktop signage make sense? Is the time limit clear?<br>• Can someone walking by understand how they can sign up to use desktops? | • Does the sign-up process necessitate any workers leaving their work desks to assist?<br>• Is this service on the FAQ/handout? |

(continued)

**TABLE 12.1**   *(continued)*

| *Work Walkthrough Questions* | *Question Specifics* | *Answers* |
|---|---|---|
| 2. [another public space] | • Is it clear to users how to use the service?<br>• Is it clear to users what is not available to them?<br>• Does signage (desktop, door, tech) make sense? Is the time limit clear?<br>• Can someone walking by understand how they can sign up to use a service? | • Who is the process owner for this space?<br>• Answering questions, handing out FAQ, monitoring sign-ups? |
| **Other Public Service Space Concerns** | | |
| Content | • A need for new opening and closing procedures given the size of space<br>• The design of new scripts for new and/or expanded services (e.g., delay on signing up for small-group study rooms)<br>• Altering orientation for new employees given new space/new space issue (new orientation, training materials)<br>• Design and updating of FAQs | • Who keeps the content up to date for FAQs and online information?<br>• How are problems, changes, and issues submitted to the creative team? |
| Training/Worker Time/ Users Informed | Tours of the new space—it is likely you will get a number of requests for visits to now-open spaces. It's your choice, but to avoid all of the individual requests—for the first month—offer a tour or two tours a day at specific times when *you* can handle and advertise these, but make sure they are offered for a limited period of time *and* that they follow the floor plan given out at circulation and reference desks. That way when you can't do the tour, the map can become a self-directed tour. | • Self-directed tours<br>• Brochure designed to be used as an audit checklist |
| Other | • Adjust scheduling for backup staff at opening and first weeks of semester for both circulation and reference<br>• Compare online information to make sure it complies with in-person space | • Services brochure<br>• Programming handout |

Sadly—our public health crises are now a part of our life, and while only a few of the six outbreaks in the last one hundred years in this generation are as serious—AIDS being the worst and, of course, a global epidemic—the COVID-19 viral transmission is based on exchanges and conditions in everyday life and thus can, over a shorter period of time, infect and kill while people are moving about at home and at work.

Oddly enough, I have been aware of pandemics for most of my life, and for this explanation, I have to reveal some personal issues about myself that have caused me to behave differently not only about myself, beginning at the very young age of twenty-five, but also about public and private spaces under my care.

I began going to our national association meetings at the beginning of my career. In my early twenties at an American Library Association conference in a large Midwestern city, I caught something from someone. And I'm not being coy; I really don't know who or where (which contributes to the feeling of helplessness), but I can track it back to normal professional parties where we went to hotel suites by vendors for large dinners with authors. In addition, I went to two parties with drinks and authors, but when I came home, I was sick and I had to come "*home* home" or back to my parents' home for care. My father, a doctor, took a quick look at my throat and said, "*Maybe* strep, but you'll be fine." My mother—a practic-

ing Christian Scientist—felt she needed to keep a close watch on me. (Yes, you read it right, so please avoid a natural reaction to the irony—as I have learned to do that and you have to as well.) But I got sicker and sicker over the weekend, and almost unable to eat and in the end even swallow—the meds really kicked in to affect me in a bad way but not to treat the problem.

Monday—early evening—I woke up to see a beam of light coming in my childhood bedroom window, and a few seconds later, a few people (visions of old friends, I think) walked in on the beam of light, past me and out the bedroom door. Within the hour, I was at the hospital with cultures taken and on IV fluids—obviously with my father—now both chagrined and concerned, but obviously now convinced he needed to treat it—but at home, as I clearly could infect others and be infected in a hospital. I was officially in quarantine.

Tuesday my father came home—midday—and very seriously sat down (across the room from me) to tell me that the culture wasn't back yet, but his *Journal of the American Medical Association* had arrived and the lead story was about Haemophilus influenza—the cause of several pandemics in history—and I had it and a bad case of it. The virus was then and continue to be a highly infectious, dangerous bacteria with six forms that, according to the CDC, was spread through respiratory droplets. You don't have to be sick to spread it, and while the older population who contracted it and children under five were dying more than others, still more infected contracted meningitis and were also losing limbs due to a variety of things including blood clots. Basically and more commonly, it was causing people's hearts to weaken, where the patient would then die of a heart attack. Sound familiar? Yes, right down to the hallucinations.

Enough said—I was sick for weeks, but of course, I lived, though I was strongly affected by the thought that someone had given it to me, who knows how—on the plane, at the conference, in meetings, at parties—and through dumb luck and living an ordinary life, I had brought it to another part of the United States and put myself and others at risk, to say the very least.

Illness and transmission continue to shape us (well me, anyway), and at thirty-seven, I woke up one morning— after a severe cold with sore throat and swollen glands— with the left side of my face paralyzed and the left side of my body greatly weakened. Although it was hard to diagnose, the doctors finally determined I had Guillain-Barré syndrome (GBS)—a condition that was moving slowing and mysteriously around and was ridiculed because of the age level affected and because it was accompanied by great fatigue (Chronic Fatigue Syndrome, and remember yuppie flu?). According to the CDC, the sickness began a few days or weeks following a respiratory or gastrointestinal viral infection.

Again, I consider myself lucky, and although many who have contracted it were partially or completely paralyzed after their outbreak, I obviously recovered and was told—among other things—that for the rest of my life, vaccinations for anything could increase the risk of the return of GBS, with primarily the paralysis returning. And if you haven't already noticed, many vaccines require you to sign a form that basically says, "We aren't to blame, but the shot can cause a variety of things, so we are warning you, don't sue," and that list contained both of my past virus experiences. So from my early thirties on, I did not take vaccines—unless required by law—and although I have felt a variety of residuals from my only two serious illnesses throughout the years, again, I consider myself extremely lucky and feel I have had far fewer and less serious situations in my life than others have had in theirs and minimal problems. But these episodes greatly affected my public behaviors and caused me to forever take certain precautions in public spaces. And although I don't have obsessive-compulsive issues regarding cleanliness, I feel I do have good judgment on a few things that others typically don't notice about me (I hope), including the following:

- I wear scarves (often daily) and open doors using the scarf to touch doorknobs.

- I shake hands and hug and kiss people on the cheek (but never on the mouth), but I use wipes and sanitizers often.
- I have learned to take great care to *not* touch my face throughout the day.
- When I fly, I don't turn the air on (even though I know federal law has revised air-circulation policies), put my scarf over my mouth and nose, and then frequently put sanitizer lightly on my nostrils and hands throughout the flight.
- I wash my hands often and often blow my nose or use a mild nasal spray—even though I don't have a cold.
- When I go to commercial service desks, I will take care not to touch many or all of the surfaces and will also not touch my face until I leave and use my sanitizer. I also always note the pen-to-borrow containers (now two), which now say "used," "clean," or something to indicate it's safe to use the pen.
- I clean my cell phone frequently (every other day and every day when I travel) and (now) use my scarf or a commercial "pull" to open doors. I also use recommended travel practices for hotel rooms, including cleaning the remote before I use it, wipes for the nightstand, and so on.
- I try to choose restaurants—more clean now than they have ever been—where the tables are farther apart and there are fewer upholstered chairs or other furniture. I also now greatly welcome "new" menus that can be cleaned more often (laminated or in plastic sleeves) or—even better—paper that can be used and then thrown away. (I typically use sanitizer after I use the menu as well.)

Additionally:

- I share my food but not my utensils, and I ask for an extra plate and set of utensils so I *can* share more safely.
- And—I don't believe I have to say this—but I don't eat birthday cake that has had the candles blown out by the celebratory crowd (whether they are family or not) or even just the one whose birthday we are celebrating (hence the rise of the one-candle cupcake for the birthday person who *can* blow out a candle—a delicious alternative, and can I have a cupcake after *every* meal?).

Admittedly, this can all clearly fit under TMI, but these are patterns I have because I have experienced things I don't want to experience again and I don't want to be a carrier. (And now, my one big change is that I take vaccines and flu shots.)

But my own behaviors are only one aspect of taking greater care, and my work goals have always included managing public and private spaces with safety in mind. Standard practices for those environments include actions that support our overall approach to taking care of ourselves and each other:

- We clean our workstations more often during our flu seasons, and—over the years—I have sent out emails/memos that remind people of the current season and times of our patron workflow and encourage them to clean more often, keep the tissues out on desks, and give users—upon request or if they ask for a tissue as well—one of our wrapped clean wipes (safe for people's faces). These practices assist us in a variety of ways: for example, one Monday some years ago, a staff member worked his circulation desk shift, touching everything of course, only to get a call at the end of his shift to be told he had very infectious poison ivy on his hands and wrists from a camping trip he had just returned from.
- When I started at my current job, I stopped the practice of allowing our users to use our work phones on reference or circulation desks (but instead direct them to the ample number of phones throughout the building). While this is less of a problem now, obviously, I recommend to workers that we clean phones at the beginning and ends of shifts as well, because users may ignore signage and use tech when we are away from the desk. (And of course, organizations typically have poor cleaning practices given the physical size and usage patterns of library spaces. To combat this, cleaning schedules and checklists for attention to detail along with larger, more in-depth cleanings are needed.)
- I methodically choose furniture for our spaces that is *not* cloth or difficult to clean and have tried to replace our cloth furniture in the libraries (we have forty-five-year-old furniture in some places and older—but, don't we all?).

Saying that all of this leads to a safer work area at all times and not just during a pandemic really isn't my point, and I can't actually make that claim—but it helps! The goal really is to recognize what new issues we have as managers of workers and spaces and the critical need for us to get ahead of dealing with the results. Our work must focus on training and education for workers and users, preventive behaviors, and ultimately prevention to mitigate the serious consequences we now know can happen. We must have *continuous* care for public and private spaces at work with more cleaning than usual; cleaning

*throughout* open hours; suggestions and guidance for users and workers to have thoughtful practices; revised customer service scripts with language reflecting safety; and new guidelines, reducing points of interaction while still providing excellent services and *not* allowing crowds or close experiences in small groups by spacing people accordingly and masking during and after recovery.

## The Pre-Pandemic Library: If We Had Been Ready

We are more than ready for the future if we just hold on to what was created in a hurry last March or more rapidly than usual during 2020 and 2021 (and note that I have focused on what I can control for my libraries). So here is the summary from every area for "ready" spaces. They should have:

- broad emergency plans in place that go beyond our disaster plans for resource recovery;
- articulated work plans for projects so workers can significantly contribute to or accomplish work in remote or "other" locations;
- enough and appropriate cleaning products for cleaning public and "office" workspaces multiple times each day (templates for workers to outline steps, sign for accountability, etc.);
- workers trained for closures;
- plans and practices for contactless services;
- floorplans ready to go to change—permanently—to a safer redesign with flexible/moveable furniture;
- public-service desk and shared workspace PPE stored for future use when serious flu seasons begin;
- longer and more directional queue lines;
- directional signs posted permanently;
- a list of ready-made signs for—when we need them—reminding people it is cold and flu season or advising people of safer distances apart;
- cross-trained workers ready to step in;
- "other" or external groups designated and trained for assistance (for smaller spaces): stakeholders (advisory board members, Friends, etc.), umbrella organization employees, peers ready to assist, and so on;
- marketing/media content (beyond signage) including news stories, emails, reporting content, data-gathering formats;
- alternate choices for backup reduced-hours service plans;
- instructions for informing closures or reduced hours for mail services, intermittent suppliers, maintenance schedules, and so on;
- awareness trees for informing users scheduled for visits, uses, meetings, and so on;

- quarantine protocols, awareness information, and spaces ready when we are open (no more carts—either by circulation or anywhere in public services—where recently-returned items can be perused for quick check out);
- library bags for carrying even one book out to decrease cloth exposure for the users, then use when it is returned;
- data-gathering packages ready to be implemented;
- research practices ready for tracking public-health or emergency-services practices in the local, state, and federal venues;
- information teams (and supporting content) for advocating for the library ready to be deployed; and
- alternate, faster, and expertise-based decision-making practices articulated and ready to be enacted.

And, in addition to all of the introspective and self-directed activities for the organization, managers and leaders need to turn to their users to become acquainted with their profiles in order to begin to or continue to meet their needs. In fact, while it is possible that we have *not* changed, it is significantly more likely that users have changed their preferences, locations, work life, leisure needs, competencies, and technologies as well as how they would like to access their resources and services.

Why? Library constituents are like any other clients, users, or members of society in that they never change in some areas and constantly change in others. Changes, however, are often realized during extreme times—such as pandemics—and some users launch and embrace changes, while others have changes thrust on them with little or no choice. To capture profiles of members of library communities—whether that community is a city, county, region, higher education setting, hospital, law firm, company, or K–12 environment—libraries should systematically scan their constituents to update for whom they are responsible and their existing and future needs.

These user changes—viewed in profiles—can be dramatic and far-reaching and include employment status, living conditions, schooling and education, tech hardware, software, and access as well as knowledge levels. The need to determine profile changes can and should cause assessments of and possible changes to current services, access to content, remote and in-person use, subscription or ownership content, and—ultimately—possible revisions of mission, goals, and outcomes. In addition, current values statements should also be reviewed to ensure the library's values—as currently stated—match users.

Finally, this monograph has a number of predications, speculations, and recommendations based on information and research from many professions, disciplines, opinions, and experts. That being said, there are a number of additional issues—some more important than others—for libraries now and into the future—that dovetail with current activities, and these drive current and upcoming budget requests, outcomes, the structure of data gathering in general, as well as changes in strategic-planning content and processes. Many of the issues are tangentially related to the pandemic, and some are not, but it wasn't possible to cover all critical issues needing attention going forward. Instead, librarians will need to be aware of the need to integrate these issues, including learning analytics for more meaningful data gathering as well as making evidence-based decisions, "open" initiatives, and a commitment to social justice and equity, diversity, and inclusion.

Finally, most managers in the beginning, midway through, and near-to-end post-pandemic experienced greatly expanded workloads and unrelenting problem solving—often in more of a vacuum than thought possible; thus, no matter the age, energy level, or health—as many emergency situations are addressed and dealt with, and we look to our new openings—there are likely to be many more managers and leaders stepping into different roles in their own or different environments, many retirements of highly experienced workers, and many workers moving up in the ranks in their library or into other spaces so that others may pick up the process to manage and lead. And that's not a bad thing.

# Appendix A

## *General Supporting Content*

I LEARNED FROM MY emergency-management research that there was and continues to be ongoing growth and change in the world of emergency-management research and information and—obviously—not only in the last decade but also significantly since the beginning of 2020. The literature of the library and information profession has also expanded—in regard to emergency management—since 9/11 somewhat, but then significantly beginning in February of 2020.

A surprising amount of information, knowledge, research, and direction about pandemics and related events is already available:

- Emergency-management print/paper resources—while continuing to be updated—have newer, more focused content on pandemic content (obviously) but also on extreme emergency management in general.
- Online emergency-management resources have continued to grow, but the breadth and range of their coverage is unprecedented. Not unlike the pre-Y2K world, almost every print/paper and online resource has a COVID or pandemic column or specialist assigned to relate to and create information. Besides the rush to provide new or quick and easy access to digital content, journal content has changed. Examples include:
  - A *Good Housekeeping* issue will have columns on cleaning spaces, cleaning vs. sanitizing, creating and maintaining work-from-home settings, and recipes for eating responsibly, and so on.
  - *Women's Wear Daily*—a trade publication of the fashion industry—will feature content on not only the impact of the pandemic on business but also sustainability of cloth and other materials likely to be used in upholstery as well as staging

programs, and unique ways to offer presentations with social distancing.
  - *Sports Illustrated* not only focuses on the effect of the pandemic on an entertainment and leisure economy but also contains articles on social distancing for crowds, safety and user bubble spaces, PPE comfort for work environments, as well as the differences in online vs. live/in-person engagement.
  - Extensive government resources have been generated not only to expand government agency general information and assistance but also to identify COVID issues from each agency's perspective with a greatly expanded CDC for each stage of the pandemic and also OSHA, FEMA, Transportation, and Homeland Security, to name just a few federal agency and information centers.
- Existing commercially available products have been identified and categorized to educate on why some products are acceptable while others are not. New commercial products have been created to meet more in-depth needs. Both existing and new products, however, exist in a roller coaster of availability, credibility, and usability.
- Existing educational programs of study not only offer intensive and in-depth content on crises or emergency management in general but also have been updated for pandemic application. Programs of study have introduced new pandemic-specific and related credentials on contact tracing, sanitizing environments, and expanded content on continuity and recovery practices.
- Professions specific and related to emergency management have increased content and altered delivery to provide for shorter, updated training as well as

revised credentialing for those already practicing in the field:

- risk-management associate in risk management (ARM designation);
- contact-tracing certifications (e.g., for public health professionals);
- leadership for remote workers/managers; and
- management content for acclimating/returning to work.

- Training is required not only for those providing services—of all types—but also for those receiving services such as training for teachers and students returning to school environments, safety and risk training for managers for all types of environments, and increased focus on the seriousness of issues such as changed communication training for directors of communication and public relations managers.
- Not only has training for organizations for employees at all levels increased in content and offerings, but also some content is now required at all levels for keeping staff safe as well as patrons, clientele, and so on. Required training is both generic as to the pandemic and safety, and also unique to settings. Most of these categories of content have already been created at level 1—that is, existing content has been revised for early "staying open," "altered services," "newly designed services," and "quick starts." These include in-person, hybrid, and remote settings:
  - offering services within physical spaces while adhering to safety;
  - new customer service scripts designed for staff to work in teams; and
  - new customer service scripts based on assessment of customers, patrons, and client needs, timelines, expectations.
- As well as:
  - external training for required behaviors in communities and environments; and
  - training for using new pandemic forms (safety, tracking, etc.) and following new procedures now required given standards and guidelines.
- Uniquely curated online information designed and maintained in the form of guides, media streams, media channels, and influencers focusing on recovery for the many as well as for their "followers" or self-selected audiences; extensive coping content beyond information in the form of humor, self-help, and do-it-yourself; and vast data and data interpretations and repurposing in dashboards, infographics, and individual as well as geographically specialized knowledge. Examples:
  - For the keyword *pandemic*, the LibGuide community identifies over three thousand pages available, while for the keyword *COVID*, there are over thirteen thousand pages.
  - YouTube media includes thousands of posted streams by individuals, many of which are humor, but most of which are Q&As, interviews, coping tips, safety ideas, and content to assist with remote school and remote work. In addition, hundreds of new and existing YouTube channels are covering or devoted to resources for dealing with pandemic issues and training for current and future activities.

- Emergency-management terminology has changed dramatically with pandemic content generating new terms and expanded meanings for existing terms for pandemic language. Almost immediately (by April 2020), new terms began to be commonly used, and now—halfway through the pandemic—multiple glossaries have been published with widely accepted terms, and already, lists of terms that are now passé have been generated. (Societal communication has been altered given not only new information but also the need to characterize the "new normal" and express thoughts and feelings more with words and tones rather than expressions—in small part—due to the need for masks.)
- Classifications and rankings of pandemic levels are widely adhered to along with common guidelines from primarily federal and state government environments.
- Existing relevant policies (and subsequent, related policy content such as procedures, etc.) have been identified and quickly updated in 2020 spring and summer.
- Legislation, guidelines, requirements, and recommendations were created (both controversial and generally accepted) for local, state, and federal venues.
- Research on the virus's surface and shelf life is extensive, and although it varies somewhat on timelines, the identification of cleaning schedules by surface is relatively fixed for active pandemic behaviors.
- Collection-development models and formulas have been articulated for many years and are diverse and—in many libraries—an ever-evolving issue. In addition to guidelines, values, and parameters for both short- and long-term collection building, librarians identify their collections in a variety of ways—to justify existing, expanded, and altered collection expenditures, areas of collection maintenance such as weeding, and guidelines for accepting donations and acquisitions of collections. Pandemic issues expand ways of identifying characteristics as well as worth and value of collections.

But more than midway through the pandemic—and *not* surprisingly given the depth and breadth of the situation—a large amount of information, knowledge, research, and direction about pandemics and related events is *not* available. What's *not* available yet, and what do professionals need to look for and begin to work on?

- Emergency-management print/paper content—while continuing to be updated—needs a *pandemic* focus for management concerns. This is primarily because, although existing extreme management content is helpful and continuity and recovery content should be able to be tailored to pandemic-level work, the majority of content does not include the permanent changes that are needed for post-pandemic spaces. These changes include floorplan redesign of furniture and public-service assistance spaces; workplace spaces; new policies and human resources content changes and additions such as a remote work infrastructure, position description revisions, customer service scripts, organizational culture assessment and rebuilding, and—among other things—building and integrating a remote and in-person workforce.

- Guides or rubrics for choosing an overall standard for public and individual workspaces are not yet available. Online emergency-management resources—although extraordinarily rich in information—pose a problem in that managers should select standard messages. And while that standard can be driven by the umbrella organization, community standards, or organizational leadership, there is no one message; rather, there are federal guidelines, community choices, institutional approaches, and adaptations. The lack of one standard and the ubiquitous media messaging mean that managers must remain knowledgeable about broad, different, or conflicting content to explain and defend—if necessary—those standards chosen for their environment. The more messaging there is, the more stress the "organization," the employees, and the users experience. Multiple, conflicting messages are divisive without clear channels for communicating and guidelines designed to structure messaging in organizations.

- Commercially available products critical for the process in creating safe environments vary dramatically in design, chemical composition, instructions for use, and availability, including shortages, hoarding, and so on. Given different standards, there are issues around marketing "promises," value, credibility, and usability of classic, altered new, and both known and unknown products. Also, many guides,

standards, and recommended resources are identified to expand practices as well as to add new processes and practices for public and workspace safety and for emergency kits for home and at work.

- Personal protective equipment varies—with no agreement of standards—and is absolutely required for safety in a variety of areas. Although there are significant federal, organizational, and professional guidelines for what and when PPE should be used—by both employees and users—organizational decision making and investment in this area are different. Concerns for this area should be among the first to be decided to clearly define choice of protective public service and staff equipment, organizational support (who buys, etc.), brands, frequency of use, and requirements for public/user and staff interactions as well as staff interactions among team members.

- Transition timelines and paradigm shifts for pandemic behaviors are too early to establish but critical to "watch" in order to reduce stress and clarify behavioral expectations. Current (during lockdown and upon opening) cleaning processes and procedures need to morph into newer, standard (credentialed), and probably less rigorous cleaning (frequency, type, and number of products) for public and workspace environments. And although halfway through a pandemic is *not* the time to standardize or relax rigor, the future for returning to work and ongoing processes will take into account data on herd-immunity timelines; expanded, longitudinal research on surface and shelf life of an active virus; and ongoing assessment with recommendations for not only materials but also frequency. In addition, users will—given their own experiences, education, and perception—choose to behave in certain ways that could include self-cleaning, continued social distancing, and generally expanded awareness of the cleanliness of facilities and the institution's practices moving forward.

- Required orientation, training, and education for staff behaviors (using internal and external training content) are not yet but must be institutionalized immediately and for the foreseeable future. Required behaviors and management expectations for staff must be integrated into a wide variety of human resources. These include dynamic documents such as workplace, team, and individual worker goals; customer service scripts; workplace working plans/schedules; and more static documents such as dress codes/workplace attire requirements and recommendations; related emergency-management documents; and more static documents such as management expectations and requirements; position descriptions; employee evaluations; and any related documents such as volunteer worker guidelines/requirements for behavior, dress, team and customer interactions, and related emergency management.

- Managers must immediately address the plethora of content—advertising, marketing, instructions, recommendations, and so on—for not only staff but also users and then assess and choose the standard information to be integrated and maintained into operations. Although libraries will maintain a broad representation of knowledge and information as part of their content pathways, specific knowledge for use for institutional *operations* will need to be vetted, selected, and curated for the library's context and then built into the organization's communication including user and staff behavioral guidelines; facilities design; labels, instructions, and signage; customer service scripts; team/internal expectations; and web design.

- Managers will continue to review, assess, and restructure as needed schedules for in-person vs. remote work. Organizations will need to decide on—for example—public service furniture and space uses, worker shifts and use of staff public workstations, and workplace behind-the-scenes spaces.

- Managers must determine acceptable terminology for internal and external discussions and exchanges/service delivery. A common terminology will drive behaviors, interpretations, policy review, and design of new procedures—as well as reduce stress and contribute to order. Common language (and thus behaviors) will serve to assist in determining how workplaces will operate and—hopefully—reflect equity in service and resource delivery as well as treatment of users and staff, and reduce feelings of fear and inadequacy for public interactions and workplace exchanges.

- Standard communication processes will reduce the chaos of conflicting messages and content regarding the identification and articulation of levels of threat. Standardized processes should be designed for how workers will follow the internal path of the organization, but they will also provide a way for employees to manage the diverse communication *they* are hearing and bringing to the workplace. Reducing this chaos is critical to provide one vision and one approach to communication in general but especially for one way to share recommendations and requirements—and in doing so—divorce choices for safety from political expression. Standard terminology can include:

  - text with a set of words/terms in subject heads that signal the goal of the communique such as *Alert*, *Update*, or *Return to Service*;
  - locations identified the same each time they are addressed with matching signage at location entry points such as "West Main Building Entry Double Doors";
  - dates/times in standard forms;
  - standard pandemic terms such as *social distancing* and *PPE*;
  - identified institutional approach (schools named safety measures after mascots, public libraries identified safety approaches in coordination with the city nomenclature) safety measures in place;
  - links identified in standard location;
  - colors, typefaces, and banners remain throughout each communique;
  - important announcements identified in a sequence such as "February 2021 Update, Week 1: Safety Required for West Main Building Entry Double Doors" and "February 2021 Update, Week 2: Safety Required for West Main Building Entry Double Doors."

- Measures of success for required and recommended behaviors must be identified, articulated, and integrated into the workplace. If an organization requires that workers follow certain guidelines, metrics must be in place to record infringements, and in the case of the pandemic, if these required activities are not adhered to, it can result in illness and death. With that in mind, managers should not only identify assessment practices with verification (observation; reports—coworkers; reports—users; self-disclosure, etc.) but also identify punitive measures. Given the seriousness of the infractions committed and verified, zero tolerance would be the most important approach to ensuring safety practices remain in place. Zero tolerance could then include: leave without pay, written reprimands, probation, and firing.

- Managers must assess legislative agendas and content (law, opinion, precedent, etc.) to interpret and determine what is appropriate for the organization. Legislation (both controversial and generally accepted) from local, state, and federal legislative environments will have to be continuously assessed and revised throughout the first, second, and third years of the end of the pandemic and post-pandemic.

- Research on the virus and pandemic issues needs to be continuously verified, and recommendations resulting from the data need to be integrated into post-pandemic organizational practices. The organization's communication plan should include a process for the intake of information, the credentialing of sources, and the choice and adoption of practices from specific channels of information. As the pandemic grew and society grew familiar with agencies of note, globally and nationally approved sources, expert credentialing, and more standard information channels in the media, organizations also gained standardized patterns and networks to rely on for infrastructure for decision making.

- Facility design for public-service workspaces and staff workspaces and work life needs to be assessed for future remodel, renovation, and new construction. The majority of libraries cannot afford to retain redesigned during-pandemic floorplans given the size of the facility and the number of users and the communities' need. In addition, library worker workspaces—already much too small in design—will eventually return to full staffing and full workdays and work schedules. With this in mind, organizations need to identify permanent changes that can contribute to worker safety, such as changes to HVAC cleaning schedules, filters, and so on; cleaning of both public and private workspaces; limiting numbers of users and workers in specific areas (meetings, programs, etc.) as well as decisions that include retaining air care such as fans and air sanitizing, as well as maintaining stricter procedures for receiving print/paper materials and the length of time delay for ongoing seclusion of materials. In addition, there needs to be signage seeking distances between or among people, in and out traffic patterns for shelves and browsing, as well as a very careful look at the placement and use of library realia in youth and family areas.

- Budgets need to be analyzed for ongoing post-pandemic behaviors to determine appropriate directions for future expenditures. Assessing budgets is a critical activity upon the immediate assignment of pandemic status and in pandemic and post-pandemic activities. Organizations should audit their expenditures to determine what dollars must continue and what needs to cease and how the organization will continue to support choices.

- Practices need to be evaluated to determine which programs and services need to be permanently altered. These activities could include:

  ◦ in-person program issues such as size of/attendance, location, types, and timelines need to be evaluated for end-of-pandemic and year 1 (at least) post-pandemic offerings, including age-level programming, instruction, cultural activities, recreational events, and so on;

  ◦ services such as testing and the pedagogy of active learning (more-than-one or self-directed, small and large group) need to be studied with research driving decision making, including reviewing data (e.g., virus spread, contact tracing, institutional reports, etc.);

  ◦ facilities usage must be assessed for social distancing and use of specific spaces such as discovery spaces, teaching spaces, small-group rooms, meeting space, and so on, needs to be studied with research driving decision making, including reviewing data (e.g., standards, transmissions, cleaning processes, etc.);

  ◦ furniture and equipment usage must be assessed for safety, cleaning processes, arrangement, and labeling or signage;

  ◦ resource usage (materials passing among employees and users) needs to be evaluated for end-of-pandemic and year 1 (at least) post-pandemic services;

  ◦ delivery of in-person operations activities for employees such as individuals, teams, and workgroups, such as training, educational coursework, office, or workspace/staff meetings; and

  ◦ collection building needs to be reviewed regarding policies and practices, to determine if materials will be acquired, accepted, stored, cleaned, and so on, in the same ways as determined by pandemic issues.

- Rebuilding the organization's culture and team is ongoing, during "out" or closure as well as critical/first-day management and leadership work. People have experienced some but certainly not all of this work. Managers and staff have not yet begun to fathom the amount of work and the length of time it will take to restore a collective positive feeling of safety in not only public spaces but also office and workspaces as well. Managers need to address content for and processes to create team building now—whether organizations are working in-person or remotely, and if organizations have *not* returned to the workplace yet, managers need to build up to a new organizational culture for transitioning the team and then putting the team back together again in a hybrid or in-person setting.

- Managers need to identify recommended training on "change." Although there is an abundance of curriculum on change, most of it does not address the magnitude of change that the pandemic has caused. Obviously, this situation has caused things to change and created not just temporary or short-term change but also long-term and, in many cases, permanent change. Transitioning employees and workers to "new" is not a one-shot situation but must be an ongoing group as well as individual approach to moving individuals and groups to positive environments.

- Ongoing management training for end-of-pandemic and post-pandemic new or newer areas should be a focus including remote management, team building, and new assessments. While there is typically never enough management training, in organizations it is important that every opportunity to grow new managers or expand manager skillsets be taken. So, although team building and assessment are often found in management training, remote management is a newer and more unknown curriculum. Post-pandemic environments can take advantage of not only newer curriculum but also the expanded experiential work that pandemic workplaces can offer.

- Ongoing leadership training for end-of-pandemic and post-COVID return should be a focus with emphasis on remote leadership and communication. Although organizations should take care to recognize and create training, education, and development opportunities for managers, they should specifically provide curriculum separate of management with a focus on leadership. In fact, just as remote management education opportunities are needed, remote leadership content is equally as critical and different. In leadership opportunities, however, as in management, experiential opportunities are possible post-pandemic.

# Appendix B

## *Supporting Content for COVID-19/Pandemic Events*

IN TODAY'S RAPIDLY CHANGING information and knowledge environment, the difficulty is often in narrowing down what specifically should be *systematically* consulted.

Although there are dozens of specific and related journals in the field of emergency management, many are technical, specific to areas (e.g., transportation, hazardous materials), hard to access (without access to research collections or professional memberships), and not applicable in a library or even a general facility setting. In the past years (many since 9/11), online aggregated information resources have grown in number, including product websites (valuable vendor education), agency content, and databases (commercial and institutional, agency, etc.). Related content has also greatly expanded, and during the pandemic, there have been few—if any—periodicals, journals, and general information resources that do *not* include pandemic and pandemic-related content. The following lists are culled from many areas and include content helpful to administrators and managers as well as the organization's pandemic coordinator or emergency-management team or workgroup—or even advisory assistance.

Of course, materials can be interlibrary-loaned but are also accessible from publisher websites, from online vendor materials, from library or association databases, or directly from association websites. Various levels of access are in play, including free, open source, partially free, fee-based, and so on.

It is critical, however, for administrators and managers to narrow down content, so although almost every publication has had a pandemic or COVID focus, the "go to" resources for critical, ongoing information and research (current, credentialed, etc.) can be found in:

- professional journals from emergency-management, disaster, and risk professions;
- journals, guides, and column content from the library and information-science profession;
- state library guides;
- online and print/paper from professional associations as well as conference proceedings;
- content from related professions or areas such as city and county management government;
- content from umbrella organization publications; education; and federal, state, regional, and local agencies;
- recognized, sanctioned, or representative global and also national organizations;
- first-responder content;
- health professions;
- travel and tourism industry information;
- K–12 education content; and
- higher education information and research.

# Appendix C

## *Recommended Resources*

---

Due to the nature of the rapidly changing pandemic, the unpredictable trajectory, and the uncharted territory created, recommended content includes dynamic web content with some basic infrastructure or more "classic" information. Users should not necessarily look at the *page* publication date, as many resources are provided in updated modes such as Libguides, blogs, wikis, and so on.

Alexander, Sally, and Mary Breighner. *Risk Management and Insurance Manual for Libraries.*
Chicago: American Library Association, 2021.

American Library Association. ALA Allied Professional Association (ALA-APA). ala-apa.org (accessed December 10, 2020).
With a focus on human resources in libraries, ALA-APA offers salary and staffing data and research as well as in-depth HR information for managers and staff in the newsletter *Library Worklife*. Managers should regularly review *Library Worklife* content on HR law, HR practice, recruitment, salaries, statistics, unions, and most—if not all—aspects of work life.

American Library Association. "Covid-19 Recovery." ala.org (accessed December 31, 2020).
Although the ALA is recommended for obvious reasons (expert contributions, all types and sizes of libraries, etc.), content is embedded throughout the association's website in a wide variety of areas. While all association resources are helpful and users can begin by reviewing type-of-library divisions, functional areas, or general disaster management, users should begin by visiting the "Covid-19 Recovery" page for links in four areas: advocacy and policy; education; data and research; and guidance content and protocols. Managers should use these resources for extensive information for reopening, distance learning, materials handling, and K–12 students for services and using libraries and virtual programming—

to name just a few areas of information. Specifically, data managers should reference:
- "Academic Librarianship in the Wake of the Coronavirus": ala.org/acre/conferences/elearning/acrlpresents (accessed January 4, 2021).
- "Coronavirus Pandemic (2019–2020) Tools|Publications|Resources": ala.org/tools/future/trends/coronavirus (accessed January 4, 2021).
- "Guidelines for Reopening Libraries during the Covid-19 Pandemic": ala.org/advocacy/intfreedom/reopeningguidelines (accessed January 4, 2021).
- "Handling Library Materials and Collections during a Pandemic": ala.org/alcts/preservationweek/resources/pandemic (accessed January 4, 2021).
- "Pandemic Preparedness: Resources for Libraries": ala.org/tools/atoz/pandemic-preparedness (accessed January 4, 2021).
- "Pandemic Resources for School Libraries": ala.org/aasl/about/pandemic (accessed January 4, 2021).
- "School Librarian Role in Pandemic Learning Conditions": ala.org/aasl/sites/ala.org.aasl/files/content/advocacy/SchoolLibrarianRolePandemic_Resources_Chart_200713.pdf (accessed January 4, 2021).

American Red Cross. redcross.org (accessed December 30, 2020).
The Red Cross website contains valuable information on food and housing challenges to support pandemic-affected populations; unique Red Cross services during the pandemic such as safety for blood donations, healthy practices and safety tips during the pandemic for workplace or home settings, dealing with stress, and assistance during emergencies occurring during the pandemic; and content for families and K–12 teachers for student safety when returning to the classroom. Managers can use the site for basic training curriculum, on-site or virtual training from Red Cross workers, as well as recommendations for employee safety in commuting/traveling to work. Local Red Cross operations also

provide services matching unique community or environmental needs, happenings, events, or activities.

Biden, Joseph R. "COVID-19—the Biden-Harris Plan to Beat COVID-19: Read the National Strategy for the COVID-19 Response and Pandemic Preparedness." Washington, DC: The White House. whitehouse.gov/priorities (accessed January 21, 2021).

A detailed, action-driven plan, providing strategies—with a science infrastructure—for stopping the expanse and effects of the COVID-19 pandemic. Institutions should access this not only as a critical resource to add to their users' pandemic resources but also to determine what the library should plan for as it recovers and assists the community in recovering.

Board of Library Commissioners, Massachusetts Libraries. "Library Space—A PLANNING RESOURCE FOR LIBRARIANS: Pandemic Considerations for Library Design." mblc.state.ma.us/programs-and-support/construction/libraryspace.php (accessed January 6, 2021).

An addendum to the library's extensive general space-planning document and explanatory web-delivered workshop, this four-page addendum has good introductory information with references back to the main document under "Flexibility—Even More Essential," "Functional, Safe Interiors," and "Enhanced Exterior Spaces." This excellent "laundry list" of recommendations includes specific HVAC technical information as well as good alternative ideas for—for example—touchless delivery. This is a great discussion starter as well as a beginning budget list for planners.

California State University. "MERLOT." merlot.org (accessed January 1, 2021).

MERLOT, the online academic community for exemplary curriculum materials, provides a variety of materials on COVID. Users can limit searches to credentialed content—recommended from other sources—and also by types of content, formats, and so on. Managers should use any commonly used search terms and will find resources putting search terms into the general search function; then if too few resources are found, they can immediately link to the search using the same terms but in "other libraries."

Centers for Disease Control and Prevention, U.S. Department of Health and Human Services. cdc.gov (accessed December 30, 2020).

Even though the CDC's roles, responsibilities, and communication were questioned in the early stages of the pandemic, the agency remains the core resource for information, knowledge, and data for decision making about the pandemic threat. In addition, their web content (articles, resource lists, toolkits, research, data, etc.) is extensive and includes critical resources for workplaces of all types and sizes, family settings or "home life," as well as in-depth, specific information for children, such as children in families, caregivers, educational environments, and so on, individuals with special needs, or those in unique situations. Keywords for the CDC website include "COVID-19" (over 100,000 references by December 31, 2020), "public spaces," "workplaces," "business," "workers," "healthcare," "non-healthcare," and specific age-level references such as "children," "kids," and "adolescents," and specifically "pandemic preparedness," to name just a few areas. Managers can consult the CDC for updated recommendations on spaces, timelines, public behaviors, worker safety, workplace safety, and other basic guidelines.

Chmara, Theresa, J.D. "Guidelines for Reopening Libraries during the COVID-19 Pandemic." Intellectual Freedom Committee, American Library Association, June 8, 2020: https://www.ala.org/advocacy/intfreedom/reopeningguidelines (Accessed September 16, 2021).

An excellent set of six questions and answers with additional links, designed to offer initial legal information regarding pandemics, access, requirements, and so on, for libraries. Managers should not miss this initial content on human resources and user operations in these unusual times. While the content has the usual disclaimer on using legal information, these answers provide a critical starting point for equitable treatment while ensuring maximum efforts for safety and security.

Disaster Recovery Journal. drj.com (accessed December 15, 2020).

A free online journal, the *Disaster Recovery Journal* provides both general/overview and specific disaster-recovery information for a wide spectrum of professions. This publication provides articles (current and archival), industry news, white papers, rules and regulations, and sample plans. Their content focus includes business continuity, disaster recovery, crisis management and communications, and risk management. Managers will get a broad range of information on current topics, pre-, during-, end-of-, and post-pandemic articles, as well as reports and sample plans (business continuity, preparedness, etc.).

EDUCAUSE. educause.org (accessed January 1, 2021).

EDUCAUSE resources are a primary support for higher education, and during the pandemic, during the end of the pandemic, and post-pandemic, managers should keep up with the association's "Covid-19" page; articles focusing on fall 2020 institutions and their individual "case study" or solutions; free fall 2020 webinars and video recordings; second-level pages on contact-tracing practices, recommendations, and apps; libraries pages such as "Libraries and Technology"; and the latest on copyright and "examples" content (in many modes) such as conference downloads and infographics like *Top IT Issues 2021: Post Pandemic Futures*.

Federal Emergency Management Administration, U.S. Department of Homeland Security. fema.gov (accessed January 1, 2021).

FEMA's homepage refers users to the partnership website coronavirus.gov as well as the FEMA information page

"Coronavirus (COVID-19) Response." This page focuses on FEMA's coordination of content from local, state, and regional sources as well as other federal content. Managers can significantly and directly benefit from workplace content, including "Coronavirus Rumor Control."

*Global Change Data Lab*, Oxford Martin Programme on Global Development. Our World in Data. ourworldindata.org (accessed December 31, 2020).

Open-source data on global issues, Our World in Data provides dynamic data on current issues with thousands of pieces of data in visual displays with analytics. Although many topics include the current pandemic situation, specific information is found under "Coronavirus Pandemic (COVID-19)." A major strength of the site—along with the sheer magnitude of statistics and other research—is its currency (dynamic with the latest data uploaded only six hours before the author visited the page on December 21, 2020).

Managers could use the website for current data on the pandemic with data parsed into question sections: the daily number of confirmed cases; daily confirmed cases and bending the curve; daily confirmed cases: when countries bend the curve; the cumulative number of confirmed cases; cumulative confirmed cases: data on rapid increase; biweekly cases: where increases and falls exist; and global cases in comparison: locations of most rapid increases as well as ideas on how to envision local data. Users can download and create their own visuals and find data on workplaces and workers in general.

Occupational Safety and Health Administration, U.S. Department of Labor. osha.gov (accessed January 1, 2021).

The entire OSHA website—always devoted to their vision of "protecting the American workforce"—has been revised to provide extensive, excellent workplace information. Managers should go here first to not only review "Standards" but also have access to legal references, interpretations, detailed PPE content, recommendations on delivery of types of services, and in-depth training designed to be used with employees as part of their required content. In addition, two critical additions to a manager's reading materials should be the free subscription to the OSHA newsletter found at dol.gov and the content delivered through OSHA RSS feeds for changes on the OSHA website in general at osha.gov.

OCLC. oclc.org (accessed January 1, 2021).

Although the library and information profession has a variety of excellent research and information environments to support pandemic decision making, OCLC has combined their exemplary content—internationally accepted research (IMLS, Battelle, OCLC, etc.)—as well as case content with best and effective practices from today's libraries to assist in global reopening. Managers should use OCLC research in general as well as resources linked from "Covid-19" and "Information and Resources to Help." The specific research from Project REALM provides data to make decisions for continuing services or reopening plans for handling materials and managing facilities.

OCLC Research, Webjunction. webjunction.org (accessed January 4, 2021).

This OCLC web content and delivery portal provides extensive in-depth content (webinars, podcasts, articles, and links to research and data) on the pandemic, COVID-19, and so on, and—although Webjunction is often primarily seen as having a public library focus—all types and sizes of libraries will find valuable information. Managers should reference their online free webinar list (almost fifty opportunities in looking at January 2021) and their homepage COVID-19 panel of resources with links to articles, events, and critical data. In addition, managers should *not* miss the news from the field with links to examples of plans of libraries for employee safety, restructuring programs, and redesigning library spaces.

Skift, Inc. skift.com (accessed January 4, 2021).

While a library manager would not normally track content on a travel industry website, Skift (translated as "transforming") was designed to provide a unified and transformative single point of entry on new and trending content on the global business. Skift, however, provides unique information on public spaces (lobbies, airports, etc.), moving among public spaces, layout/design and furniture needed for public spaces, and excellent customer service perspectives for not only customer–organization relationship but also contactless interactions. Managers assessing how their spaces should look, reviewing trends on temporary and longer-term flexibility of public space settings, and those making decisions on protecting frontline staff interacting with clients will benefit from Skift.

Todaro, Julie. *Emergency Preparedness for Libraries*, 2nd ed. Lanham, MD: Rowman & Littlefield, 2020.

At the heart of any effective response to emergencies is the organization inherent in the basics of emergency management. Using this 2020 monograph provides many specifics just on libraries in the context of the broader topic of overall preparedness. This monograph also includes a variety of examples for problem solving, examples by type of library, forms for use throughout events, and tools to use to assist managers and employees in dealing with all sizes and types of activities. Managers will find the following content helpful:

- Scenarios by type of library (all types are included) provide extensive "rollouts" of the application of planning documents. (Note: Cases are designed with "answers." This is a standard technique in educational settings that are asynchronous and self-directed, or business settings, due to the fact that in the absence of being able to move readers through issues to solutions, the steps with possible answers are outlined for managers to use with employees or peers.)
- Emergency-management planning steps are outlined in detail (planning, prevention, response/business continuity, and recovery).

- Day 1 and day 2 content provides the quick starts applicable to all levels and types of emergency events.
- Multiple paradigm shifts—applicable to all types of libraries and library functions, resources, and services—provide in-depth, detailed examples and are designed to be easily replicated.

U.S. Department of Health and Human Services. hhs.gov (accessed January 1, 2021).

The U.S. Department of Health and Human Services focus is on safety for families, homes, children (in all settings), and medical information for personal safety and assistance. Pandemic content for children, families, and caregivers includes new guidelines for virtual visits for social workers, links to content on pandemic assistance and children with special needs, content on learning from home, behavioral recommendations and how to talk with children about infectious diseases, pregnancy and COVID, housing issues for those with children related to homelessness, seeking spaces while children learn online, and childcare. Managers should consult recommendations on information sharing, personal safety, and families as well as guidelines for changing interactions for families seeking assistance or working with social workers, childcare, and so on.

U.S. General Services Administration, Technology Transformation Service. usa.gov (accessed January 1, 2021).

USA.gov—a search engine designed to search all federal agencies—provides a single search into all federal agency information. While this search engine includes more commonly used agency content, since all government entities are searchable, agencies such as the Environmental Protection Agency and additional online resources such as Ready.gov are discoverable. Managers can find many resources through this tool, and the most successful searches limit using specific terms, specific agencies, and dates as well as keywords such as "guide," "toolkit," "playbook," and "handbook."

White House, Centers for Disease Control and Prevention, U.S. Department of Homeland Security, and Federal Emergency Management Administration. coronavirus.gov (accessed December 31, 2020).

This partnership website provides the latest White House coronavirus taskforce information with basic guidelines and links to a variety of other federal government online content. In addition to these resources, however, are links to YouTube channel media streams from leaders in the pandemic fight such as Dr. Anthony Fauci. Managers should use this content to determine the latest federal guidelines for assistance in guiding staff in social distancing, identification of symptoms, and where to get treatment as well as other information for business and workplace environments. Clearly managers must adhere to HIPAA when assisting staff; however, managers can easily refer staff to basic government information—in cooperation with organization or umbrella institution HR departments.

World Health Organization, United Nations. who.int (accessed December 29, 2020).

A specialized agency of the United Nations since 1948, the World Health Organization (WHO) is the agency tasked with the responsibility for monitoring and gathering data on international public health. The WHO, very much in the news since spring of 2020, maintains an extensive data-driven web environment. Besides providing this dashboard of information, this organization has provided global data (and links to other content) on information, science timelines, chronological leadership communication and decision making, advice for healthcare workers, risk management, and recovery resources. Managers should use the WHO's extensive, annotated timeline data and longitudinal charts to speculate on second-level or even third-level planning as well as visit "Situational Reports." Managers should then access WHO's interactive learning platform—OpenWHO—(see "Courses"), which offers free online courses on a variety of aspects of health emergencies. Designed for first responders, primarily, there are several core training courses applicable for any public service workers. In addition, all courses are available in a wide variety of languages.

YouTube. youtube.com (accessed January 1, 2021).

YouTube searches are successful with common emergency-management keyword searches; however, the strength of YouTube lies in the users' ability to parse out what they need given delimiters under "Search," then "Filter." Filter categories, combined with user search terms—such as using the search term *COVID training* with the delimiter *channel*—provides an extensive list of training videos for managers to use with their employees. Media content could be limited by date, and that—coupled with terms such as *curriculum* or *training curriculum*—can be further identified by loading date, length, and intended audiences. Managers have a wealth of information available, and faced with an extensive list, they can search by known agencies for credentialed materials. A successful search—for example—would be "CDC COVID employee training materials."

In addition to web-based content with some print/paper content, there are apps and other online collections in related fields.

## Apps

There are a myriad of apps available in emergency management in general as well as apps specific to the current pandemic environment. They are designed to assist in dealing with all aspects of the pandemic. These apps—both fee and free—support the contact-tracing process, testing, locating COVID support resources, diagnosis, treatment, aggregate and offer data, transmission information, exposure notification, and recovery, to name just a few areas. As with other issues, institutions, agencies, businesses, and different professions have their own—typically free—apps, while other apps are created and sold for general use. Obviously apps can be vetted as other resources are, such as based on—for example—authoring credentials. USA.gov maintains an A-to-Z one-stop landing page for "mobile apps" where any federal agency or departmental apps can be found.

### Databases

Library collections are designed to provide extensive content to support academic programs (education environments), general consumer content (public environments), and unique, special access (often restricted to specific targeted association members or employees of an agency).

Although there are dozens of curated content products and tools, the following list is narrowed to those collections or databases of resources specifically on disaster and emergency management, with some free and others commercial or subscription content. The following list includes general topic (heavily used, considered premier in breadth and depth), science or health subscription databases with extensive pandemic and COVID-19 information, several databases on emergency management and agency and institutional datasets, selected content with federal agency information, and the public health profession's research and reporting. (Several of these specialized limited-use collections are freely available on the web, accessible by signing up, a combination of free and fee and subscription only. Users seeking content not readily available should also note that many of these are available through state agencies as well as large educational institutions where access is possible through user status, guest status, or possible community, area, or network-driven card-only access.)

In addition, many online collections provide streamlined access to topical content through "front"-page recommended search terms, above-banner links, added tabs above search windows, additions to advanced searches, curated content pathways, and content organized and labeled for specific users such as "family," "supervisors," and "health professionals." (All content was last accessed by the author on December 30, 2020.)

- Business Continuity and Disaster Recovery Reference Center (www.ebsco.com/products/research-databases/business-continuity-disaster-recovery-reference-center): The reference center covers all aspects of business continuity and disaster recovery,

including risk evaluation, emergency preparedness, and crisis communications.
- CINAHL Complete—Cumulative Index to Nursing and Allied Health Literature (www.ebsco.com/products/research-databases/cinahl-complete): CINAHL is a definitive research database for nursing and allied health professionals in a readable, easily understandable format. It provides access to thousands of full-text journals and indexed journals, evidence-based care sheets, curriculum and lessons, continuing education modules, and research instruments.
- Disaster Lit: Resource Guide for Disaster Medicine and Public Health (www.nlm.nih.gov/dimrc/disasterinfo.html): Disaster Lit offers the National Library of Medicine's management research center with thousands of in-depth articles, research projects, and sample plans and templates. This database contains links to disaster medicine and public health documents available on the internet at no cost. Documents include expert guidelines, research reports, conference proceedings, training classes, factsheets, websites, databases, and similar materials selected from over seven hundred organizations for a professional audience.
- Health Source: Consumer Edition (www.ebsco.com/products/research-databases/health-source-consumer-edition): This consumer-designed web content provides authoritative health information and wellness practices on current practices and policies.
- *Journal of Homeland Security and Emergency Management* (degruyter.com and hsdl.org): The journal offers research articles regarding homeland security and emergency management as well as news, reviews, and editorials. Many articles are freely available with registration. The agency also offers the Homeland Security Digital Library, an online database with an in-depth collection of homeland security policy and strategy documents, including presidential directives, theses, and reports from universities, organizations, and state and local agencies. (Note: Access is limited by the Department of Homeland Security. State employees with standard state email addresses can register for remote access to this database by clicking on the "Request an Individual HSDL Account" link on the database home page.)
- MetaLib GPO (metalib.gpo.gov): MetaLib searches multiple U.S. federal government databases, retrieving reports, articles, and citations.
- SafetyLit (www.safetylit.org): SafetyLit offers abstracts and citations for reports, charts, data, and articles on an individual's health.

## Vendor/Member-Based Organizations

Vendor content plays a unique role in today's continuing-education marketplace. So, although vendors have always provided goals and instructions for using their products, the expansion of overall education has greatly enhanced the "knowledge-gathering" opportunities for librarians. In fact, made available from vendor websites are YouTube videos, YouTube channels, blogs, podcasts, data, charts, graphs, and point-of-use training instructions. Managers should seek and share vendor links to valuable—typically free—information.

# Index

# About the Author

**Dr. Julie Todaro** is a librarian and consultant in libraries and nonprofit environments. She has managed and worked in a variety of types and sizes of libraries in her career, including academic, public, and school libraries. Her career includes academic dean and library manager, graduate school library educator, consultant, and trainer, and she has experience as a children's librarian in a public library and is a certified all-levels school librarian. Todaro has an MSIS from the University of Texas School of Information, Austin, and a DLS from Columbia University in New York City.

She is dean of Austin Community College (ACC) with 40k+ enrollments, eleven libraries, and technical services serving seven central Texas counties and school districts. As dean of the award-winning library services, Julie manages 145+ employees, including 36 full-time faculty librarians, 30+ hourly academic librarians, 4–5 hourly instruction librarians, 35+ full-time classified staff, and 35+ hourly classified employees.

Julie is a frequent keynote speaker, trainer, and presenter at local, state, and national conferences and staff development days. She has presented for institutional and library administrative teams, library cooperatives, governing and advisory boards, and institutes on professionalism; general and executive management; general, executive, and association leadership; and communication, marketing, public relations, and advocacy. She has presented on mentoring for nonprofits and the role of mentorship in development and fundraising. She has consulted for all types and sizes of libraries across the country on designing organizational structures, organizational climate, and change management; designing facilities; twenty-first-century services; operational and strategic planning; communication, public relations, and marketing; community partnerships; customer service;

value, benefit, worth, and impact; and measurement, assessment, and accountability.

Todaro was the Association of College and Research Libraries (ACRL) 2007–2008 president and the American Library Association (ALA) 2016–2017 president, where—as the first community college president—her presidential initiative focused on professional expertise. At ALA, Todaro served as co-chair and member of four presidential initiatives and member and chair of ACRL's Institute for Information Literacy. Todaro received the 1996 Texas Library Association (TLA) Librarian of the Year Award and the 1999 YWCA Austin Educator of the Year Award, and she was the 2001 TLA president. She was also honored by TLA with a 2012 Lifetime Achievement Award and with the 2020 TLA Distinguished Service Award. She also received the 2005 *Austin Business Journal*'s Profiles in Power award and her LLAMA journal "The Truth Is Out There" column received a LLAMA certificate of recognition.

Julie has authored dozens of articles, chapters, and columns—for all types and sizes of libraries—and has written three books on emergency management (two editions), library management, and leadership and mentorship and has coauthored a handbook on customer services. Her books include *Mentoring A to Z* (ALA/Neal-Schuman); *Library Management for the Digital Age: A New Paradigm* (Rowman and Littlefield); and *Emergency Preparedness in Libraries* (Government Institute, with a fall 2019 second edition); and she coauthored with Texas State Librarian and Archives Commission's (TSLAC) Mark Smith *Training Library Staff and Volunteers to Provide Extraordinary Customer Service* (Neal-Schuman).

Her other work over the past three decades focuses on designing and using evidence-based decision-making practices and includes content on "Collaborating,

Partnering, Cooperating: The Good, the Bad, and the Future," "Staffing Issues for the 21st Century," "Integrating Learning with Work: Designing the 21st-Century Learning Library," and "Cutting Edge Redux: New and 'Used' Programs and Services with a 21st-Century Spin." Since 1994, she has been curriculum designer/presenter for the foundation content for TSLAC's Small Public Library Management Series (planning, change, budgeting, marketing, etc.) and was the creator, curriculum designer, and presenter for TLA's A-to-Z Training for Support Staff 2014–2020 and TLA's Executive Leadership Immersion program 2016–2019.